Forgotten
Tales and Vanished Trails

BY THEODORE ROOSEVELT

JIM CASADA, Editor

Going to Water.

From Scribner's Magazine.

Forgotten
Tales and Vanished Trails

THEODORE ROOSEVELT

*Edited and Compiled
with an Introduction and Notes
By Jim Casada*

Skyhorse Publishing

Skyhorse Publishing books may be purchased in bulk at special discounts for sales promotion, corporate gifts, fund-raising, or educational purposes. Special editions can also be created to specifications. For details, contact the Special Sales Department, Skyhorse Publishing, 307 West 36th Street, 11th Floor, New York, NY 10018 or info@skyhorsepublishing.com.

Skyhorse® and Skyhorse Publishing® are registered trademarks of Skyhorse Publishing, Inc.®, a Delaware corporation.

Visit our website at www.skyhorsepublishing.com.

10 9 8 7 6 5 4 3

Library of Congress Cataloging-in-Publication Data is available on file.

Cover design by Victoria Bellavia
Cover photo courtesy of the public domain

ISBN: 978-1-62873-796-7
Ebook ISBN: 978-1-62914-051-3

Printed in China

Table of Contents

ACKNOWLEDGMENTS

INTRODUCTION

A NOTE ON SELECTION AND ORGANIZATION

PART I. A SPORTSMAN IN THE MAKING
THE NEED OF TRAINED OBSERVATION   4
COURSING THE PRONGBUCK   9
PRONGHORN   14

PART II. IN SEARCH OF THE STRENUOUS LIFE
LITERATURE OF AMERICAN BIG-GAME HUNTING   20
TALES TOLD BY A RANCH FIRESIDE: WOLFISH MARAUDERS   24
TALES TOLD BY A RANCH FIRESIDE: A MAN-KILLING BEAR   29
HUNTING IN THE CATTLE COUNTRY   33
THE BEAR'S DISPOSITION   50
ON THE LITTLE MISSOURI   53

PART III. A SPORTSMAN IN HIS PRIME
GRAND CANYON SPEECH, 1903   65
THREE CAPITAL BOOKS OF THE WILDERNESS   66
SMALL COUNTRY NEIGHBORS   73
IN THE LOUISIANA CANEBREAKS   85
WOLF-COURSING   98
TURKEY   102
WAPITI   105
BISON   110
CARIBOU   113
PUMA   116
ROCKY MOUNTAIN GOAT   117
PRAIRIE CHICKEN   120

PART IV. SPORTING WAYS IN LATER DAYS
    FREDERICK COURTENEY SELOUS   126
    MY LIFE AS A NATURALIST   130
    A COUGAR HUNT ON THE RIM OF THE GRAND CANYON   137
    HARPOONING DEVILFISH   150

PART V. READINGS, REFLECTIONS, AND REMINISCENCES
    OUR VANISHING WILD LIFE   168
    JOHN MUIR: AN APPRECIATION   171
    A NATIONAL PARK SERVICE   173
    THE CONSERVATION OF WILD LIFE   175
    THE AMERICAN HUNTER-NATURALIST   182
    A HUNTER-NATURALIST IN EUROPE AND AFRICA   186

BIBLIOGRAPHY

Acknowledgments

A number of individuals have assisted or encouraged me during the compilation of this work. The concept of the Theodore Roosevelt Classics Library came from Les Adams' fertile mind. His daughter, Amanda, has been a patient and persuasive taskmaster, guiding or goading me, whichever was needed, throughout the project. To Les and Amanda, along with the other fine folks at Palladium Press, I can only acknowledge what a pleasure it is to work with true professionals. Much the same can be said of Katharine Wiencke, copyeditor par excellence, who ferrets out my errors and polishes my prose in exemplary fashion. The staff at Winthrop University's Dacus Library has been helpful in procuring material through interlibrary loan and has assisted me in other aspects of my research efforts.

As always, there are debts of gratitude to my family, bastions of support amidst the constant uncertainty of the writing life. My parents gave me a love of literature and the outdoors, Mom as a librarian and Dad as a sportsman. Each passing year enhances my awareness of just what treasures these gifts were. This is the first book I have completed since my mother's passing, and any time I delve into a tale well told, memory's fond reflections help me turn the pages. Finally, to my wife, Ann, my daughter, Natasha, and my son-in-law, Eric, I tender heartfelt thanks for the patience and understanding that have made not only the present work, but all my literary labors, possible.

Introduction

Theodore Roosevelt has fascinated me since my boyhood. As a youngster growing up in the North Carolina high country, I avidly read everything relating to hunting and fishing that I could lay my hands on. The library in Bryson City was a small one, but fortunately the collection included several of Roosevelt's outdoor-related works. Along with the writings of authors such as Robert Ruark, Archibald Rutledge, Havilah Babcock, and Nash Buckingham, they vicariously took me to fields of sporting dreams. Yet early on, realization dawned that Roosevelt was a different man from the other writers who were among my favorites. Those authors were all staunch sons of the Southern soil, while Roosevelt was a "damn yankee." More significantly, Roosevelt had a tremendous impact not only as a writer but as a soldier, politician, diplomat, reformer, and visionary.

He was, in short, a true Renaissance man, and his advocacy of what he styled the "strenuous life" had tremendous appeal. Doubtless some of that appeal derived from my upbringing, a rearing in which constant adherence to a solid work ethic figured prominently. For a boy, though, the fact that a man who had become president could also be a noted hunter and naturalist had an irresistible attraction. I read and reread the books available to me — *African Game Trails, Outdoor Pastimes of an American Hunter,* and *Ranch Life and the Hunting-Trail.* Indeed, the only work I read more was one that probably stands as the most popular book on the outdoors ever written by an American: Robert Ruark's *The Old Man and the Boy* (1957). After all, Ruark was a fellow Tarheel, and as someone who was fortunate enough to have a grandfather as a sporting mentor, it was certainly easy for me to identify with his timeless tales of a boy growing up under similar guidance.

In time, however, my opinion of Ruark altered. He remains, to my way of thinking, an unexcelled sporting scribe, but as a human being he was in many ways a miserable failure. His personal life was a shambles, he drank himself to death before reaching the age of fifty — no one with an iota of common sense could call him a role model. On the other hand, appreciation of Roosevelt grows as one comes to know more of the man and his career. Such was the case as the starstruck perspective of a boy gave way to the more mature and cautious reflections of an adult.

My life's path led me to a first career as a historian (writing on the outdoors being my second and present vocation), and most of my in-depth research focused on pioneering explorers, sportsmen, and colonial civil servants. Time and again the personal papers of explorers such as Sir Harry H. Johnston and Frederick C. Selous, other archives, and obscure publications reminded me of Roosevelt. So omnipresent was mention of the man in writings by and about those interested in Africa during the years before World War I that I decided to renew my perusal of his work. In some senses, this anthology is an outgrowth of those efforts, although there have been other manifestations of my interest in Roosevelt.

Almost two decades ago, for example, when named a distinguished professor by the university where I taught, I chose Roosevelt as the subject of an annual speech to the institution's honor students. The man and his milieu lay outside my primary field of study, British imperial history, but it seemed that one could offer nothing finer to the best and brightest among college students than a glimpse of his approach to life. Certainly to me, for whom the natural world has always been of surpassing significance, the fact that outdoor-related experiences loomed so large in Roosevelt's life has been highly inspirational. I suspect that others who read this work, and its predecessors in the Theodore Roosevelt Classics Library, will concur in wholehearted fashion. With that by way of background, let us now take a fuller look at the career of this remarkable man, with particular attention being devoted to his evolution as a hunter, naturalist, and conservationist.

****

Theodore Roosevelt, Jr., was born on October 27, 1858, in New York City. His parents were comfortably well off, living in an upscale area of the city and regularly taking extended summer vacations in the country. It might be stretching matters a tad to suggest that young Theodore was born with a silver spoon in his mouth, but unquestionably he enjoyed many of the advantages associated with affluence. However, from a tender age Theodore (he loathed the nickname "Teddy," which was not accorded him until he was a prominent national figure), for all the wealth and privilege that was his birthright, faced adverse circumstances.

He was a victim of recurrent and severe asthma attacks, and so sickly was the lad that he did not attend public schools. Instead, tutors were hired by the family, and there was the occasional stint in private schools. As a result, his education was a bit of a hodgepodge, although there can be no denying his intellectual powers. Always an insatiable reader, he enjoyed Joel Chandler Harris' Uncle Remus stories, *Robinson Crusoe,* and most any romantic tale of history or adventure.

The love of literature came in considerable measure from his mother and her sister, Anna, who read to him on a regular basis. His father also influenced his namesake's development significantly and in many ways. One example that stands out is from a trip abroad, after a strenuous hike in the Alps. The elder Roosevelt had noticed that outdoor exercise seemed to help his son's asthma, but he also worried about the boy's frailty. Eventually, in a straightforward manner, he presented his son with the facts of life as he saw them: "Theodore, you have the mind but you have not the body, and without the help of the body the mind cannot go as far as it should. You must make your body. It is hard drudgery to make one's body, but I know you will do it." Never one to shrink from a challenge, Teedie (as the family nicknamed him) henceforth devoted himself to physical exercise and conditioning in an admirable fashion. "I'll make my body," he vowed, and the strenuous life so often associated with Roosevelt began. Wrestling, boxing, horseback riding, hiking, camping, climbing, rowing, swimming, and, most of all, hunting became lifelong obsessions. These endeavors also had a significant psychological effect. As he strengthened and increasingly proved able to overcome attacks of asthma and bronchial problems, his confidence grew exponentially.

"My father was the best man I ever knew," Roosevelt would later write. "He combined strength and courage with gentleness, tenderness, and great unselfishness." To some degree, all of these qualities, but particularly strength and courage, made up the elder Roosevelt's legacy to his son. On the other hand, Theodore senior found far too little time for sport or other leisure pursuits, and most of his son's biographers have suggested that the father's preoccupation with work contributed to a premature death.

Theodore senior had only tangential interests in the outdoors. He did a bit of hunting with his sons in Oyster Bay and on the occasional family outing, and during an extended vacation abroad in 1872–1873, they hunted birds in Egypt. Yet he owned some lovely guns, including a set of percussion pistols from W. W. Greener, the noted British gunmaker, and a pinfire 12-gauge shotgun made by Lefaucheux. The former carried the monogram *TR,* which the son would eventually adopt. In the pages that follow, Theodore junior is frequently referred to simply as TR.

The origins of TR's interest in hunting and natural history can be readily discerned. The highly romantic adventure novels of Mayne Reid, works on African exploration such as those by Dr. David Livingstone and

Roualeyn Gordon-Cumming, and a boy's typical fascination with nature all contributed. His real mentor in this field, however, was his uncle, Robert Barnwell Roosevelt. Uncle Robert lived next door, and he was a recognized authority on a variety of outdoor subjects. He wrote several well-respected books on fishing and ichthyology, as well as *Game Birds of the Coasts* and *Florida and the Game Water Birds,* and also served on the New York Fish and Game Commission for the better part of two decades. In addition, Robert Roosevelt was quite active in politics. Indeed, in practical matters, as opposed to philosophical outlook, he may well have been a more meaningful mentor to TR than his father.

In his preteen and teenage years, Roosevelt hunted whenever he could and pursued studies in natural history, in which ardor more than offset any tendencies toward amateurishness. With an eye to the grandiose that would never leave him, he established the Roosevelt Museum of Natural History in a corner of his bedroom, with a seal's skull as the centerpiece of his exhibit. He also maintained a diary, some index to the near compulsion to commit words to paper that would characterize him his entire life, and his entries were as careful as his spelling was capricious.

A trip to Europe in 1869, followed by another in 1872–1873, influenced him a great deal, and the family's summertime escapes from the stifling confines of the city were for him periods of joy. Other important developments took place as he entered the troubled times of teenagedom. In the late summer of 1871, he went on a camping, fishing, and shooting trip in the Adirondacks and White Mountains. In company with his cousin West and others, he caught trout, canoed, shot air guns, and had ample opportunity to observe a variety of wildlife. The following year came the discovery that he was exceptionally nearsighted. Eyeglasses opened up a new world for him, both figuratively and literally, and it seems somehow appropriate that the revelation of his myopia came after he had been given a gun (the aforementioned Lefaucheux 12 gauge). Before being fitted with glasses, he could not even see the targets at which others shot, but once fitted, he remarked that he had had "no idea how beautiful the world was."

That same year, Roosevelt underwent some formal training in natural history (his teacher was John G. Bell, a noted authority who had worked with John James Audubon) and began a program of intense reading on the subject, a program that would continue until his death. He delighted in the Egyptian portion of the family's 1872–1873 vacation, shooting a wide variety of the birds along the Nile, and a Christmas present of a double-barreled breech-loading shotgun added to his joy. By the time the family returned home in the fall of 1873, the precocious fifteen-year-old was intent on embracing the "vigor of life" as best he could. He now fully appreciated the Roman adage that a sound mind and a sound body went together, and further ventures afield in 1874 and 1875 gave him welcome chances to focus on both *mens* and *corpus*.

During that same period, he set about preparing himself for admission to Harvard University, and under the stern tutelage of Arthur Cutler he made excellent progress. When he entered the most venerable and prestigious of all American universities in the fall of 1876, he already possessed many of the characteristics that would mark his adult life. Increasingly self-confident, always hardworking, loquacious, and often combative, he was far removed from the label of weakling that had haunted him in earlier days. The fact that he earned a Phi Beta Kappa key while at Harvard attests to his intellect and powers of application, but from the standpoint of his development in the areas embraced by the present work, it was vacation trips into the Maine wilderness that shaped the budding hunter-naturalist.

These ventures provided both surcease of sorrow at the death of his father late in 1877 and a test of his manhood. His guide and outfitter for these trips was a Maine lumberman, Bill Sewall, who picked up extra income by taking parties of hunters into the wilderness around his Island Falls home. Sewall was a consummate woodsman of the "Nessmuk" (George Washington Sears) school, and the trip that Roosevelt took with him from September 7 to 26, 1878, proved to be a real watershed in the young man's life.

In the course of the adventure, as one of Roosevelt's most perceptive biographers, H. W. Brands, remarked in *T. R.: The Last Romantic* (1997), Sewall demonstrated that "the rugged and the refined could coexist." The pair took to one another almost immediately, thanks in no small measure to common interests and a shared outlook on life. Deeply versed in just the sort of literature TR enjoyed, Sewall had himself been a sickly youth. He would initially serve as a mentor to TR in the ways of woodcraft, and in time he also became a cross between a father figure and an older brother. In that capacity, he would fill the role as an everyman sounding board for Roosevelt as long as he lived.

Never mind that TR, by his own account, shot so poorly that he bemoaned, "I am disgusted with myself." Sewall's first impression of the untested young man as "a thin, pale youngster with bad eyes and a weak heart" would have led him to expect general ineptitude, but to his surprise and eventual delight, TR insisted on nonstop, dawn-to-dusk activity every day. In some senses, this initial Maine journey saw the boy become a man, and TR returned to Cambridge and his studies at Harvard with an improved sense of self-confidence.

Two subsequent hunting outings in Maine, in March 1879 and from August 23 to September 24 of that same year, strengthened the bond between Sewall and TR, and the lessons learned during these long sojourns in the wilderness would serve TR well in years to come. This would be especially true during the time he spent ranching and hunting in the Dakota Badlands. Meanwhile, the backwoods experiences correlated with striking success at Harvard. When he graduated in 1880, he ranked well toward the top of his class, and his extracurricular activities attested to the breadth of his interests. During his years at the university, TR was welcomed into the ranks of the exclusive Porcellian Club and also belonged to the Hasty Pudding Club and the O.K. Society. He was an active participant in the Natural History Society, served as editor of the *Harvard Advocate,* and somehow found time to follow a strict regimen of physical training and teach Sunday school at the Cambridge Episcopal Church.

The time was at hand to deal with momentous matters — graduate study, a career path, and possibly marriage. However, TR first went on an extended hunting trip, this time in company with his brother, Elliott. This escape to the wilds and engagement in manly pursuits would become a prominent feature of TR's adult life (despite the fact that in this instance the trip was undertaken against the strong advice of his physician, who expressed concerns about a weak heart). On this occasion and on many subsequent ones when faced by pressures in his personal or political life, TR would find that the solitude of the wild world, perhaps shared with a close companion such as Elliott, was the ideal situation in which to clear his mind and make critical decisions.

During this particular trip, the brothers hunted upland birds and small game. TR treated himself to a new shotgun, and he got his first taste of the West, a region that would draw him for the remainder of his existence. When he and Elliott returned to the family's Oyster Bay home at the end of September, TR assuredly felt a sense of inner peace and readiness to face whatever the future might bring.

Upon his return, Roosevelt plunged into adult life in typically ebullient fashion. On his twenty-second birthday he married Alice Hathaway Lee, whom he had met while at Harvard, and the couple settled in New York City, where he began studies as a law student at Columbia University. He completed work on the first of what would be many books, *The Naval War of 1812* (1882), began active participation in the Republican Club of New

York City, and took a European tour with his new bride. Election to the New York State Assembly soon followed (TR had left Columbia), and he plunged headlong into controversy surrounding financial and judicial irregularities connected with the Manhattan Elevated Railway. Soon he would be seen as a major voice for reform, and for the next three decades, outdoor experiences were for the most part precious times to be sampled and savored between the demands of politics, diplomacy, writing, and military pursuits.

Yet there was never any doubt about what held priority of place in TR's mind. He wrote to H. H. Gorringe, a retired U. S. naval officer who contemplated joining him on an 1883 trip to the Little Missouri River, "I am fond of politics, but fonder still of a little big game hunting." Reaching this conclusion required no great degree of introspection. His remark was simply a statement of reality, and TR's sentiments on this score would continue unchanged. As Paul Russell Cutright noted in the preface to his important book, *Theodore Roosevelt: The Naturalist* (1956), "Roosevelt began his life as a naturalist, and he ended it as a naturalist. Throughout a half century of strenuous activity his interest in wildlife, though subject to ebb and flow, was never abandoned at any time."

In the autumn of 1883, plagued by a return of his old nemesis, asthma, and desperately in need of some relief from the tiring grind of politics, Roosevelt decided to go on a hunting trip in the Dakota Badlands. He shot a buffalo, albeit only after varied misadventures including dealing with inclement weather and his indifferent marksmanship. Yet to TR, obstacles were ever a welcome challenge, and he was a complete stranger to the word *quit.* As he repeatedly commented to his companion and guide on the trip, Joe Ferris, "It's dogged as does it." In the end, the taciturn Ferris, a tough little man who initially harbored serious doubts regarding the toughness of his client, altered his opinion. He described TR as "a plumb good sort," and for Ferris that was the highest compliment.

Roosevelt's initial exposure to the Badlands had a dramatic impact on him, and for the ensuing decade he would be torn between the West and the East, between a life lived close to nature and one at the heart of national affairs. Before he boarded the train for the return home, he had set in motion plans to buy a ranch, Chimney Butte, in the Badlands. His intent was to begin raising cattle, and he invested a substantial sum in livestock. By the time he returned, on June 9, 1884, his life had changed dramatically. His wife and mother died within hours of one another on February 14, 1884. Alice died from a kidney disease, two days after childbirth, and his mother, affectionately known as Mittie, succumbed to typhoid fever. It was the lowest point of Roosevelt's life. His diary for the day shows a black *X* followed by a single sentence: "The light has gone out of my life."

In reality, TR was far too resilient and possessed of too strong a character for even twin disasters of this magnitude to cause him to remain inactive for long. At this sad juncture in his life, the Badlands afforded him a refuge. On the day his wife and mother were buried, he wrote in his journal: "For joy or for sorrow my life has now been lived out." He left the State Assembly and suffered mightily for a time. Within four months, however, he was back in the Dakota Territory, and soon he bought a second ranch, which he named Elkhorn because shed elk antlers were plentiful on its acreage. He even managed to persuade his old Maine guide and mentor, Bill Sewall, to come west and manage the ranch.

Soon he was, by his own judgment, "well hardened," and the prairie wildflowers and singing birds of spring lifted his spirits. He took a solitary trip, perhaps in search of himself and perhaps because he "wanted to sce if I could not do perfectly well without a guide." The experience was an inspiring one: "I felt as absolutely free as a man could feel; . . . I do not mind loneliness; and I enjoyed the trip to the utmost."

So much was this the case, in fact, that he undertook a more ambitious outing, a hunting trip to Wyoming. Until he went on his great African safari, this would be TR's longest and most ambitious outdoor adventure. The trip lasted seven weeks and gave Roosevelt a great deal of satisfaction. He and members of his party took six elk, seven deer, three grizzlies, and 109 head of various "small game," with the daily bag being duly recorded in his diary. Roosevelt could justifiably feel, at the conclusion of the arduous adventure, that he had become an able, even accomplished, outdoorsman. With the trip in the Bighorns behind him, it was once more time to look back to the East and the responsibilities of public service, which were a family tradition, and his destiny. As R. L. Wilson wrote, in *Theodore Roosevelt — Outdoorsman* (1971), "His heart belonged to the West, his mind to the East."

From 1883 through 1886, Roosevelt would spend just over a year in the Badlands, for political affairs and other matters increasingly claimed his attention in New York. Yet he already had the raw material that would result in two of his most moving and enduring books, *Hunting Trips of a Ranchman* (1885) and *Ranch Life and the Hunting-Trail* (1888). Portions of *The Wilderness Hunter* (1893) also draw on his experiences in these years. In these books — and in the early books published by the Boone and Crockett Club that he coedited with George Bird Grinnell, as well as in periodicals — he wrote vividly of bears and wolves, elk and antelopes, together with giving readers a real feel for the hardiness and hardship that were integral parts of ranching. He was already an authority on western fauna, and the region's wildness and primitive loveliness had left an indelible impression on him. The same was true of its inhabitants. When, in *Hunting Trips of a Ranchman,* he described cowboys as "sinewy, hardy, [and] self-reliant," saying that "their life forces them to be both daring and adventurous, and the passing over their heads of a few years leaves printed on their faces certain lives which tell of dangers quietly confronted and hardships uncomplainingly endured," he was waxing wistful about a style of life he greatly admired. Small wonder that he left this period of his life with a determination to preserve the West that had laid hold of a corner of his soul. It is a measure of his determination that Roosevelt would, to a greater degree than any other American, be responsible for protecting this western wonderland.

Sadly, major setbacks in his personal life continued to haunt Roosevelt. The winter of 1886–1887 in the Badlands was one of the most severe on record. He lost most of his cattle, and when he visited the ranch in the spring of 1887, he saw scenes of utter devastation. He took the only road truly open to him and abandoned the ranch life that held such personal appeal but that emptied his purse. Yet his love affair with the region was a lasting one, and soon he would offer, in his four-volume *The Winning of the* West (1889–1896), a paean to the West that is of scholarly importance even today. As a contemporary reviewer wrote, the work was "natural, simple, and picturesque" with "chapters of singular felicity."

The ensuing decade would be one of the most sedentary periods of Roosevelt's life. Yet the years leading up to his career-shaping exploits with the Rough Riders at San Juan Hill were anything but devoid of outdoor activity. In December 1887, he hosted a dinner that resulted in the founding of the Boone and Crockett Club, and he wrote the organization's constitution, with the concept of fair chase being at the heart of its philosophy. Another primary aim of the club, one redolent of Roosevelt's thinking, was conservation of big game animals and their habitat.

A year earlier he had married Edith Kermit Carow, and soon they were the parents of a bevy of boisterous youngsters. The children, born over a span of eleven years in the late 1880s and the 1890s, gave him great joy and the perfect excuse for short, satisfying escapes to nature. In time he would introduce each of the four boys to hunting and wilderness ways, and all of the children (TR's first wife had borne a daughter, as had Edith) were instilled with an appreciation for nature. The boys would become skilled hunters and, not surprisingly, surer shots than their myopic father.

Quentin was killed in World War I when only 21 years of age, and Archibald suffered serious wounds in both World War I and World War II. Kermit, who died in Alaska in 1943, transcended his father in his breadth of geographical experience, and both he and Theodore junior (actually Theodore Roosevelt III but always known as Theodore junior) were active members and officers of the Boone and Crockett Club.

Growing up at the home TR had acquired for his rambunctious brood, Sagamore Hill, the children had elbow room aplenty. Their father, on the other hand, found himself more and more at the center of the nation's affairs in Washington. In 1888 he resumed an active role in politics, campaigning for the successful presidential candidate, Benjamin Harrison. This led to an appointment to the Civil Service Commission that would be continued under President Grover Cleveland. Still, even in this period in which earning a living took on increasing importance (his Dakota ranching investments had eaten up most of his inheritance), he managed to go on at least one hunt each year. These outings took him to British Columbia, the Rockies, his old haunts in the Badlands, the Yellowstone River region, and elsewhere. Out of these experiences came, among other writings, *The Wilderness Hunter,* arguably the finest of TR's hunting books. In it he made "a plea for manliness and simplicity and delight in a vigorous outdoor life." To read the work is to realize that the author was a man who had experienced and who understood the subjects about which he wrote.

In 1895, he left his position with the Civil Service Commission to become New York City's police commissioner. It was a lateral career move, indicative more than anything else of how Washington had begun to pall. The new post also bore some promise of adventure — not the outdoor kind to which Roosevelt was accustomed, but rather an opportunity for meaningful reforms. He worked like a Trojan, relishing the challenge presented to him. Incorruptible and fearless, Roosevelt managed to step on plenty of political toes as police commissioner, including those of the entrenched Thomas "Boss" Platt. The fact that Platt was a fellow Republican mattered not one whit to Roosevelt, and TR's honesty and flair for the dramatic began to catch the eye of the common man.

Acceptance in April 1897 of the position of assistant secretary of the Navy under President William McKinley gave him even greater prominence. Yet it was the Spanish-American War and the acceptance of a lieutenant colonel's commission in a volunteer cavalry regiment that would place him squarely in the national eye. The regiment, which came to be known as the Rough Riders, drew men of the sort TR liked best, "a splendid set of men," as he described them. When Roosevelt led the Rough Riders in the assault on San Juan Hill, he called it "the great day of my life." In many ways it was, despite the fact that the conflict was in truth a minor one, referred to in the title of one history as "the splendid little war."

It was certainly splendid for Roosevelt, because the recognition and renown it brought him opened the road to the White House. Election as governor of New York followed almost immediately, and in that post he was an effective reformer and fiscal conservative. Although he was anything but keen on the nomination, he agreed (before his term was out) to join the William McKinley ticket as the Republican candidate for vice president. The Republicans won, an assassin's bullet struck McKinley in September 1901, and suddenly the White House was home to a devoted hunter.

Even though the last few years had seen Roosevelt do far less hunting than he would have liked, he was afield when he got news of the anarchist's having shot McKinley. As president, TR would find a surprising amount of time to hunt, mixing escapes to the wild with trust-busting, reform on many fronts, diplomatic initiatives that led to the "great rapprochement" with England, and much more. His first hunt as president took him to Mississippi, where to his lasting chagrin he found that his guide, the highly experienced bear hunter Holt Collier, had captured a bear and bound it in ropes, to await a killing shot. TR bluntly refused to be a part of such a charade, and from this the "Teddy" bear fad was born. He was disgusted with the whole affair, and it would be a source of embarrassment for the remainder of his life. Nonetheless, from that time forward his name would be associated with bears.

Other aspects of his two terms as president (he was elected in his own right after completing McKinley's term) that were associated with sport and conservation were much more satisfying. These included an outing in Yosemite with the great naturalist John Muir and a similar trip to Yellowstone with another noted conservationist, John Burroughs. The latter's *Camping & Tramping with Roosevelt* (1907) offers particularly useful insight into this meeting of kindred minds. More significant, however, were TR's concrete accomplishments in terms of promoting conservation. He founded the Forest Service and persuaded Gifford Pinchot to serve as its first director, signed bills creating five new national parks, established game reserves and the National Bison Range, and in general made Americans aware of the importance of protecting wildlife and habitat. As R. L. Wilson wrote, "Had Roosevelt done nothing else as President, his greatness would still have been ensured by what he did in conservation."

TR hunted regularly during his presidency — taking a wild turkey in Virginia, a bear in Louisiana; coursing after wolves, coyotes, and foxes in several states; killing rattlesnakes and wolves in Oklahoma; and chasing bears and bobcats in Colorado. He also regularly entertained Boone and Crockett Club compatriots at the White House, along with eminent foreign hunters such as the great British big game hunter Fred Selous.

As his second term in office moved toward an end, Roosevelt increasingly thought about a grand African safari. His papers reveal correspondence with a remarkable number of individuals who were intimately familiar with the Dark Continent. In addition to Selous, these included J. H. Patterson, author of the chilling *The Man-Eaters of Tsavo and Other East African Adventures* (1907); R. J. Cuninghame, a fellow hunter-naturalist; the noted American naturalist Carl Akeley; and Edward North Buxton, author of several highly respected works on big game, including *Two African Trips* (1902) and *Short Stalks; Or Hunting Camps North, South, East, and West* (1892). Selous and Buxton helped immeasurably in planning the trip, and Roosevelt found plenty of financial supporters.

Andrew Carnegie helped subsidize the safari, and TR contracted with *Scribner's Magazine* to write a series of articles that would eventually become a book. The magazine offered the princely sum of $50,000 for the articles, plus royalties from the book. Roosevelt also worked out an arrangement with the Smithsonian Institution to collect specimens for it, thereby stifling in large measure those who had criticized the forthcoming safari as little more than a progress of slaughter. The safari, which got under way in 1909 after months of the type of meticulous preparation one would expect from a man with TR's devotion to detail, would be the high point of his hunting life.

It was a success from beginning to end, despite irritating attention from the press of the sort reminiscent of today's paparazzi. Accompanied by his son Kermit, he bagged Africa's Big Five (lion, leopard, buffalo, elephant, and rhinoceros), along with a variety of less dangerous game. His experiences are fully detailed in *African Game Trails* (1910) and the two-volume *Life-Histories of African Game Animals* (with Edmund Heller; 1914). *National Geographic* magazine, in a lengthy review of the former work, said that Africa's "sights . . . are described so vividly and accurately that even the most quiet and unimaginative citizen . . . can easily picture the extraordinary contact which remains so fixed in Mr. Roosevelt's mind." *National Geographic* termed the book "the strongest and best work of literature Mr. Roosevelt has yet written," saying it constituted "an unusual contribution to science, geography, literature, and adventure."

The magnitude of the expedition's collection can only be described as amazing. Altogether, TR and those who accompanied him collected 4,897 mammals, some 2,000 reptiles, 500 fish, and 4,000 birds, not to mention numerous invertebrates. The overall holding, portions of which can still be studied at the Smithsonian, remains one of the most important of its kind.

The triumphant progress through Europe that followed the safari (Edith met her husband and son at Khartoum and toured with them through Europe) was a bittersweet experience. After the wilds of Africa and constant communing with nature in its most primitive and raw forms, it was hectic in the extreme to be always in demand in civilized society. TR traveled to Norway to make his belated acceptance speech for the 1906 Nobel Peace Prize (awarded for his efforts in ending the Russo-Japanese War), spoke at Oxford University and the Sorbonne, visited the mercurial German kaiser Wilhelm, and met royalty and dignitaries in most of the European capital cities. He wound up his tour by attending, as President Taft's chosen emissary, the funeral of King Edward VII.

A hale and hearty Roosevelt was 51 years of age when he returned home. He found the Republican Party in turmoil. Taft had proven an ineffectual president, indecisive, vacillating, and prone to take the path of least resistance rather than make hard decisions. TR was appalled at the state of affairs, especially when he found that Gifford Pinchot had been dismissed as chief forester and the goals of the Republican Party's progressives sacrificed on the altar of expediency and economic interest. He broke openly with Taft and announced, with regard to the 1912 presidential nomination, "My hat is in the ring."

He campaigned with characteristic vigor, although he was shot by a fanatic in Milwaukee. Even though the bullet lodged near his right lung, after penetrating his coat, glasses case, and speech, TR refused to go immediately to the hospital. Stubborn and determined as ever, he delivered an impassioned address, holding his audience enthralled as he promoted what he styled the New Nationalism. He then spent a fortnight convalescing at Sagamore Hill, after which he gave a rousing speech at Madison Square Garden, just before the election. He lost to Woodrow Wilson, the Democratic nominee, but far outdistanced Taft. This defeat effectively ended his political career.

TR then turned to writing his autobiography, contributing to *Scribner's Magazine* and the *Outlook,* and putting his papers in order. He went on a cougar hunt in the Grand Canyon as well, in company with his sons Archibald and Quentin and his nephew Nicholas. The four also crossed the Navajo desert and camped in the wilds of Colorado. This trip would be his next-to-last North American big game hunt.

In 1913, TR lost all vestiges of sight in his left eye, which had been injured years earlier in a boxing match. The loss, however, did nothing to diminish his enthusiasm for the outdoors or determination to live an active life. Instead, he began planning an exploration of Brazil's fabled River of Doubt — a "last chance to be a boy," as he put it. He consulted with officials at the American Museum of Natural History, asked acquaintances in South America to help with arrangements, and contacted experts in South American wildlife. Since Roosevelt's son Kermit was already employed in Brazil, it was logical that he be included in the party. No detail regarding firearms or other equipment was overlooked.

The journey was, as TR wrote in his account of it (*Through the Brazilian Wilderness* [1914]), "a thorough success." The party mapped the river, a tributary of the Amazon that was later renamed Rio Roosevelt; collected thousands of birds, mammals, and fish; and hunted jaguars and other South American game. However, the hunting paled in comparison with that in Africa, and the heat and humidity took a considerable toll. Roosevelt was injured in a canoe accident, and when the party emerged from the jungle, he was lame and completely worn out and had lost over thirty-five pounds.

He had only ten days to recuperate, not nearly enough time, before setting out for Spain to attend Kermit's wedding. Age was beginning to tell, and he also watched the deteriorating European situation with dismay. In September 1915, TR traveled to the woods of Quebec, and, as he wrote, "there befell me one of the most curious and interesting adventures with big game that have ever befallen me." He was charged by a bull moose and reluctantly shot it (he had already taken one moose) at a range of less than ten yards.

His beloved sister, Anna Roosevelt Cowles, later commented that she "saw evidence for the first time that this mighty human dynamo is working with a somewhat diminished energy." Indeed, TR had confided to her that this hunting trip might well be his last, saying he had no desire to be "taken care of," and those words proved prophetic. He realized that his once vast physical powers and incredible determination were beginning to wane. In the years that remained to him, Roosevelt sorted through his mementos of a sporting life, worked on the impressive trophy room at Sagamore Hill, organized his extensive library, and continued his longtime habit of corresponding with other hunters and naturalists.

While enjoying these leisurely pursuits, he watched developments of the Great War with growing concern. An unabashed Anglophile, he criticized President Wilson's waffling and advocated the need for America to ready itself for war. He sensed that the United States would be drawn into the conflict, and he brought his considerable literary powers to bear in preaching what he considered the neglected gospel of preparedness. When the United States finally entered the war, General John J. Pershing's American Expeditionary Force included all four of TR's sons, and the old Bull Moose and hero of San Juan bid them farewell, reluctantly remaining behind at Sagamore Hill.

The war brought tragedy to the Roosevelt family. Quentin died in aerial combat late in the war, and his passing moved TR in profound fashion. "Only those are fit to live who do not fear to die," he wrote, "and none are fit to die who have shrunk from the joy of life." There could be no adequate preparation for this tragic event, although Roosevelt confessed to King George V that when his boys left for the European theater, "we did not expect to see all of them come back." James Amos, Roosevelt's beloved butler and bodyguard, said the death of "Quinikins" left Roosevelt "a changed man. He was eating his heart out."

The grief was intensified, if that was possible, by the fact that his son's death came shortly after TR had had an attack of jungle fever, a holdover from his earlier adventures in the tropics. The attack left him with limited mobility and some deafness. His physicians even went so far as to warn him that he might spend the remainder of his life in a wheelchair. He courageously shrugged off their pronouncements, saying, "All right, I can work that way." And work he did through much of 1918. In fact, after the Democratic Party took a thrashing in the fall elections and the Republicans were left holding a majority in both the House and the Senate, he even began thinking of a run for president in 1920. It was not to be.

Late in 1918 he was once more quite ill. The diagnosis was inflammatory rheumatism, but biographer H. W. Brands suggested that the real problem was probably parasites remaining from his Amazon trip "that were undetectable by contemporary medical tests." For a few days in the new year there were hints of his old energy, and on January 5 he worked a full eleven hours. At bedtime, though, he told Edith he had "such a strange feeling." In the wee hours of the morning, after TR had slept quietly for several hours, his faithful factotum, James Amos, noticed he had stopped breathing. Roosevelt's son Archibald, home recuperating from wounds suffered in battle on the western front, cabled his brothers: "The old lion is dead."

Thus ended what TR had called (and what *Scribner's* would entitle a collection of his speeches and essays) "the great adventure." He described those "who have dared the Great Adventure" as "the torch-bearers." Without question, for virtually all of his life Roosevelt had belonged in the front rank of the torch-bearers. Nowhere was that more obvious than in his efforts as a hunter, naturalist, and advocate of protecting the nation's natural resources.

Roosevelt remains the only American president to have had a true sense of the importance of balancing human and environmental needs. He knew nature intimately and cherished the natural world with fervor while communicating its wonders with verve and vigor. He was an advocate of conservation, not preservation, believing that forests and fields, wildlife and wild wonders should be used intelligently to serve humankind. He left a lasting and romantic legacy, one that places today's lovers of nature, whether their outlook is that of Thoreau or of hunters like Davy Crockett and Daniel Boone, in his debt. He lived, with incredible fullness, the strenuous life in which he so staunchly believed. The essence of that life remains one that we can share, in our national forests and national parks, with their fish-filled streams and game-rich forests, and in our wildlife refuges and bird sanctuaries, teeming with creatures of the air, water, and land. "To know him was to love him," said John Burroughs when he learned of Roosevelt's death.

Even today, a full fourscore years and more later, Roosevelt's legacy inspires us even as his joie de vivre invigorates us. To read the selections from his works that follow, together with the material offered in the earlier books in this Library, is to savor that inspiration and share that invigoration at the hands of a masterful writer.

Jim Casada

ROCK HILL, SOUTH CAROLINA

A Note on Selection and Organization

Theodore Roosevelt was a prolific writer throughout virtually all of his adult life, and the subjects he covered ranged as widely as his multifaceted endeavors. The outdoor and sporting life ran as a bright and constant thread through the fabric of his career, and his pursuits afield were the core around which his articles and books were built. As members of this Library already realize, Roosevelt wrote on hunting and what he fondly styled the "strenuous life" with power and poignancy. Many of his books, perhaps most notably *African Game Trails* and *Outdoor Pastimes of an American Hunter,* have become enduring classics. Others languished in relative obscurity until the advent of the Theodore Roosevelt Classics Library. The least-appreciated part of his oeuvre as a sporting or outdoor scribe is his contributions to magazines and anthologies.

To be sure, some of Roosevelt's work for popular periodicals was eventually incorporated in his books. For example, most of what was to become *African Game Trails* first saw the light of day as a series of articles in *Scribner's Magazine.* Nonetheless, a considerable number of writings by Roosevelt heretofore have not appeared in book form, or, in the case of pieces that did so appear, were published as parts of anthologies. Accordingly, the selections included here are those that focus in some fashion on Roosevelt's outdoor interests and that are not readily found (if at all) in book form.

Each piece included in this volume is identified according to its original place of publication, and if I have knowledge of its subsequently having been reprinted, that bibliographical information is given as well. Brief editorial commentary, intended to provide a backdrop for the subject of the article, introduces the individual selections. Fuller editorial input begins each of the anthology's five parts, with the arrangement following a somewhat loose chronological scheme.

PART I

A Sportsman in the Making

Introductory Note

It can be said that from a quite tender age, Theodore Roosevelt was a sportsman in the making. He evinced a keen interest in all aspects of natural history; he early realized that hunting and other activities afield required grit and stamina, qualities he possessed in abundance; and he found life in the open an ideal antidote for a youthful frailty that came from chronic asthma. His fondest recollections of childhood revolved around outdoor adventure, with the family's frequent retreats to the country giving him great pleasure. As he would later write:

> In the country we children ran barefoot much of the time, and the seasons went by in a round of uninterrupted and enthralling pleasures — supervising the haying and harvesting, picking apples, hunting frogs successfully and woodchucks unsuccessfully, gathering hickory-nuts and chestnuts for sale to patient parents, building wigwams in the woods, and sometimes playing Indians in too realistic a manner by staining ourselves (and incidentally our clothes) in liberal fashion with poke-cherry juice.

Interestingly, Theodore Roosevelt, Sr., was not a keen sportsman. While he occasionally joined his sons in hunting game during their adolescence, he cannot really be viewed as his son's sporting mentor. Instead, TR became a hunter through his youthful fascination with natural history. Both sport and the study of wildlife would become lifelong passions. In the three pieces offered here, we see the manner in which natural history and sport were inextricably intertwined in Roosevelt the hunter.

TR realized that solid woodcraft loomed large in hunting success, and the observational skills he had nurtured from boyhood served him well in this regard. Indeed, Roosevelt was never more than a mediocre shot at best, and his eyesight was a distinct liability in the hunting field. Yet he more than offset these potentially significant shortcomings through dogged persistence and heavy reliance on his understanding of game behavior and habitat. The wisdom he offers in these pieces, and this is especially true of the essay that opens the book, is timeless. As a contemporary of Roosevelt's who was known as the Dean of American Campers once wrote: "In the school of the outdoors there is no graduation day." Those words might well have been a sporting motto for TR.

****

*Roosevelt was always a staunch advocate of careful, even meticu-
lous, observation. Most likely he cultivated this approach because he
considered it essential to the making of a competent naturalist. After
all, he lived in an age when talented amateurs made some of the
most significant contributions to knowledge of natural history. He
cultivated friendships with many such individuals, and three of them,
the Englishmen Frederick C. Selous and Abel Chapman, along with
John Muir, figure prominently elsewhere in the present work. In this
short piece, which originally appeared in* Outing *magazine (vol. 37
[1900–1901]: 631–633), Roosevelt makes a convincing case for
trained observation in a hunter. As a hunter, from his first tentative
footsteps afield through the crowning achievement of his grand
African safari and beyond, it would be his most important and dis-
tinguishing characteristic.*

THE NEED OF TRAINED OBSERVATION

EVERY hunter *ought* to be a field naturalist, and *must* be an observer, if he is to be a hunter in anything but name. His observations
will deal primarily with the animals he pursues, but if he is wise,
they will also cover a wide range of other subjects. The professed naturalist owes much to his sporting brother. This, of course is especially true
as regards big game, and, indeed, as regards all the rarer quadrupeds
which vanish before the advent of civilization. It is a real misfortune
when a man who has exceptional opportunities for observing the wild life
of these creatures fails to take advantage of his opportunities, for too often
they have vanished by the time the trained scientific man comes upon the
field. Moreover, the latter is apt to be absorbed with his observations of
the numerous lesser forms of animal life, which stay in the land, and the
records concerning which therefore do not have the same value. It is for
this reason, by the way, that the big game hunter who has scientific aspirations should not lose his sense of perspective, so to speak, and neglect
the work which he alone can do, for the sake of that which can be done at
any time by any of those who may follow in his footsteps. Thus in Dr.
Donaldson Smith's recent record of his noteworthy explorations in Africa
there are appendices devoted to catalogues of beetles and botanical specimens. This is all very well in its way, but it is not one-thousandth part as
important from the larger scientific standpoint, as would have been a full
and accurate account by the Doctor of the life history, and indeed the

physical peculiarities of the rhinoceros, with which he was brought into such intimate and often unpleasant contact. It is not so important as a full and detailed account of such incidents as the fighting between the lions and hyenas, of which he was an eye witness.

Every big game hunter ought to be an observer. If he keeps a record of his observations, one of his first experiences will be to find that they seemingly conflict with those of some other observer equally competent. If he is hasty he will conclude that the other observer is not telling the truth; and the public at large will conclude that they cannot both be right. Now, of course, it is perfectly possible that they both are right; and it is possible, on the other hand, that while each has seen a part of the truth, he has not seen all. In any observation of this kind there are varying factors. In the first place, two men may not see the same thing alike; and in the next place, one man may not see the same thing quite alike on two different days; while finally, two animals of the same kind may act utterly different, or one may act differently at different times, or all of those who dwell in one place, or who are observed at one season, may behave very differently from those that dwell in other places, or are seen under other circumstances.

When these conditions are set forth in print, they seem such obvious truisms as hardly to be worth putting down. But as a matter of fact they are continually forgotten in practice. Even a trained observer will make mistakes, and those, who, though eager and interested, have no special training or knowledge, are sure to err much more frequently. Besides, the language which one person uses to convey a somewhat unfamiliar idea, may to another person convey this idea in a totally different form. For instance, at one time I was a great deal in the cattle country, and in the spring time, out on the treeless wastes, I frequently came across sage fowl. On a still, clear morning at dawn I would often hear the love notes of the male and, going toward them, have had to travel a very long distance before coming in sight of the bird himself. The impression gradually fixed itself upon my mind that there was a considerable volume of sound, which I described as "booming;" and at first I was rather impatient of correction when a friend of wide experience insisted that it ought rather to be described as clucking, and was by no means a powerful noise. Yet I afterwards became convinced that my friend was, in the main, right, and that my impressions of the sound were due less to the sound itself than to the stillness, the loneliness, and the uninterrupted, measureless expanse of the surroundings. In another matter connected with this same bird, the difference in certain observations was due not to anything in me or the surroundings, but to a variation in the habits of the bird. I had always found sage fowl far away from trees, on desolate flats, where there could be no ranches. But in 1892, near the head waters of the upper Missouri, I came upon them more than once in parties right by the river, among the small cottonwoods, and on at least one occasion, so near the garden of a settler that I was for a moment doubtful whether they were not domesticated.

Wherever any man has the opportunity to observe but a few individuals of any species, and of course when his observations are hurried, there is every chance for a conflict of testimony. For instance, I recall two friends, each with about an equal experience in shooting our large bears. One has been repeatedly charged, and has a most wholesome respect for the grizzly's prowess. The other, who has killed an even larger number, has never seen the grizzly display anything but abject cowardice, and down in the bottom of his heart I think, he regards all tales to the contrary as impinging somewhat on fancy.

In my own experience I have generally found the mountain sheep to be a very difficult animal to bag, far more so than deer or elk. One of the hands on my ranch, however, who had killed several, always insisted that the direct reverse was the case, and that, as he expressed it, they were "dumber" than deer. Another friend who was accustomed to European chamois, not only considered the big horn by comparison a stupid, but also by comparison, even a bad climber—a statement I found very hard to believe. In the United States from the days of the earliest explorers to the present time, the big horn has always been, as his name implies, a mountain sheep; but his giant kinsfolk of Asia are often not climbers at all, dwelling on huge plateaus, level or rolling, and with little or no cover.

It is quite impossible to reconcile some conflicting statements made even by the most eminent authorities. I suppose that all of us who care for a hunter's life have read, with peculiar interest, the exploits of our fortunate brethren who have shot in that grandest of all the world's hunting grounds, Africa, and the most enthralling chase is naturally the chase of dangerous game. African hunters are agreed that the lion, elephant, rhinoceros and buffalo are the four kinds of game, the pursuit of which must be considered as dangerous. But when the question is as to which is the most dangerous, every variety of opinion is forthcoming. We must, of course, disregard absolutely the untrustworthy writers, who practice a melodrama degenerating into opera bouffe, like Girard, whose accounts of lion hunting in Algeria are almost pure romance (in striking contrast to the admirable descriptions of that great French hunter, M. Foa). But even when we examine the writings of men who have the highest claims to serious consideration, we are met by irreconcilable differences of opinion, and even differences of fact. Taking four such men, all with wide experience with all the kinds of dangerous African game, Mr. Selous considers the lion by far the most dangerous; Mr. Jackson ranks the buffalo first; Sir Samuel Baker insists upon the elephant; and Mr. Drummond gives the palm to the rhinoceros. Of the rhinoceros, by the way, Messrs. Selous and Jackson speak almost with contempt. Again, take the hyena. Most writers on African sport treat the hyena as an exceedingly cowardly and harmless animal. But some of those who write of Somaliland and the north, not only treat of its ravages among the flocks, but also of its frequently preying upon men, and I have already alluded to Mr. Smith's account of its prowess even against the lion.

Closely allied animals certainly show marvelous differences of conduct in different localities. It is hard to give any satisfactory reason for the undoubted fact that throughout Asia, and in many parts of Europe, the wolf is often a dangerous foe to human life; whereas, in America such an event as an attack by a wolf upon a human being is almost unknown. On the other hand, the big American bear, until much molested by hunters, was undoubtedly far more to be dreaded by man than any Asiatic or European bear. Yet another puzzle is offered by the fact that in America the black bear, almost everywhere, outlasts the wolf as settlements advance, while in Europe the reverse is the case. It is not easy to see why a comparatively clumsy animal like the bear, which is less prolific than the wolf, should outlast it. Yet such is undoubtedly the case throughout our Atlantic States.

Turning from big game, let me take an example among our own familiar birds. To many people, including myself, the voice of the Western meadow lark has a peculiar charm. It happened that my early associations with the Eastern meadow lark were such that I rarely heard more than its chatter, and not the plaintive song-note which I have since grown to love. But to me the Western meadow lark is an incomparably better singer. Yet I have seen the opposite opinion upheld, even in a journal like *The Auk*. I wonder how much association really has to do with our appreciation of bird songs? A great deal undoubtedly, as witness particularly the cases of the old-world nightingale and sky lark. These are extreme examples of birds with a literary reputation so great that hardly one man in a hundred who writes of them does anything but accept what other writers have already said of them.

It must remain true always that the surroundings inevitably influence any observer's judgment and appreciation. For instance, any hunter will probably at once assent to the statement that the love challenge of the bull elk, heard, as it so often is, on a frosty night in the mountains, echoing down through the pines, is one of the most musical of all nature's major sounds. But if heard close by, or in a zoölogical garden, it loses almost every element of attraction.

This same elk, or, to give him his proper name, Wapiti, affords a very curious instance of an entirely trustworthy and well qualified observer being utterly mistaken in his judgement. The late General Dodge was one of our best writers upon sport in the plains and among the Rockies in the old days. He observed elk by the thousand under all conditions. Yet he actually believed that the elk was a mild-mannered beast and that the males hardly ever fought among themselves! To most of us it seems incomprehensible that even a day's experience, where there is any large mixed herd of elk, should not convince any man of the exact contrary. Wapiti bulls fight together even more freely than black tail or white tail bucks, and are also more apt to turn upon outside enemies.

Then there are entirely different problems in observation; problems concerning the seemingly unaccountable differences two similar species will display under like conditions. Why is it that among the grouse of the plains, the largest of all those found within our boundaries, the sage grouse is the tamest? While among the grouse of the woods, the spruce grouse, which is the smallest, is the tamest? The ruffed grouse is tame also, in out-of-the-way localities, but he is never guilty of such utter folly as the stupid, handsome little spruce grouse. Is the tameness of the white goat when compared with the mountain sheep a parallel case? Or does the white goat become as wary as the sheep when equally persecuted? My own experience would lead me to answer the latter question in the negative; but I should much like to have the judgment of men who have seen more of both animals.

I have here mentioned only a few instances where there is need of trained observation among hunters and hunter naturalists. Each man should school himself to accuracy of observation. And yet each man should remember that not only he himself may err, but that the same animal may act in an entirely different manner under different conditions, or indeed under the same conditions. Some of the seemingly inexplicable differences in the character and habits of different creatures which I have mentioned above are doubtless due to differences in the observer, and equally without doubt some of them are due to variation in the animal itself, this variation being either individual, seasonal or local. Only by numerous observations taken by keen and trained observers would it be possible to reconcile or explain these differences. Only when such observers are sufficiently numerous will we ever get really satisfactory life histories of the rarer and more interesting wild beasts; and surely the production of such a life history is better worth while than mere hunting either with gun or camera—good in itself though this mere hunting may be.

****

As a founding and influential member of the Boone and Crockett Club, Roosevelt figured prominently in the early efforts of this venerable organization (which today, well over a century after its founding, is as active and influential as ever). Indeed, it is generally accepted that the concept of such an organization, intended both to function as a clearinghouse for big game records and to bring men of kindred interests together for social and intellectual interchange, originated at a dinner in December 1887 when Roosevelt broached the subject. From the outset he contributed to the club in a significant fashion. This included writing and serving in an editorial capacity for a number of the club's early publications. This piece, which is based on his experiences hunting antelopes (or pronghorns) in the Badlands as a young man, is a good case in point. It comes from American Big-Game Hunting: The Book of the Boone and Crockett Club *(New York: Forest and Stream Publishing, 1893; pp. 129–139), which he coedited with George Bird Grinnell. That work also appeared the same year in Edinburgh, Scotland, under the imprint of David Douglas. The book has been reprinted at least twice: it was reissued in 1901 by the original publisher and then in 1983, in a limited edition of 450 copies, by the Boone and Crockett Club. Fuller details of this and other Boone and Crockett Club publications can be obtained from M. L. Biscotti's* American Sporting Book Series *(Madison, Ohio: Sunrise Publishing Company, 1994).*

COURSING THE PRONGBUCK

THE prongbuck is the most characteristic and distinctive of American game animals. Zoölogically speaking, its position is unique. It is the only hollow-horned ruminant which sheds its horns. We speak of it as an antelope, and it does of course represent on our prairies the antelopes of the Old World, and is a distant relative of theirs; but it stands apart from all other horned animals. Its position in the natural world is almost as lonely as that of the giraffe.

The chase of the prongbuck has always been to me very attractive, but especially so when carried on by coursing it with greyhounds. Any man who has lived much in the cow-country, and has wandered about a good deal over the great plains, is of course familiar with this gallant little beast, and has probably had to rely upon it very frequently for a supply of fresh meat. On my ranch it has always been the animal which yielded us most of the fresh meat we had in the spring and summer. Of course at such times we killed only bucks, and even these only when we positively needed the flesh.

In all its ways and habits the prongbuck differs as much from deer and elk as from goat and sheep. Now that the buffalo has gone, it is the only game really at home on the wide plains. It is a striking-looking little creature, with its big bulging eyes, single-pronged horns, and the sharply contrasted coloration of its coat; this coat, by the way, being composed of curiously course and brittle hair. In marked contrast to deer, antelope never seek to elude observation; all they care for is to be able to see themselves. As they have good noses and wonderful eyes, and as they live by preference where there is little or no cover, shots at them are usually obtained only at far longer range than is the case with other game; and yet, as they are easily seen, and often stand looking at the hunter just barely within very long rifle-range, they are always tempting their pursuer to the expenditure of cartridges. More shots are wasted at antelope than at any other game. They would be even harder to secure were it not that they are subject to fits of panic, folly, or excessive curiosity, which occasionally put them fairly at the mercy of the rifle-bearing hunter.

Prongbucks are very fast runners indeed, even faster than deer. They vary greatly in speed, however, precisely as is the case with deer; in fact, I think that the average hunter makes altogether too little account of this individual variation among different animals of the same kind. Under the same conditions different deer and antelope vary in speed and wariness, exactly as bears and cougars vary in cunning and ferocity. When in perfect condition a full-grown buck antelope, from its strength and size, is faster and more enduring than an old doe; but a fat buck, before the rut has begun, will often be pulled down by a couple of good greyhounds much more speedily than a flying yearling or two-year-old doe. Under favorable circumstances, when the antelope was jumped near by, I have seen one overhauled and seized by a single first-class greyhound; and, on the other hand, I have more than once seen a pronghorn run away from a whole pack of just as good dogs. With a fair start, and on good ground, a thoroughbred horse, even though handicapped by the weight of a rider, will run down an antelope; but this is a feat which should rarely be attempted, because such a race, even when carried to a successful issue, is productive of the utmost distress to the steed.

Ordinary horses will sometimes run down an antelope which is slower than the average. I had on my ranch an under-sized old Indian pony named White Eye, which, when it was fairly roused, showed a remarkable turn of speed, and had great endurance. One morning on the round-up, when for some reason we did not work the cattle, I actually ran down an antelope in fair chase on this old pony. It was a nursing doe, and I came over the crest of a hill, between forty and fifty yards away from it. As it wheeled to start back, the old cayuse pricked up his ears with great interest, and the minute I gave him a sign was after it like a shot. Whether, being a cow-pony, he started to run it just as if it were a calf or a yearling trying to break out of the herd, or whether he was overcome by dim reminiscences of buffalo-hunting in his Indian youth, I know not. At any rate, after the doe he went, and in a minute or two I found I was drawing up to it. I had a revolver, but of course did not wish to kill her, and so got my rope ready to try to take her alive. She ran frantically, but the old pony, bending level to the ground, kept up his racing lope and closed right in beside her. As I came up she fairly bleated. An expert with the rope would have captured her with the utmost ease; but I missed, sending the coil across her shoulders. She again gave an agonized bleat, or bark, and wheeled around like a shot. The cow-pony stopped almost, but not quite, as fast, and she got a slight start, and it was some little time before I overhauled her again. When I did I repeated the performance, and this time when she wheeled she succeeded in getting on some ground where I could not follow, and I was thrown out.

I have done a good deal of coursing with greyhounds at one time or another, but always with scratch packs. The average frontiersman seems to have an inveterate and rooted objection to a dog with pure blood. If he gets a greyhound, his first thought is to cross it with something else, whether a bull mastiff, or a setter, or a foxhound. There are a few men who keep leashes of greyhounds of pure blood, bred and trained to antelope-coursing, and who do their coursing scientifically, carrying the dogs out to the hunting-grounds in wagons and exercising every care in the sport; but these men are rare. The average man who dwells where antelope are sufficiently abundant to make coursing a success, simply follows the pursuit at odd moments, with whatever long-legged dogs he and his neighbors happen to have; and his methods of coursing are apt to be as rough as his outfit. My own coursing has been precisely of this character. At different times I have had on my ranch one or two high-class greyhounds and Scotch deerhounds, with which we have coursed deer and antelope, as well as jack-rabbits, foxes, and coyotes; and we have usually had with them one or two ordinary hounds, and various half-bred dogs. I must add, however, that some of the latter were very good. I can recall in particular one fawn-colored beast, a cross between a greyhound and a foxhound, which ran nearly as fast as the former, though it occasionally yelped in shrill tones. It could also trail well, and was thoroughly game; on one occasion it ran down and killed a coyote single-handed.

On going out with these dogs, I rarely chose a day when I was actually in need of fresh meat. If this was the case, I usually went alone with the rifle; but if one or two other men were at the ranch, and we wanted a morning's fun, we would often summon the dogs, mount out horses, and go trooping out to the antelope-ground. As there was a good deer-country between the ranch bottom and the plains where we found the prongbuck, it not infrequently happened that we had a chase after blacktail or whitetail on the way. Moreover, when we got out to the ground, before sighting antelope, it frequently happened that the dogs would jump a jackrabbit or a fox, and away the whole set would go after it, streaking through the short grass, sometimes catching their prey in a few hundred yards, and sometimes having to run a mile or so. In consequence, by the time we reached the regular hunting-ground, the dogs were apt to have lost a good deal of their freshness. We would get them in behind the horses and creep cautiously along, trying to find some solitary prongbuck in a suitable place, where we could bring up the dogs from behind a hillock, and give them a fair start after it. Usually we failed to get the dogs near enough for a good start; and in most cases their chases after unwounded prongbuck resulted in the quarry running clean away from them. Thus the odds were greatly against them; but, on the other hand, we helped them wherever possible with the rifle. We often rode well scattered out, and if one of us put up an antelope, or had a chance at one when driven by the dogs, he would always fire, and the pack were saved from the ill effects of total discouragement by so often getting these wounded beasts. It was astonishing to see how fast an antelope with a broken leg could run. If such a beast had a good start, and especially if the dogs were tired, it would often lead them a hard chase, and the dogs would be utterly exhausted after it had been killed; so that we would have to let them lie where they were for a long time before trying to lead them down to some streambed. If possible, we carried water for them in canteens.

There were red-letter days, however, in which our dogs fairly ran down and killed antelope—days when the weather was cool, and when it happened that we got our dogs out to the ground without their being tired by previous runs, and found our quarry soon, and in favorable places for slipping the hounds. I remember one such chase in particular. We had at the time a mixed pack, in which there was only one dog of my own, the others being contributed from various sources. It included two greyhounds, a rough-coated deerhound, a foxhound, and the fawn-colored crossbred mentioned above.

We rode out in the early morning, the dogs trotting behind us; and, coming to a low tract of rolling hills, just at the edge of the great prairie, we separated and rode over the crest of the nearest ridge. Just as we topped it, a fine buck leaped up from a hollow a hundred yards off, and turned to look at us for a moment. All the dogs were instantly spinning toward him down the grassy slope. He apparently saw those at the right, and, turning, raced away from us in a diagonal line, so that the left-hand greyhound, which ran cunningly and tried to cut him off, was very soon almost alongside. He saw her, however—she was a very fast bitch—just in time, and, wheeling, altered his course to the right. As he reached the edge of the prairie, this alteration nearly brought him in contact with the crossbred, which had obtained a rather poor start, on the extreme right of the line. Around went the buck again, evidently panic-struck and puzzled to the last degree, and started straight off across the prairie, the dogs literally at his heels, and we, urging our horses with whip and spur, but a couple of hundred yards behind. For half a mile the pace was tremendous, when one of the greyhounds made a spring at his ear, but, failing to make good his hold, was thrown off. However, it halted the buck for a moment, and made him turn quarter round, and in a second the deerhound had seized him by the flank and thrown him, and all the dogs piled on top, never allowing him to rise.

Later in the day we again put up a buck not far off. At first it went slowly, and the dogs hauled up on it; but when they got pretty close, it seemed to see them, and letting itself out, went clean away from them almost without effort.

Once or twice we came upon bands of antelope, and the hounds would immediately take after them. I was always rather sorry for this, however, because the frightened animals, as is generally the case when beasts are in a herd, seem to impede one another, and the chase usually ended by the dogs seizing a doe, for it was of course impossible to direct them to any particular beast.

It will be seen that with us coursing was a homely sport. Nevertheless we had very good fun, and I shall always have enjoyable memories of the rapid gallops across the prairie, on the trail of a flying prongbuck.

****

This piece originally appeared in volume 2 of The Encyclopaedia of Sport *(New York: G. P. Putnam, 1898; pp. 137–138), edited by Hedley Peek, earl of Suffolk and Berkshire, and F. G. Aflalo. Although its publication came at a later point in Roosevelt's life, it appears here to offer contrast with the previous piece. Whereas* Coursing the Pronghorn *is devoted to specific hunting experiences,* Pronghorn *is a general look at the animal and how it is hunted.*

PRONGHORN

The prongbuck (*Antilocapra americana*) is almost universally known in America as "antelope"; yet it is, in reality, not an antelope at all, but a very peculiar beast which zoologically stands in a position as unique as that of the giraffe, being the only hollow-horned ruminant which annually sheds its horns.

Pronghorns were formerly found all over the great plains of western North America from the Mississippi to the Pacific, and from Northern Mexico to the Saskatchewan. Like all other big game, their numbers have been very much reduced. They hold their own, of course, far better than great beasts like the bison and wapiti, where the conditions are similar: in many places where all three were formerly abundant the pronghorn is now the only survivor, though sadly thinned in numbers. But he is, when left to himself, purely a beast of the prairie and the open plains, and like all such beasts he vanishes far more quickly than those that dwell in the shelter of the tangled forests; the white-tail deer always outlasts him.

When much persecuted, pronghorns are driven into rough and even into wooded country, but their chosen ground is the open grassland. In power of eyesight they far surpass deer, and their noses are good. In consequence, they are very difficult to stalk; for they are always found far from cover. Their tactics are just the reverse of those of white-tail deer. The white-tail's one object is to avoid observation; he trusts to sheltering himself so that the hunter will not see him. The pronghorn doesn't care in the least whether he is seen or not, and indeed is usually found in some conspicuous position where he challenges attention: for all that he wishes is to be sure that he sees everything within half a mile or more. Formerly it was possible to take advantage of the curiosity of the prongbuck and lure him toward the hunter by means of a red handkerchief, or something similar; but there are very few regions nowadays where the game is so unsophisticated. At present pronghorns are usually killed by fair stalking. They are also sometimes followed on horseback with the rifle, and they afford the best sport of all when regularly coursed with greyhounds.

Stalking antelope is very different work from still-hunting deer, wapiti, and moose, or climbing after mountain sheep and goats. More than any of these sports it necessitates skill in the use of the long-range rifle, the shots being customarily taken at standing objects, a rather long distance off. There is no need for the noiseless stealth of the hunter who follows his quarry through thick woods, and though long walks over the rough prairie grass give plenty of exercise, they are, of course, wholly free from the difficulty and fatigue of mountaineering. But there is much need to show the stalker's skill in the actual approach to the game. If the pronghorn once sees the hunter, the latter's chances are gone, unless the quarry suffers from one of those queer, freakish fits which occasionally attack it. The hunter must spy out the land with such care as surely to get the first glimpse of the animals he is after. He may see them either feeding or lying down, for they graze and rest at all hours of the day. Once seen, I think the lying down animal is easier to approach, because it cannot see so far, and, moreover, it is not continually shifting its position and thereby increasing its chance of destroying the benefit of the very little shelter the hunter has. At first sight, it seems impossible to stalk anything on the plains, for to all appearance there is no cover whatever. Nevertheless, in most places the ground is not really perfectly flat. There are slight rolls, making very gentle hillocks and valleys; and there are small watercourses which here and there make cut banks, though only a few inches in height. Often a band of pronghorns will be in an entirely impossible position— indeed, I think I may say that this is generally the case; but if carefully watched and followed they are apt, sooner or later, to get into some position where it is possible to approach within long rifle range. A good part of the stalk must be made on hands and knees, and the remainder flat on one's stomach, hitching along by means of the elbows. Occasionally, of course, the animals are found in places where the hunter can get a close shot, but ordinarily they must be killed at long range. In consequence, they are usually shot at a much greater distance that any other American game, and from this it follows as a corollary that more cartridges are expended for every head bagged than in any other kind of hunting.

Pronghorns can run away from any ordinary horse; but when once they have taken their line of flight they hate to swerve from it, and advantage can often be taken of this peculiarity, by riding at an angle to their course, to get a shot at them.

When I did my first shooting on the plains, fifteen years ago, there was plenty of other game, and I rather looked down on pronghorns; but for the last five or six years I have followed them to the exclusion of everything, except an occasional deer or sheep, on the few occasions when I have been able to get out to my ranch.

For a fuller account of their habits and chase I would refer to my books, *The Wilderness Hunter*, *Hunting Trips of a Ranchman*, and *Ranch Life and the Hunting Trail*, and also to the chapters I have written on the subject in the three volumes of the Boone and Crockett Club.

PART II

In Search of the Strenuous Life

Introductory Note

Throughout adulthood, Roosevelt pursued sport whenever and wherever possible. His youthful experiences as a naturalist, and the years he spent in the Dakota Badlands, fostered a love of the outdoors and hunting that bordered on obsession. Certainly a corner of TR's soul belonged to the natural world, and the six pieces offered in this section provide considerable insight in that regard. They touch on a variety of subjects, all of which he held near and dear.

An inveterate reader (like many talented writers), Roosevelt consistently kept abreast of all that was new and noteworthy in the literature of sport and natural history. Furthermore, quite early in his career he began corresponding with individuals both in the United States and abroad who had interests similar to his own. Anyone who consults his voluminous personal papers soon realizes that the exchange of letters with persons such as Fred Selous and Abel Chapman gave him great pleasure as well as keeping him current of the latest developments in the naturalist world. "Literature of American Big-Game Hunting" is the result of an early TR foray into review-essay writing, which he later would engage in regularly.

TR also immensely enjoyed the art of storytelling. He was a master of the form, whether done by a cozy fireside, as the titles of two of the following pieces suggest, or offered through a literary medium. We see Roosevelt the rancher dealing with wolves and a man-killing bear, and the fact that ranching was in many senses little more than an excuse to hunt becomes manifest in other works included here. All these efforts are vintage Roosevelt, full of activity and animation of the sort in which he reveled. TR was always an outspoken advocate of the strenuous life, and as these selections demonstrate, he practiced what he preached.

While some biographers have argued he was so caught up in love of the chase that it affected his career, probably precisely the opposite holds true. In hunting and evening chats around remote hearths, in bone-tiring jaunts on horseback and endless hours spent in rugged terrain, Roosevelt found a much-needed balance to the cares of politics and the professional world. In that regard, it might also be worth noting that other American presidents — among them George Washington, Thomas Jefferson, Ulysses S. Grant, Grover Cleveland, Herbert Hoover, Dwight Eisenhower, and Jimmy Carter — have sought release through hunting and fishing. It is just that Roosevelt, typically, hunted as he did everything that meant anything to him — with matchless enthusiasm. Evidence of that enthusiasm is abundantly obvious in the tales that follow.

****

This piece appeared, unsigned, in American Big-Game Hunting: The Book of the Boone and Crockett Club *(New York: Forest and Stream Publishing, 1893; pp. 319–325), edited by Theodore Roosevelt and George Bird Grinnell. Anyone conversant with TR's writing will readily recognize his distinctive, often flamboyant style. In just a few pages, he presents an overview of some of the most important American writers on the outdoors. Interestingly, most of TR's analysis is as true today as it was more than a century ago. T. S. Van Dyke's* The Still Hunter *remains a "must read" for anyone interested in whitetails, and Henry David Thoreau and to a lesser degree John Burroughs are still held in high esteem as natural historians.*

LITERATURE OF AMERICAN BIG-GAME HUNTING

Throughout the pioneer stages of American history, big-game hunting was not merely a pleasure, but a business, and often a very important and in fact vital business. At different times many of the men who rose to great distinction in our after history took part in it as such: men like Andrew Jackson and Sam Houston, for instance. Moreover, aside from these pioneers who afterward won distinction purely as statesmen or soldiers, there were other members of the class of professional hunters—men who never became eminent in the complex life of the old civilized regions, who always remained hunters, and gloried in the title—who, nevertheless, through and because of their life in the wilderness, rose to national fame and left their mark on our history. The three most famous instances of this class are Daniel Boone, David Crockett, and Kit Carson: men who were renowned in every quarter of the Union for their skills as gamehunters, Indian-fighters, and wilderness explorers, and whose deeds are still stock themes in the floating legendary lore of the border. They stand for all time as types of the pioneer settlers who won our land: the bridge-builders, the road-makers, the forest-fellers, the explorers, the land-tillers, the mighty men of their hands, who laid the foundations of this great commonwealth.

Moreover, the class of men who follow hunting not as a business, but as the most exhilarating and health-giving of all pastimes, has always existed in this country from the very foundation of the republic. Washington was himself fond of rifle and shot-gun, and a skilled back-woodsman; and he was also, when at his Mount Vernon home, devoted to the chase of the gray fox with horse, horn, and hound. From that time to this the sport-loving planters of the South have relished hunting deer, bear, fox, and wildcat with their packs of old-fashioned hounds; while many of the bolder spirits in the new West have always been fond of getting time for a hunt on the great plains or in the Rockies. In the Northeastern States there was formerly much less heed paid to, or love felt for, the wilder kind of sports; but the feeling in their favor has grown steadily, and indeed has never been extinct. Even in this part of the country, many men of note have been, like Webster, devotees of the fishing-rod, the shot-gun, or the rifle; and of late years there has been a constantly increasing number of those who have gone back to the old traditions of the American stock on this continent, and have taken delight in the wild sports of the wilderness.

Yet there have been fewer books written by Americans about life in the American wilderness and the chase of American big game than one would suppose, — or at least fewer books which are worth reading and preserving; for there does not exist a more dismal species of literature than the ordinary cheap sporting volume. This paucity of good books is, however, not unnatural. In a new country, where material needs are very pressing, the men who do the things are apt to be more numerous than those who can write well about them when done. This is as it should be. It is a good thing to write books, but it is a better thing still to do the deeds which are worth being written about. We ought to have both classes, and highest of all comes he who belongs to both; but if we had to choose between them, we would of course choose the doer rather than the writer.

Nevertheless the writer's position is very important; and there is no delusion more hopeless than the belief of many excellent people to the effect that the man who has done most is necessarily he who can write best. The best books are those written by the rare men who, having actually done the things, are also capable of writing well about them when done. It is as true of hunting-books as of those relating to graver matters, that in very many cases he whose experiences are best worth recording is himself wholly unable to record them. No amount of experience and observation can supply the lack of the literary gift. Many of the old hunters tried their hands at making books, but hardly a volume they produced is worth preserving, save possibly as material which some better writer may handle at a future time. Boone wrote, or rather allowed a small pedant to write for him, a little pamphlet on his early wanderings in Kentucky; but its only value is derived from the fact that for certain of the events in early Kentucky history it is the sole contemporaneous authority. The biography published by or for Davy Crockett is somewhat better, but it is hard to say what parts of it are authentic and what not. Of course, a comparatively uneducated man may by some rare chance possess the true literary capacity; and the worst of all writers is the half-educated man, especially he who takes the newspapers as models whereon to found his style; while the mere pedant who takes his language solely from books and the schoolroom is but slightly better. But, taken as a rule, it may be stated that the man who writes well about life in the wilderness must not only have had long and thorough acquaintance with that life, but must also have had some good literary training.

There have been a few excellent books written by Americans upon the wilderness life and the wilderness game of this continent. Elliott's "South Carolina Field Sports" is a very interesting and entirely trustworthy record of the sporting side of existence on the old Southern plantations, and not only commemorates how the planters hunted bear, deer, fox, and wildcat in the cane-brakes, but also gives a unique description of harpooning the devil-fish in the warm Southern waters. General Marcy wrote several volumes upon life on the plains before the civil war, and in them devoted one or two chapters to different kinds of plains game. The best book upon the plains country, however, is Colonel Richard Irving Dodge's "Hunting Grounds of the Great West," which deals with the chase of most kinds of plains game proper.

Judge Caton, in his "Antelope and Deer of America," gave a full account of not only the habits and appearance, but the methods of chase and life histories of the prongbuck, and of all the different kinds of deer found in the United States. Dr. Allen, in his superb memoir on the bisons of America, and Hornaday, in his book upon the extermination of that species, have rendered similar service for the vast herds of shaggy-maned wild cattle which have vanished with such singular and melancholy rapidity during the lifetime of the present generation. Mr. Van Dyke's "Still-Hunter" is a noteworthy book which, for the first time, approaches the still-hunter and his favorite game, the deer, from what may be called the standpoint of the scientific sportsman. It is one of the few hunting-books which should really be studied by the beginner because of what he can learn therefrom in reference to the hunter's craft. The Century Co.'s magnificent volume "Sport with Gun and Rod" contains accounts of the chase of most of the kinds of American big game, although there are two or three notable omissions, such as the elk, the grizzly bear, and the white goat. Lieutenant Schwatka, in his "Nimrod in the North," has chapters on hunting the polar bear, the musk-ox, and the arctic reindeer.

All of the above hunting-books should be in the library of every American lover of the chase. Aside from these volumes, which deal specifically with big-game hunting, there are others touching on kindred subjects connected with wild life and adventure in the wilderness which should also be mentioned. Of course all the records of the early explorers are of special and peculiar interest. Chief among the books of this sort are the volumes containing the records of the explorations of Lewis and Clark; the best edition being that prepared by the ornithologist Coues, who has himself had much experience of life in the wilder regions of the West. Catlin's books have a special merit of their own. The faunal natural histories, from the days of Audubon and Bachman to those of Hart Merriam, must likewise be included; and, in addition, no lover of nature would willingly be without the works of those masters of American literature who have written concerning their wanderings in the wilderness, as Parkman did in his "Oregon Trail," and Irving in his "Tour on the Prairies"; while the volumes of Burroughs and Thoreau have of course a unique literary value for every man who cares for outdoor life in the woods and fields and among the mountains.

****

Consummate predators, wolves have always been a source of great fascination. In Roosevelt's time, the attitude that a good wolf was a dead wolf overwhelmingly prevailed. Things have changed dramatically, with the attempted reintroduction of red wolves into the Great Smoky Mountains National Park and of gray wolves into Yellowstone National Park. One constant remains, however: wolves generate great interest from humans. Roosevelt knew as much when he wrote this piece for the June 22, 1893, edition of an immensely popular publication for boys, the Youth's Companion *(the story appeared on p. 318). In it he hints at having had some personal experiences with wolves, but the heart of the tale derives from stories he garnered from others.*

TALES TOLD BY A RANCH FIRESIDE:
WOLFISH MARAUDERS

A round my ranch the wolves molest full-grown animals but seldom, and never, so far as I know, attack or threaten human beings. They often kill calves and colts, and in one or two rare instances I have known of their hamstringing and tearing to pieces cows and steers. Westward of the Rockies, however, from the great main divide of the continent to the coast-line of British Columbia, Washington and Oregon, the wolves are larger and fiercer.

Our plains wolf is usually called the buffalo wolf, and varies from gray to white in color. The great timber wolf which haunts the deep forests of the northern Rockies and the coast ranges resembles ours in color, but has better, and on the whole darker, fur; is a longer-legged, longer-toothed, more sinewy beast.

In winter the timber wolves become very bold, and then sometimes attack man. Whenever the snow is on the ground they become dangerous to the settlers' live stock. Sometimes singly, but more often in twos or threes, they will boldly assail the largest horse or horned animal. Unlike the panther they rarely make their main attack at the throat, preferring to hamstring their prey and then tear out the flanks and stomach.

A settler in northern Idaho once told me of the damage a small party of these great wolves inflicted on him, and the way in which he finally got rid of them.

His little outlying farm was situated in the heart of a great pine and spruce forest well up in the mountains. There were some beaver meadows along the banks of the stream by which his log house stood, and there were open glades in the valleys and on the hillsides, while a stump-dotted clearing surrounded his cabin.

He had put up a log barn and farm-yard corral; and his live stock consisted of a horse, a mare with her colt, a yoke of oxen for plowing his grain land, and a milch cow, together with four powerful dogs accustomed to battle with wild beasts.

Early one winter the wolves made their first descent upon him. The milch cow had been left out to pick up her living in the woods during the daytime, as it was certain that she would return at night to her calf in the yard. On the day in question, however, she did not come back; and early the next morning the settler started out to look for her, taking his dogs with him.

A mile from the house, in an open glade, the dogs suddenly struck the trail of some wild beast of a dangerous kind, as was indicated by the bristling of their hair and their low growling. This trail led up the mountain, but the settler called his dogs away from it and forced them to follow it back the other way until he came to a little glade, in which lay the remains of the cow.

There the ground was very much torn up, and in the soft soil were the footprints of several huge timber wolves. Following their tracks where they left the cow the settler soon discovered that there were three of them.

He came back that night and sat up in the clear, cold moonlight to get a shot at the marauders if they returned; but the cunning beasts circled around, got his wind and made off without giving him a chance at them. No animal is more difficult to outwit than one of these great wolves.

After this he carefully housed his stock at night and watched it during the day, keeping even the dogs from wandering of into the forest. One clear, cold day he took out his oxen to haul in some logs from a couple of miles up the mountain. On his second trip down some accident occurred which made it necessary for him to leave the yoke of steers hitched to a tree, and go back to the house for some tools.

He had no idea that there was any danger in thus leaving the animals, for it did not occur to him that the wolves would dare to make an assault in open daylight where he had been passing and repassing along the road.

He went down to the cabin, got the axe and whatever tools were needed, and returned toward the oxen with one of his dogs frisking beside him.

On nearing the place where the oxen had been left, the dog suddenly pricked up its ears and raced off ahead of him. Stopping for a moment to listen, he heard up the mountain-side a crashing and struggling in the bushes and a savage growling and snarling, and instantly knew that his poor steers had been attacked by the wolves.

Shouting at the top of his voice, he ran up toward the place and soon heard the clamorous baying of the dog. On reaching a bend in the road he saw before him a scene of destruction.

The three wolves had come down the road and suddenly assailed the oxen, which, yoked as they were to a heavy sledge, and in addition tied to a tree, were unable to either escape or to make any resistance. The savage beasts had overthrown them and torn them terribly, although in their frantic dying struggles the oxen had overturned the sledge and smashed many of the neighboring saplings and small trees.

When the man came up, the three wolves were ravening on the warm flesh, while the dog, at some distance off, was baying and afraid to come near them.

The wolves at first seemed inclined to resist the man's approach. His rifle had been left in the sledge, and was lying overturned in the snow some thirty feet from the wolves, so that he had only his axe.

He advanced toward them, shouting and brandishing his weapon, and the dog, taking courage, went on slightly ahead of him. Two of the wolves slunk slowly off; the third, a huge gray beast, stood with its forepaws on one of the oxen, glaring at him and declining to leave.

The settler came on to within ten yards and then skirted around to where his rifle lay in the snow, keeping a sharp lookout on the wolf for fear it might jump on him. On picking up the rifle he found that the snow had caked in the lock, and for a moment or two he was busy putting it in order.

During this time the great gray wolf wrenched the fore shoulder from the ox and trotted off with it into the forest. The two others then slouched along the edge of the clearing to join their comrade; but the settler was in time, by a quick shot, to take partial vengeance by breaking the back of the rearmost of the three.

The dog rushed forward and shook the dying beast and then, excited by the blood, dashed into the forest after the two others. He had not gone a hundred yards before the man heard him yell in agony, and hurrying toward him through the snow, found him lying with his throat and flanks cut open.

Evidently as soon as the two wolves had got out of rifle-shot they had turned savagely on the unfortunate dog and killed him.

The settler, furious at his loss and misfortune, instantly went down to the nearest neighbor to borrow two large steel bear-traps, which he intended to set by some bait.

Three nights afterward one of his enemies bearded him on his very threshold; for as one of the dogs was walking from the barn over to the house just after nightfall a great wolf suddenly galloped out of the darkness, overthrew and throttled the dog in the twinkling of an eye, though it was a large and strong beast, and started to drag the animal into the bushes.

The two remaining dogs, however, rushed forward to the rescue of their comrade, and as the man appeared at the same moment, the wolf sullenly drew off into the thicket. Immediately the man set one of the iron traps by the body of the dead dog, and went back into his house.

In an hour afterward the wolf returned. The carcass had been left not a hundred yards from the hut, and the spring of the trap and the savage growl of pain of the wolf were both distinctly audible.

Seizing a torch and his axe, the settler threw open the door and rushed out with his dogs, which raced ahead. As he ran up toward the trap a furi-

ous worrying and snarling told him that the trapped wolf was being throttled by the comrades of the dead dog.

On reaching the scene of conflict the torch showed the wolf held firmly by one forepaw, and yet holding his own fairly well against the two
powerful dogs, both of which he had wounded. However, they had him
fast, one by the side of the neck and the other by the flank, and the settler
put an end to the conflict with his axe.

After this he believed he was safe, as he did not suppose that the third
wolf would linger around the neighborhood where the other two had been
killed. For six weeks, indeed, he saw no sign of it. Then one day he came
across the huge footprints of the robber in the snow, where it had been
walking around and around the house. Again it went off and did not come
back until early in the spring.

This wolf was, as he saw by the tracks, the largest of the three—probably the one which had stood on the body of the ox and defied him as he
approached. The game had been driven by the snow from the neighboring mountains, and evidently the brute was very hungry.

One morning early the settler decided to go down the mountain, and
accordingly saddled his horse. In putting on the bridle the horse for some
reason took fright at him, broke off and ran away up the wood road. He
followed it at once.

After going half a mile he topped a slight rise and saw the horse in a
beaver meadow, some six hundred yards ahead. As he saw it he also
noticed a great gray figure come galloping out of the spruce woods
through the snow toward the unfortunate animal.

The horse saw his foe at the same moment, and started down the road
on a desperate run. But before he could get under way the wolf galloped
alongside and seized it by the outstretched hock with such violence that
the teeth met clean through the sinews, and the horse was brought down
on his haunches.

It gave a piercing whinny of despair, and the wolf let go for a moment.
But the instant the horse again attempted to start off it was seized by the
other hock and completely hamstrung. Before the man could come up its
flank was torn open and its life was extinct. Nevertheless the settler drove
off the wolf before it had a chance to snatch more than a mouthful or two.

He brought out the mare and dragged the saddle horse down to his
cabin, where he left it outside the door, intending to use it as bait the following day. That same evening, however, the wolf, evidently maddened
with hunger, visited the farm-house.

It was just dusk, and the mare and her colt were in the corral, when the great gray beast crept up to the outside and leaped suddenly over the high stockade to get at the colt, which ran frantically toward the mare. As the wolf followed, the mare, wheeling around, lashed out with her hind legs and struck him squarely in the face, breaking his lower jaw.

The scuffle had called out the dogs, which rushed furiously to the rescue. The wolf turned and galloped toward the stockade, but stunned by the mare's blow, he missed his jump the first time and fell backward. As he rose one of the dogs seized him by the ham.

He fought savagely, but with his broken under jaw he could do little damage. When the settler, roused by the tumult, rushed in with his rifle, it was to find the last one of the three beasts which had done him so much damage dying under the fangs of the dogs.

****

Mountain men gave the grizzly bear monikers such as "Old Ephraim" or simply "griz." They had a healthy respect for these massive, unpredictable creatures, and with good reason. Even today grizzlies can be deadly, and, as I can personally attest, any type of encounter with one is traumatic. (I once spent a night up a tree at the headwaters of Wyoming's Thorofare River, with a grizzly having free range of my camp.) Here Roosevelt relates the tale of a man-killer.

*Man-killing beasts always make for gripping reading. Those familiar with the books of Jim Corbett, who made a career of ending the career of man-eating tigers in India, will be well aware of this. Similarly, a recent movie (*The Ghost and the Darkness*) was based on J. H. Patterson's classic,* The Man-Eaters of Tsavo and Other East African Adventures. *The story printed here originally appeared on page 354 of the July 13, 1893, issue of the* Youth's Companion. *The piece also appears in* American Bears: Selections from the Writings of Theodore Roosevelt *(1983), edited by Paul Schullery. The short but scintillating tale is early evidence of TR's lasting fascination with bears, as members of the Roosevelt Classics Library will know from having read chapters in* The Wilderness Hunter *("The Black Bear" and "Old Ephraim, the Grisly Bear"), which was first published in the same year as this article. His first piece on the subject, however, was "Old Ephraim" in* Hunting Trips of a Ranchman *(1885).*

TALES TOLD BY A RANCH FIRESIDE:
A MAN-KILLING BEAR

The grizzly bear is without doubt the most formidable wild beast of North America, and the most dangerous antagonist to man. It must not be supposed, however, that the grizzly is likely to attack man unprovoked; though in the old days, at the beginning of the present century, the first trappers and hunters who crossed the great plains and the Rockies found these huge bears very fierce and aggressive.

But the advent of the white hunter, and later the introduction of the large-bored, breechloading rifle, soon worked a radical change in bear nature. The grizzlies of to-day do not eagerly assail and molest travellers as their forefathers did in the days of Lewis and Clark, and of the hardy adventurers who followed in the footsteps of these first explorers.

Yet even now bears are occasionally found which will assail men in certain circumstances. A she-bear with cubs, if the cubs are menaced, will often charge with reckless fury at any brute or human foe, although it is often the case that even a she-bear will flee with abject cowardice from an attack, leaving her cubs to their fate.

If a bear is suddenly surprised, where he sees no means of escape, he will often attack a man simply through dread or to get out of the way.

Finally there are a very few wicked and crafty old bears which will attack from sheer malice.

Almost every trapper past middle age who has spent his life in the wilderness has stories to tell about exceptionally savage bears of this kind. One of these stories was told in my ranch-house one winter evening by an old mountain hunter, clad in fur cap, buckskin hunting-shirt and leather trousers, who had come to the ranch at nightfall, when the cow-boys were returning from their day's labor.

The old fellow, who was known by the nickname of "Buckskin," had camped for several months in the Bad Lands but a score of miles away from my ranch. Most of his previous life had been spent among the main chains of the Rockies. After supper the conversation drifted to bears, always a favorite subject of talk in frontier cabins, and some of my men began to recount their own adventures with these great, clumsy-looking beasts.

This at once aroused the trapper's interest. He soon had the conversation to himself, telling us story after story of the bears he had killed and the escapes he had met with in battling against them.

In particular he told us of one bear which, many years before, had killed the partner with whom at the time he was trapping.

The two men were camped in a high mountain valley in northwestern Wyoming, their camp being pitched at the edge of a "park country"—that is, a region where large glades and groves of tall evergreen-trees alternate.

They had been trapping beaver, the animal which, on account of its abundance and the value of the fur, was more eagerly followed than any other by the old-time plains and mountain trappers. They had with them four shaggy pack-ponies, such as most of these hunters use, and as these ponies were not needed at the moment, they had been turned loose to shift for themselves in the open glade country.

Late one evening three of the ponies surprised the trappers by galloping up to the camp-fire and there halting. The fourth did not make his appearance. The trappers knew that some wild beast must have assailed the animals and had probably caught one and caused the others to flee for protection toward the place which they had learned to associate with safety.

Before dawn the next morning the two men started off to look for the lost horse. They skirted several great glades, following the tracks of the ponies that had come to the fire the previous evening. Two miles away, at the edge of a tall pine wood, they found the body of the lost horse, already partially eaten.

The tracks round about showed that the assailant was a grizzly of uncommon size, which had evidently jumped at the horses just after dusk, as they fed up to the edge of the woods. The owner of the horse decided to wait by the carcass for the bear's return, while old Buckskin went off to do the day's work in looking after traps, and the like.

Buckskin was absent all day, and reached camp after nightfall. His friend had come in ahead of him, having waited in vain for the bear. As there was no moon he had not thought it worth while to stay by the bait during the night.

The next morning they returned to the carcass and found that the bear had returned and eaten his full, after which he had lumbered off up the hillside. They took up his tracks and followed him for some three hours; but the wary old brute was not to be surprised. When they at last reached the spot where he had made his bed, it was only to find that he must have heard them as they approached, for he had evidently left in a great hurry.

After following the roused animal for some distance they found they could not overtake him. He was in an ugly mood, and kept halting every mile or so to walk to and fro, bite and break down the saplings, and paw the earth and dead logs; but in spite of this bullying he would not absolutely await their approach, but always shambled off before they came in sight.

At last they decided to abandon the pursuit. They then separated, each to make an afternoon's hunt and return to camp by his own way.

Our friend reached camp at dusk, but his partner did not turn up that evening at all. However, it was nothing unusual for either one of the two to be off for a night, and Buckskin thought little of it.

Next morning he again hunted all day, and returned to camp fully expecting to see his friend there, but found no sign of him. The second night passed, still without his coming in.

The morning after, the old fellow became uneasy and started to hunt him up. All that day he searched in vain, and when, on coming back to camp, there was still no trace of him, he was sure that some accident had happened.

The next morning he went back to the pine grove in which they had separated on leaving the trail of the bear. His friend had worn hob-nail boots instead of moccasins, and this made it much easier to follow his tracks. With some difficulty the old hunter traced him for some four miles, until he came to a rocky stretch of country, where all sign of the footprints disappeared.

However, he was a little startled to observe footprints of a different sort. A great bear, without doubt the same one that had killed the horse, had been travelling in a course parallel to that of the man.

Apparently the beast had been lurking just in front of his two pursuers the day they followed him from the carcass; and from the character of the "sign" Buckskin judged that as soon as he separated from his friend, the bear had likewise turned and had begun to follow the trapper.

The bear had not followed the man into the rocky piece of ground, and when the old hunter failed in his efforts to trace up his friend, he took the trail of the bear instead.

Three-quarters of a mile on, the bear, which had so far been walking, had broken into a gallop, the claws making deep scratches here and there in the patches of soft earth. The trail then led into a very thick and dark wood, and here the footprints of the man suddenly reappeared.

For some little time the old hunter was unable to make up his mind with certainty as to which one was following the other; but finally, in the decayed mold by a rotten log, he found unmistakable sign where the print of the bear's foot overlaid that of the man. This put the matter beyond doubt. The bear was following the man.

For a couple of hours more the hunter slowly and with difficulty followed the dim trail.

The bear had apparently not cared to close in, but had slouched along some distance behind the man. Then in a marshy thicket where a mountain stream came down, the end had come.

Evidently at this place the man, still unconscious that he was followed, had turned and gone upward, and the bear, altering his course to an oblique angle, had intercepted him, making his rush just as he came through a patch of low willows. The body of the man lay under the willow branches beside the brook, terribly torn and disfigured.

Evidently the bear had rushed at him so quickly that he could not fire his gun, and had killed him with its powerful jaws. The unfortunate man's body was almost torn to pieces. The killing had evidently been done purely for malice, for the remains were uneaten, nor had the bear returned to them.

Angry and horrified at his friend's fate, old Buckskin spent the next two days in looking carefully through the neighboring groves for fresh tracks of the cunning and savage monster. At last he found an open spot of ground where the brute was evidently fond of sunning himself in the early morning; and to this spot the hunter returned before dawn the following day.

He did not have long to wait. By sunrise a slight crackling of the thick undergrowth told him that the bear was approaching. A few minutes afterward the brute appeared. It was a large beast with a poor coat, its head scarred by teeth and claw marks gained in many a combat with others of its own kind.

It came boldly into the opening and lay down, but for some time kept turning its head from side to side so that no shot could be obtained.

At last, growing impatient, the hunter broke a stick. Instantly the bear swung his head around sidewise, and in another moment a bullet crashed into its skull at the base of the ear, and the huge body fell limply over on its side, lifeless.

****

The reader of this piece initially gets the impression that Roosevelt did relatively little hunting while vainly attempting to make a go of it as a rancher. However, delving deeper, here or elsewhere, the reader gradually comes to realize that hunting meant at least as much to TR as the daily drudgery of raising cattle in hardscrabble country. Indeed, more than one biographer has suggested that hunting offered him an escape from personal tragedies, and at no time was this more true than during the period of his life that produced grist for TR's literary mill that eventually resulted in The Wilderness

Hunter *(1893) and* Ranch Life and the Hunting-Trail *(1888).*

The current piece is a fairly extensive overview of more than a decade of hunting in the West, with information on all aspects of the sporting experience — guns and cartridges, game and tactics, woodsmanship and individual hunts. The piece first appeared in Hunting in Many Lands: The Book of the Boone and Crockett Club *(New York: Forest and Stream Publishing, 1895; pp. 278–317), edited by Theodore Roosevelt and George Bird Grinnell. This was the second work the pair had edited for the club, and today it is exceedingly rare, fetching prices of several hundred dollars on the out-of-print market. It was reprinted by the Boone and Crockett Club in 1986 in two forms — a limited clothbound edition of 500 copies and a paperbound edition of 2,000 copies.*

HUNTING IN THE CATTLE COUNTRY

The little hunting I did in 1893 and 1894 was while I was at my ranch house, or while out on the range among the cattle; and I shot merely the game needed for the table by myself and those who were with me. It is still possible in the cattle country to kill an occasional bighorn, bear or elk; but nowadays the only big game upon which the ranchman of the great plains can safely count are deer and antelope. While at the ranch house itself, I rely for venison upon shooting either blacktail in the broken country away from the river, or else whitetail in the river bottoms. When out on the great plains, where the cattle range freely in the summer, or when visiting the line camps, or any ranch on the heads of the longer creeks, the prongbuck furnishes our fresh meat.

In both 1893 and 1894 I made trips to a vast tract of rolling prairie land, some fifty miles from my ranch, where I have for many years enjoyed the keen pleasure of hunting the prongbuck. In 1893 the pronghorned bands were as plentiful in this district as I have ever seen them anywhere. A friend, a fellow Boone and Crockett man, Alexander Lambert, was with me; and in a week's trip, including the journey out and back, we easily shot all the antelope we felt we had any right to kill; for we only shot to get meat, or an unusually fine head.

In antelope shooting more cartridges are expended in proportion to the amount of game killed than with any other game, because the shots are generally taken at long range; and yet, being taken in the open, there is usually a chance to use four or five cartridges before the animal gets out of sight. These shots do not generally kill, but every now and then they do; and so the hunter is encouraged to try them, especially as after the first shot the game has been scared anyway, and no harm results from firing the others.

In 1893, Lambert, who was on his first hunt with the rifle, did most of the shooting, and I myself fired at only two antelope, both of which had already been missed. In each case a hard run and much firing at long ranges, together with in one case some skillful maneuvering, got me my game; yet one buck cost nine cartridges and the other eight. In 1894 I had exactly the reverse experience. I killed five antelope for thirty-six shots, but each one that I killed was killed with the first bullet, and in not one case where I missed the first time did I hit with any subsequent one. These five antelopes were shot at an average distance of about 150 yards. Those that I missed were, of course, much further off on an average, and I usually emptied my magazine at each. The number of cartridges spent would seem extraordinary to a tyro; and a very unusually skillful shot, or else a very timid shot who fears to take risks, will of course make a better showing per head killed; but I doubt if men with much experience in antelope hunting, who keep an accurate account of the cartridges they expend, will see anything out of the way in the performance. During the thirteen years I have hunted in the West I have always, where possible, kept a record of the number of cartridges expended for every head of game killed, and of the distances at which it was shot. I have found that with bison, bears, moose, elk, caribou, bighorn and white goats, where the animals shot at were mostly of large size and usually stationary, and where the mountainous or wooded country gave chance for a close approach, the average distance at which I have killed the game has been eighty yards, and the average number of cartridges expended per head slain three: one of these representing the death shot and the others standing either for misses outright, of which there were not very many, or else for wounding game which escaped, or which I afterward overtook, or for stopping cripples or charging beasts. I have killed but one cougar and two peccaries, using but one cartridge for each; all three were close up. At wolves and coyotes I have generally had to take running shots at very long range, and I have killed but two for fifty cartridges. Blacktail deer I have generally shot at about ninety yards, at an expenditure of about four cartridges apiece. Whitetail I have killed at shorter range; but the shots were generally running, often taken under difficult circumstances, so that my expenditure of cartridges was rather larger. Antelope, on the other hand, I have on the average shot at a little short of 150 yards, and they have cost me about nine cartridges apiece. This, of course, as I have explained above, does not mean that I have missed eight out of nine antelope, for often the entire nine cartridges would be spent at an antelope which I eventually got. It merely means that, counting all the shots of every description fired at antelope, I had one head to show for each nine cartridges expended. Thus, the first antelope I shot in 1893 cost me ten cartridges, of which three hit him, while the seven that missed were fired at over 400 yards' distance while he was running. We saw him while we were with the wagon. As we had many miles to go before sunset, we cared nothing about frightening other game, and, as we had no fresh meat, it was worth while to take some chances to procure it. When I first fired, the prongbuck had already been shot at and was in full flight. He was beyond all reasonable range, but some of our bullets went over him and he began to turn. By running to one side I got a shot at him at a little over 400 paces, as he slowed to a walk, bewildered by the firing, and the bullet broke his hip. I missed him two or three times as he plunged off, and then by hard running down a water course got a shot at 180 paces and broke his shoulder, and broke his neck with another bullet when I came up. This one was shot while going out to the hunting ground. While there, Lambert killed four or five; most of the meat we gave away. I did not fire again until on our return, when I killed another buck one day while we were riding with the wagon.

The day was gray and overcast. There were slight flurries of snow, and the cold wind chilled us as it blew across the endless reaches of sad-colored prairie. Behind us loomed Sentinel Butte, and all around the rolling surface was broken by chains of hills, by patches of bad lands, or by isolated, saddle-shaped mounds. The ranch wagon jolted over the uneven sward, and plunged in and out of the dry beds of the occasional water courses; for we were following no road, but merely striking northward across the prairie toward the P. K. ranch. We went at a good pace, for the afternoon was bleak, the wagon was lightly loaded, and the Sheriff, who was serving for the nonce as our teamster and cook, kept the two gaunt, wild-looking horses trotting steadily. Lambert and I rode to one side on our unkempt cow ponies, our rifles slung across the saddle bows.

Our stock of fresh meat was getting low and we were anxious to shoot something; but in the early hours of the afternoon we saw no game. Small parties of horned larks ran along the ground ahead of the wagon, twittering plaintively as they rose, and occasional flocks of longspurs flew hither and thither; but of larger life we saw nothing, save occasional bands of range horses. The drought had been very severe and we were far from the river, so that we saw no horned stock. Horses can travel much further to water than cattle, and, when the springs dry up, they stay much further out on the prairie.

At last we did see a band of four antelope, lying in the middle of a wide plain, but they saw us before we saw them, and the ground was so barren of cover that it was impossible to get near them. Moreover, they were very shy and ran almost as soon as we got our eyes on them. For an hour or two after this we jogged along without seeing anything, while the gray clouds piled up in the west and the afternoon began to darken; then, just after passing Saddle Butte, we struck a rough prairie road, which we knew led to the P. K. ranch—a road very faint in places, while in others the wheels had sunk deep in the ground and made long, parallel ruts.

Almost immediately after striking this road, on topping a small rise, we discovered a young prongbuck standing off a couple of hundred yards to one side, gazing at the wagon with that absorbed curiosity which in this game so often conquers its extreme wariness and timidity, to a certain extent offsetting the advantage conferred upon it by its marvelous vision. The little antelope stood broadside, too, gazing at us out of its great bulging eyes, the sharply contrasted browns and whites of its coat showing plainly. Lambert and I leaped off our horses immediately, and I knelt and pulled the trigger; but the cartridge snapped, and the little buck, wheeling around, cantered off, the white hairs on its rump all erect, as is always the case with the pronghorn when under the influence of fear and excitement. My companion took a hasty, running shot, with no more effect than changing the canter into a breakneck gallop; and, though we opened on it as it ran, it went unharmed over the crest of rising ground in front. We ran after it as hard as we could pelt up the hill, into a slight valley, and then up another rise, and again got a glimpse of it standing, but this time further off than before; and again our shots went wild.

However, the antelope changed its racing gallop to a canter while still in sight, going slower and slower, and, what was rather curious, it did not seem much frightened. We were naturally a good deal chagrined at our shooting and wished to retrieve ourselves, if possible; so we ran back to the wagon, got our horses and rode after the buck. He had continued his flight in a straight line, gradually slackening his pace, and a mile's brisk gallop enabled us to catch a glimpse of him, far ahead and merely walking. The wind was bad, and we decided to sweep off and try to circle round ahead of him. Accordingly, we dropped back, turned into a slight hollow to the right, and galloped hard until we came to a series of low buttes, when we turned more to the left; and, when we judged that we were about across the antelope's line of march, leaped from our horses, threw the reins over their heads, and left them standing, while we stole up the nearest rise; and, when, close to the top, took off our caps and pushed ourselves forward, flat on our faces, to peep over. We had judged the distance well, for we saw the antelope at once, now stopping to graze. Drawing back, we ran along some little distance nearer, then drew up over the same rise. He was only about 125 yards off, and this time there was no excuse for my failing to get him; but fail I did, and away the buck raced again, with both of us shooting. My first two shots were misses, but I kept correcting my aim and holding further in front of the flying beast. My last shot was taken just as the antelope reached the edge of the broken country, in which he would have been safe; and almost as I pulled the trigger I had the satisfaction of seeing him pitch forward and, after turning a complete somersault, lie motionless. I had broken his neck. He had cost us a good many cartridges, and, though my last shot was well aimed, there was doubtless considerable chance in my hitting him, while there was no excuse at all for at least one of my previous misses. Nevertheless, all old hunters know that there is no other kind of shooting in which so many cartridges are expended for every head of game bagged.

As we knelt down to butcher the antelope, the clouds broke and the rain fell. Hastily we took off the saddle and hams, and, packing them behind us on our horses, loped to the wagon in the teeth of the cold storm. When we overtook it, after some sharp riding, we threw in the meat, and not very much later, when the day was growing dusky, caught sight of the group of low ranch buildings toward which we had been headed. We were received with warm hospitality, as one always is in a ranch country. We dried our steaming clothes inside the warm ranch house and had a good supper, and that night we rolled up in our blankets and tarpaulins, and slept soundly in the lee of a big haystack. The ranch house stood in the winding bottom of a creek; the flanking hills were covered with stunted cedar, while dwarf cottonwood and box elder grew by the pools in the half-dried creek bed.

Next morning we had risen by dawn. The storm was over, and it was clear and cold. Before sunrise we had started. We were only some thirty miles from my ranch, and I directed the Sheriff how to go there, by striking east until he came to the main divide, and then following that down till he got past a certain big plateau, when a turn to the right down any of the coulees would bring him into the river bottom near the ranch house. We wished ourselves to ride off to one side and try to pick up another antelope. However, the Sheriff took the wrong turn after getting to the divide, and struck the river bottom some fifteen miles out of his way, so that we reached the ranch a good many hours before he did.

When we left the wagon we galloped straight across country, looking out from the divide across the great rolling landscape, every feature standing clear through the frosty air. Hour after hour we galloped on and on over the grassy seas in the glorious morning. Once we stopped, and I held the horses while Lambert stalked and shot a fine prongbuck; then we tied his head and hams to our saddles and again pressed forward along the divide. We had hoped to get lunch at a spring that I knew of some twelve miles from my ranch, but when we reached it we found it dry and went on without halting. Early in the afternoon we came out on the broad, tree-clad bottom on which the ranch house stands, and, threading our way along the cattle trails, soon drew up in front of the gray, empty buildings.

Just as we were leaving the hunting grounds on this trip, after having killed all the game we felt we had a right to kill, we encountered bands of Sioux Indians from the Standing Rock and Cheyenne River reservations coming in to hunt, and I at once felt that the chances for much future sport in that particular district were small. Indians are not good shots, but they hunt in great numbers, killing everything, does, fawns and bucks alike, and they follow the wounded animals with the utmost perseverance, so that they cause great destruction to game.

Accordingly, in 1894, when I started for these same grounds, it was with some misgivings; but I had time only to make a few days' hunt, and I knew of no other accessible grounds where prongbuck were plentiful. My foreman was with me, and we took the ranch wagon also, driven by a cowboy who had just come up over the trail with cattle from Colorado. On reaching our happy hunting grounds of the previous season, I found my fears sadly verified; and one unforeseen circumstance also told against me. Not only had the Indians made a great killing of antelope the season before, but in the spring one or two sheep men had moved into the country. We found that the big flocks had been moving from one spring pool to another, eating the pasturage bare, while the shepherds whom we met—wild-looking men on rough horses, each accompanied by a pair of furtive sheep dogs—had taken every opportunity to get a shot at antelope, so as to provide themselves with fresh meat. Two days of fruitless hunting in this sheep-ridden region was sufficient to show that the antelope were too scarce and shy to give us hope for sport, and we shifted quarters, a long day's journey, to the head of another creek; and we had to go to yet another before we found much game. As so often happens on such a trip, when we started to have bad luck we had plenty. One night two of the three saddle horses stampeded and went back straight as the crow flies to their home range, so that we did not get them until on our return from the trip.

On another occasion the team succeeded in breaking the wagon pole; and, as there was an entire absence of wood where we were at the time, we had to make a splice for it with the two tent poles and the picket ropes. Nevertheless it was very enjoyable out on the great grassy plains. Although we had a tent with us, I always slept in the open in my buffalo bag, with the tarpaulin to pull over me if it rained. On each night before going to sleep, I lay for many minutes gazing at the extraordinary multitude of stars above, or watching the rising of the red moon, which was just at or past the full.

We had plenty of fresh meat—prairie fowl and young sage fowl for the first twenty-four hours, and antelope venison afterward. We camped by little pools, generally getting fair water; and from the camps where there was plenty of wood we took enough to build the fires at those where there was none. The nights were frosty, and the days cool and pleasant, and from sunrise to sunset we were off riding or walking among the low hills and over the uplands, so that we slept well and ate well, and felt the beat of hardy life in our veins.

Much of the time we were on a high divide between the two creek systems, from which we could see the great landmarks of all the regions roundabout—Sentinel Butte, Square Butte and Middle Butte, far to the north and east of us. Nothing could be more lonely and nothing more beautiful than the view at nightfall across the prairies to these huge hill masses, when the lengthening shadows had at last merged into one and the faint glow of the red sun filled the west. The rolling prairie, sweeping in endless waves to the feet of the great hills, grew purple as the evening darkened, and the buttes loomed into vague, mysterious beauty as their sharp outlines softened in the twilight.

Even when we got out of reach of the sheep men we never found antelope very plentiful, and they were shy, and the country was flat, so that the stalking was extremely difficult; yet I had pretty good sport. The first animal I killed was a doe, shot for meat, because I had twice failed to get bucks at which I emptied my magazine at long range, and we were all feeling hungry for venison. After that I killed nothing but bucks. Of the five antelope killed, one I got by a headlong gallop to cut off his line of flight. As sometimes happens with this queer, erratic animal, when the buck saw that I was trying to cut off his flight he simply raced ahead just as hard as he knew how, and, as my pony was not fast, he got to the little pass for which he was headed 200 yards ahead of me. I then jumped off, and his curiosity made him commit the fatal mistake of halting for a moment to look round at me. He was standing end on, and offered a very small mark at 200 yards; but I made a good line shot, and, though I held a trifle too high, I hit him in the head, and down he came. Another buck I shot from under the wagon early one morning as he was passing just beyond the picketed horses. The other three I got after much maneuvering and long, tedious stalks.

In some of the stalks, after infinite labor, and perhaps after crawling on all fours for an hour, or pulling myself flat on my face among some small sagebrush for ten or fifteen minutes, the game took alarm and went off. Too often, also, when I finally did get a shot, it was under such circumstances that I missed. Sometimes the game was too far; sometimes it had taken alarm and was already in motion. Once in the afternoon I had to spend so much time waiting for the antelope to get into a favorable place that, when I got up close, I found the light already so bad that my front sight glimmered indistinctly, and the bullet went wild. Another time I met with one of those misadventures which are especially irritating. It was at midday, and I made out at a long distance a band of antelope lying for their noon rest in a slight hollow. A careful stalk brought me up within fifty yards of them. I was crawling flat on my face, for the crest of the hillock sloped so gently that this was the only way to get near them. At last, peering through the grass, I saw the head of a doe. In a moment she saw me and jumped to her feet, and up stood the whole band, including the buck. I immediately tried to draw a bead on the latter, and to my horror found that, lying flat as I was, and leaning on my elbows, I could not bring the rifle above the tall, shaking grass, and was utterly unable to get a sight. In another second away tore all the antelope. I jumped to my feet, took a snap shot at the buck as he raced round a low-cut bank and missed, and then walked drearily home, chewing the cud of my ill luck. Yet again in more than one instance, after making a good stalk upon a band seen at some distance, I found it contained only does and fawns, and would not shoot at them.

Three times, however, the stalk was successful. Twice I was out alone; the other time my foreman was with me, and kept my horse while I maneuvered hither and thither, and finally succeeded in getting into range. In both the first instances I got a standing shot but on this last occasion, when my foreman was with me, two of the watchful does which were in the band saw me before I could get a shot at the old buck. I was creeping up a low washout, and, by ducking hastily down again and running back and up a side coulee, I managed to get within long range of the band as they cantered off, not yet thoroughly alarmed. The buck was behind, and I held just ahead of him. He plunged to the shot, but went off over the hill crest. When I had panted up to the ridge, I found him dead just beyond.

One of the antelope I killed while I was on foot at nightfall, a couple of miles from the wagon; I left the shoulders and neck, carrying in the rest of the carcass on my back. On the other occasion I had my horse with me and took in the whole antelope, packing it behind the saddle, after it was dressed and the legs cut off below the knees. In packing an antelope or deer behind the saddle, I always cut slashes through the sinews of the legs just above the joints; then I put the buck behind the saddle, run the picket rope from the horn of the saddle, under the belly of the horse, through the slashes in the legs on the other side, bring the end back, swaying well down on it, and fasten it to the horn; then I repeat the same feat for the other side. Packed in this way, the carcass always rides perfectly steady, and can not, by any possibility, shake loose. Of course, a horse has to have some little training before it will submit to being packed.

The above experiences are just about those which befall the average ranchman when he is hunting antelope. To illustrate how much less apt he is to spend as many shots while after other game, I may mention the last mountain sheep and last deer I killed, each of which cost me but a single cartridge.

The bighorn was killed in the fall of 1894, while I was camped on the Little Missouri, some ten miles below my ranch. The bottoms were broad and grassy, and were walled in by rows of high, steep bluffs, with back of them a mass of broken country, in many places almost impassable for horses. The wagon was drawn up on the edge of the fringe of tall cottonwoods which stretched along the brink of the shrunken river. The weather had grown cold, and at night the frost gathered thickly on our sleeping bags. Great flocks of sandhill cranes passed overhead from time to time, the air resounding with their strange, musical, guttural clangor.

For several days we had hunted perseveringly, but without success, through the broken country. We had come across tracks of mountain sheep, but not the animals themselves, and the few blacktail which we had seen had seen us first and escaped before we could get within shot. The only thing killed had been a whitetail fawn, which Lambert had knocked over by a very pretty shot as we were riding through a long, heavily-timbered bottom. Four men in stalwart health and taking much outdoor exercise have large appetites, and the flesh of the whitetail was almost gone.

One evening Lambert and I hunted nearly to the head of one of the creeks which opened close to our camp, and, in turning to descend what we thought was one of the side coulees leading into it, we contrived to get over the divide into the coulees of an entirely different creek system, and did not discover our error until it was too late to remedy it. We struck the river about nightfall, and were not quite sure where, and had six miles' tramp in the dark along the sandy river bed and through the dense timber bottoms, wading the streams a dozen times before we finally struck camp, tired and hungry, and able to appreciate to the full the stew of hot venison and potatoes, and afterward the comfort of our buffalo and caribou hide sleeping bags. The next morning the Sheriff's remark of "Look alive, you fellows, if you want any breakfast," awoke the other members of the party shortly after dawn. It was bitterly cold as we scrambled out of our bedding, and, after a hasty wash, huddled around the fire, where the venison was sizzling and the coffee-pot boiling, while the bread was kept warm in the Dutch oven. About a third of a mile away to the west the bluffs, which rose abruptly from the river bottom, were crowned by a high plateau, where the grass was so good that over night the horses had been led up and picketed on it, and the man who led them up had stated the previous evening that he had seen what he took to be fresh footprints of a mountain sheep crossing the surface of a bluff fronting our camp. The footprints apparently showed that the animal had been there since the camp had been pitched. The face of the cliff on this side was very sheer, the path by which the horses scrambled to the top being around a shoulder and out of sight of camp.

While sitting close up around the fire finishing breakfast, and just as the first level sunbeams struck the top of the plateau, we saw on this cliff crest something moving, and at first supposed it to be one of the horses which had broken loose from its picket pin. Soon the thing, whatever it was, raised its head, and we were all on our feet in a moment, exclaiming that it was a deer or a sheep. It was feeding in plain sight of us only about a third of a mile distant, and the horses, as I afterward found, were but a few rods beyond it on the plateau. The instant I realized that it was game of some kind I seized my rifle, buckled on my cartridge belt, and slunk off toward the river bed. As soon as I was under the protection of the line of cottonwoods, I trotted briskly toward the cliff, and when I got to where it impinged on the river I ran a little to the left, and, selecting what I deemed to be a favorable place, began to make the ascent. The animal was on the grassy bench, some eight or ten feet below the crest, when I last saw it; but it was evidently moving hither and thither, sometimes on this bench and sometimes on the crest itself, cropping the short grass and browsing on the young shrubs. The cliff was divided by several shoulders or ridges, there being hollows like vertical gullies between them, and up one of these I scrambled, using the utmost caution not to dislodge earth or stones.

Finally I reached the bench just below the sky line, and then, turning to the left, wriggled cautiously along it, hat in hand. The cliff was so steep and bulged so in the middle, and, moreover, the shoulders or projecting ridges in the surface spoken of above were so pronounced, that I knew it was out of the question for the animal to have seen me, but I was afraid it might have heard me. The air was absolutely still, and so I had no fear of its sharp nose. Twice in succession I peered with the utmost caution over shoulders of the cliff, merely to see nothing beyond save another shoulder some forty or fifty yards distant. Then I crept up to the edge and looked over the level plateau. Nothing was in sight excepting the horses, and these were close up to me, and, of course, they all raised their heads to look. I nervously turned half round, sure that if the animal, whatever it was, was in sight, it would promptly take the alarm. However, by good luck, it appeared that at this time it was below the crest on the terrace or bench already mentioned, and, on creeping to the next shoulder, I at last saw it—a yearling mountain sheep—walking slowly away from me, and evidently utterly unsuspicious of any danger. I straightened up, bringing my rifle to my shoulder, and as it wheeled I fired, and the sheep made two or three blind jumps in my direction. So close was I to the camp, and so still was the cold morning, that I distinctly heard one of the three men, who had remained clustered about the fire eagerly watching my movements, call, "By George, he's missed; I saw the bullet strike the cliff." I had fired behind the shoulders, and the bullet, of course going through, had buried itself in the bluff beyond. The wound was almost instantaneously fatal, and the sheep, after striving in vain to keep its balance, fell heels over head down a crevice, where it jammed. I descended, released the carcass and pitched it on ahead of me, only to have it jam again near the foot of the cliff. Before I got it loose I was joined by my three companions, who had been running headlong toward me through the brush ever since the time they had seen the animal fall.

I never obtained another sheep under circumstances which seemed to me quite so remarkable as these; for sheep are, on the whole, the wariest of game. Nevertheless, with all the game there is an immense amount of chance in the chase, and it is perhaps not wholly uncharacteristic of a hunter's luck that, after having hunted faithfully in vain and with much hard labor for several days through a good sheep country, we should at last have obtained one within sight and earshot of camp. Incidentally I may mention that I have never tasted better mutton, or meat of any kind, than that furnished by this tender yearling.

In 1894, on the last day I spent at the ranch, and with the last bullet I fired from my rifle, I killed a fine whitetail buck. I left the ranch house early in the afternoon on my favorite pony, Muley, my foreman riding with me. After going a couple of miles, by sheer good luck we stumbled on three whitetail—a buck, a doe and a fawn—in a long winding coulee, with a belt of timber running down its bottom. When we saw the deer, they were trying to sneak off, and immediately my foreman galloped toward one end of the coulee and started to ride down through it, while I ran Muley to the other end to intercept the deer. They were, of course, quite likely to break off to one side, but this happened to be one of the occasions when everything went right. When I reached the spot from which I covered the exits from the timber, I leaped off, and immediately afterward heard a shout from my foreman that told me the deer were on foot. Muley is a pet horse, and he enjoys immensely the gallop after game; but his nerves invariably fail him at the shot. He stood snorting beside me, and finally, as the deer came in sight, away he tore—only to go about 200 yards, however, and stand and watch us with his ears pricked forward until, when I needed him, I went for him. At the moment, however, I paid no heed to Muley, for a cracking in the brush told me the game was close, and in another moment I caught the shadowy outlines of the doe and the fawn as they scudded through the timber. By good luck, the buck, evidently flurried, came right on the edge of the woods next to me, and, as he passed, running like a quarter horse, I held well ahead of him and pulled the trigger. The bullet broke his neck and down he went—a fine fellow with a handsome ten-point head, and fat as a prize sheep; for it was just before the rut. Then we rode home, and I sat in a rocking-chair on the ranch house veranda, looking across the river at the strangely shaped buttes and the groves of shimmering cottonwoods until the sun went down and the frosty air bade me to go in.

I wish that members of the Boone and Crockett Club, and big game hunters generally, would make a point of putting down all their experiences with game, and with any other markworthy beasts or birds, in the regions where they hunt, which would be of interest to students of natural history; noting any changes of habits in the animals and any causes that tend to make them decrease in numbers, giving an idea of the times at which the different larger beasts became extinct, and the like. Around my ranch on the Little Missouri there have been several curious changes in the fauna. Thus, magpies have greatly decreased in number, owing, I believe, mainly to the wolf-hunters. Magpies often come around carcasses and eat poisoned baits. I have seen as many as seven lying dead around a bait. They are much less plentiful than they formerly were. In this last year,

1894, I saw one large party; otherwise only two or three stragglers. This same year I was rather surprised at meeting a porcupine, usually a beast of the timber, at least twenty miles from trees. He was grubbing after sagebrush roots on the edge of a cut bank by a half-dried creek. I was stalking an antelope at the time, and stopped to watch him for about five minutes. He paid no heed to me, though I was within three or four paces of him. Both the luciver, or northern lynx, and the wolverine have been found on the Little Missouri, near the Killdeer Mountains, but I do not know of a specimen either that has been killed there for some years past. The blackfooted ferret was always rare, and is rare now. But few beaver are left; they were very abundant in 1880, but were speedily trapped out when the Indians vanished and the Northern Pacific Railroad was built. While this railroad was building, the bears frequently caused much trouble by industriously damming the culverts.

With us the first animal to disappear was the buffalo. In the old days, say from 1870 to 1880, the buffalo were probably the most abundant of all animals along the Little Missouri in the region that I know, ranging, say, from Pretty Buttes to the Killdeer Mountains. They were migratory, and at times almost all of them might leave; but, on the whole, they were the most abundant of the game animals. In 1881 they were still almost as numerous as ever. In 1883 all were killed but a few stragglers, and the last of these stragglers that I heard of as seen in our immediate neighborhood was in 1885. The second game animal in point of abundance was the blacktail. It did not go out on the prairies, but in the broken country adjoining the river it was far more plentiful than any other kind of game. It is greatly reduced in numbers now. Blacktail were not much slaughtered until the buffalo began to give out, say in 1882; but they are probably now not a twentieth as plentiful as they were in that year. Elk were plentiful in 1880, though never anything like as abundant as the buffalo and the blacktail. Only straggling parties or individuals have been seen since 1883. The last I shot near my ranch was in 1886; but two or three have been shot since, and a cow and calf were seen, chased and almost roped by the riders on the round-up in the fall of 1893. Doubtless one or two still linger even yet in inaccessible places. Whitetail were never as numerous as the other game, but they have held their own well. Though they have decreased in numbers, the decrease is by no means as great as of the blacktail, and a good many can be shot yet. A dozen years ago probably twenty blacktail were killed for every one whitetail; now the numbers are about equal. Antelope were plentiful in the old days, though not nearly so much so as buffalo and blacktail. The hunters did not molest them while the buffalo and elk lasted, and they then turned their attention to blacktails. For some years after 1880 I think the pronghorn in our neighborhood positively increased in numbers. In 1886 I thought them more plentiful than I had ever known them before. Since then they have decreased, and in the last two years the decrease has been quite rapid. Mountain sheep were never very plentiful, and during the last dozen years they have decreased proportionately less than any other game. Bears have decreased in numbers, and have become very shy and difficult to get at; they were never plentiful. Cougars were always very scarce.

There were two stages of hunting in our country, as in almost all other countries similarly situated. In 1880 the Northern Pacific Railroad was built nearly to the edge of the Bad Lands, and the danger of Indian war was totally eliminated. A great inrush of hunters followed. In 1881, 1882, and 1883 buffalo, elk and blacktail were slaughtered in enormous numbers, and a good many whitetail and prongbuck were killed too. By 1884 the game had been so thinned out that hide hunting and meat hunting had ceased to pay. A few professional hunters remained, but most of them moved elsewhere, or were obliged to go into other business. From that time the hunting has chiefly been done by the ranchers and occasional small grangers. In consequence, for six or eight years the game about held its own—the antelope, as I have said above, at one time increasing; but the gradual increase in the number of actual settlers is now beginning to tell, and the game is becoming slowly scarcer.

The only wild animals that have increased with us are the wolves. These are more plentiful now than they were ten years ago. I have never known them so numerous or so daring in their assaults on stock as in 1894. They not only kill colts and calves, but full-grown steers and horses. Quite a number have been poisoned, but they are very wary about taking baits. Quite a number also have been roped by the men on the round-up who have happened to run across them when gorged from feeding at a carcass. Nevertheless, for the last few years they have tended to increase in numbers, though they are so wary, and nowadays so strictly nocturnal in their habits, that they are often not seen. This great increase, following a great diminution, in the number of wolves along the Little Missouri is very curious. Twenty years ago, or thereabouts, wolves were common, and they were then frequently seen by every traveler and hunter. With the advent of the wolfers, who poisoned them for their skins, they disappeared, the disappearance being only partly explicable, however, by the poisoning. For a number of years they continued scarce; but during the last four or five they have again grown numerous, why I cannot say. I wish that there were sufficient data at hand to tell whether they have decreased during these four or five years in neighboring regions, say in central and eastern Montana. Another curious feature of the case is that the white wolves, which in the middle of the century were so common in this region, are now very rare. I have heard of but one, which was seen on the upper Cannon Ball in 1892. One nearly black wolf was killed in 1893.

I suppose all hunters are continually asked what rifles they use. Any good modern rifle is good enough, and, after a certain degree of excellence in the weapon is attained, the difference between it and a somewhat better rifle counts for comparatively little compared to the difference in the skill, nerve and judgment of the men using them. Moreover, there is room for a great deal of individual variation of opinion among experts as to rifles. I personally prefer the Winchester. I used a .45-75 until I broke it in a fall while goat-hunting, and since then I have used a .45-90. For my own use I consider either gun much preferable to the .500 and .577 caliber double-barreled Express for use with bears, buffalo, moose and elk; yet my brother, for instance, always preferred the double-barreled Express; Mr. Theodore Van Dyke prefers the large bore, and Mr. H. L. Stimson has had built a special .577 Winchester, which he tells me he finds excellent for grizzly bears. There is the same difference of opinion among men who hunt game on other continents than ours. Thus, Mr. Royal Carroll, in shooting rhinoceros, buffalo and the like in South Africa, preferred big, heavy English double-barrels; while Mr. William Chanler, after trying these same double-barrels, finally threw them aside in favor of the .45-90 Winchester for use even against such large and thick-hided beasts as rhinoceros. There was an amusing incident connected with Mr. Chanler's experiences. In a letter to the London *Field* he happened to mention that he preferred, for rhinoceros and other large game, the .45-90 Winchester to the double-barrel .577, so frequently produced by the English gun makers. His letter was followed by a perfect chorus of protests in the shape of other letters by men who preferred the double-barrel. These men had a perfect right to their opinions, but the comic feature of their letters was that, as a rule, they almost seemed to think that Mr. Chanler's preference of the .45-90 repeater showed some kind of moral delinquency on his part; while the gun maker, whose double-barrel Mr. Chanler had discarded in favor of the Winchester, solemnly produced tests to show that the bullets from his gun had more penetration than those from the Winchester— which had no more to do with the question than the production by the Winchester people of targets to show that this weapon possessed superior accuracy would have had. Of course, the element of penetration is only one of twenty entering into the question; accuracy, handiness, rapidity of fire, penetration, shock—all have to be considered. Penetration is useless after a certain point has been reached. Shock is useless if it is gained at too great expense of penetration or accuracy. Flatness of trajectory, though admirable, is not as important as accuracy, and when gained at a great expense of accuracy is simply a disadvantage. All of these points are admirably discussed in Mr. A. C. Gould's "Modern American Rifles." In the right place, a fair-sized bullet is as good as a very big one; in the wrong place, the big one is the best; but the medium one will do more good in the right place than the big one away from its right place; and if it is more accurate it is therefore preferable.

Entirely apart from the merit of guns, there is a considerable element of mere fashion in them. For the last twenty years there has been much controversy between the advocates of two styles of rifles—that is, the weapon with a comparatively small bore and long, solid bullet and a moderate charge of powder, and the weapon of comparatively large bore with a very heavy charge of powder and a short bullet, often with a hollow end. The first is the type of rifle that has always been used by ninety-nine out of a hundred American hunters, and indeed it is the only kind of rifle that has ever been used to any extent in North America; the second is the favorite weapon of English sportsmen in those grandest of the world's hunting grounds, India and South Africa. When a single-shot rifle is not used, the American usually takes a repeater, the Englishman a double-barrel. Each type has some good qualities that the other lacks, and each has some defects. The personal equation must always be taken into account in dealing with either; excellent sportsmen of equal experience give conflicting accounts of the performances of the two types. Personally, I think that the American type is nearer right. In reading the last book of the great South African hunter, Mr. Selous, I noticed with much interest that in hunting elephants he and many of the Dutch elephant hunters had abandoned the huge four and eight bores championed by that doughty hunter, Sir Samuel Baker, and had adopted precisely the type of rifle which was in almost universal use among the American buffalo hunters from 1870 to 1883— that is, a rifle of .45 caliber, shooting 75 grains of powder and a bullet of 550 grains. The favorite weapon of the American buffalo hunter was a Sharps rifle of .45 caliber, shooting about 550 grains of lead and using ordinarily 90 to 110 grains of powder—which, however, was probably not as strong as the powder used by Mr. Selous; in other words, the types of gun were identically the same. I have elsewhere stated that by actual experience the big double-barreled English eight and ten bores were found inferior to Sharps rifle for bison-hunting on the Western plains. I know nothing about elephant or rhinoceros shooting; but my own experience with bison, bear, moose and elk has long convinced me that for them and for all similar animals (including, I have no doubt, the lion and tiger) the .45-90 type of repeater is, on the whole, the best of the existing sporting rifles for my own use. I have of late years loaded my cartridges not with the ordinary rifle powder, but with 85 grains of Orange lightning, and have used a bullet with 350 grains of lead, and then have bored a small hole, taking out 15 or 20 grains, in the point; but for heavy game I think the solid bullet better. Judging from what I have been told by some of my friends, however, it seems not unlikely that the best sporting rifle will ultimately prove to be the very small caliber repeating rifle now found in various forms in the military service of all countries—a caliber of say .256 or .310, with 40 grains of powder and a 200-grain bullet. These rifles possess marvelous accuracy and a very flat trajectory. The speed of the bullet causes it to mushroom if made of lead, and gives it great penetration if hardened. Certain of my friends have used rifles of this type on bears, caribou and deer; they were said to be far superior to the ordinary sporting rifle. A repeating rifle of this type is really merely a much more perfect form of the repeating rifles that have for so long been favorites with American hunters.

But these are merely my personal opinions; and, as I said before, among the many kinds of excellent sporting rifles turned out by the best modern makers each has its special good points and its special defects; and equally good sportsmen, of equally wide experience, will be found to vary widely in their judgment of the relative worth of the different weapons. Some people can do better with one rifle and some with another, and in the long run it is "the man behind the gun" that counts most.

****

This is yet another selection from an anthology published by the Boone and Crockett Club and edited by Roosevelt and his good friend and fellow sportsman-naturalist George Bird Grinnell. In this instance the selection comes from Trail and Camp-Fire: The Book of the Boone and Crockett Club *(New York: Forest and Stream Publishing, 1897; pp. 230–237), the third volume in the anthology series and the last with which TR would be involved as an editor (Grinnell would serve as editor or coeditor of a further four books). This short piece includes several of TR's personal encounters with bruins — both grizzlies and black bears — and is written with his customary verve and flair. It was previously reprinted in* American Bears: Selections from the Writings of Theodore Roosevelt *(1983), edited by Paul Schullery.*

THE BEAR'S DISPOSITION

My own experience with bears tends to make me lay special emphasis upon their variation in temper. There are savage and cowardly bears, just as there are big and little ones; and sometimes these variations are very marked among bears of the same district, and at other times all the bears of one district will seem to have a common code of behavior which differs utterly from that of the bears of another district. Readers of Lewis and Clark do not need to be reminded of the great difference they found in ferocity between the bears of the Upper Missouri and the bears of the Columbia River drainage system; and those who have lived in the Upper Missouri country nowadays know how widely the bears that still remain have altered in character from what they were as recently as the middle of the century.

This variability has been shown in the bears which I have stumbled upon at close quarters. On but one occasion was I ever regularly charged by a grizzly. To this animal I had given a mortal wound, and without any effort at retaliation he bolted into a thicket of what, in my hurry, I thought was laurel (it being composed in reality I suppose of thick-growing berry bushes). On my following him up and giving him a second wound, he charged very determinedly, taking two bullets without flinching. I just escaped the charge by jumping to one side, and he died almost immediately after striking at me as he rushed by. This bear charged with his mouth open, but made very little noise after the growl or roar with which he greeted my second bullet. I mention the fact of his having kept his mouth open, because one or two of my friends who have been charged have informed me that in their cases they particularly noticed that the bear charged with his mouth shut. Perhaps the fact that my bear was shot through the lungs may account for the difference, or it may simply be another example of individual variation.

On another occasion, in a windfall, I got up within eight or ten feet of a grizzly, which simply bolted off, paying no heed to a hurried shot which I delivered as I poised unsteadily on the swaying top of an overthrown dead pine. On yet another occasion, when I roused a big bear from his sleep, he at the first moment seemed to pay little or no heed to me, and then turned toward me in a leisurely way, the only sign of hostility he betrayed being to ruffle up the hair on his shoulders and the back of his neck. I hit him square between the eyes, and he dropped like a pole-axed steer.

On another occasion I got up quite close to and mortally wounded a bear, which ran off without uttering a sound until it fell dead; but another of these grizzlies, which I shot from ambush, kept squalling and yelling every time I hit him, making a great rumpus. On one occasion one of my cow hands and myself were able to run down on foot a she grizzly bear and her cub, which had obtained a long start of us, simply because of the foolish conduct of the mother. The cub—or more properly the yearling, for it was a cub of the second year—ran on far ahead, and would have escaped if the old she had not continually stopped and sat up on her hind legs to look back at us. I think she did this partly from curiosity, but partly also from bad temper, for once or twice she grinned and roared at us. The upshot of it was that I got within range and put a bullet in the old she, who afterwards charged my companion and was killed, and we also got the yearling.

Another young grizzly which I killed dropped to the first bullet, which entered its stomach. It then let myself and my companion approach closely, looking up at us with alert curiosity, but making no effort to escape. It was really not crippled at all, but we thought from its actions that its back was broken, and my companion foolishly advanced to kill it with his pistol. The pistol, however, did not inflict a mortal wound, and the only effect was to make the young bear jump to its feet as if unhurt, and race off at full speed through the timber; for though not full-grown it was beyond cubhood, being probably about eighteen months old. By desperate running I succeeded in getting another shot, and more by luck than anything else knocked it over, this time permanently.

Black bear are not, under normal conditions, formidable brutes. They are not nearly so apt to charge as is a wild hog; but if they do charge and get home they will maul a man severely, and there are a number of instances on record in which they have killed men. Ordinarily, however, a black bear will not charge at all, though he may bluster a good deal. I once shot one very close up which made a most lamentable outcry, and seemed to lose its head, its efforts to escape resulting in its bouncing about among the trees with such heedless hurry that I was easily able to kill it. Another black bear, which I also shot at close quarters, came straight for my companions and myself, and almost ran over the white hunter who was with me. This bear made no sound whatever when I first hit it, and I do not think it was charging. I believe it was simply dazed, and by accident ran the wrong way, and so almost came into collision with us. However, when it found itself face to face with the white hunter, and only four or five feet away, it prepared for hostilities, and I think would have mauled him if I had not brained it with another bullet; for I was myself standing but six feet or so to one side of it.

Ordinarily, however, my experience has been that bears were not flurried when I suddenly came upon them. They impressed me as if they were always keeping in mind the place toward which they wished to retreat in the event of danger, and for this place, which was invariably a piece of rough ground or dense timber, they made off with all possible speed, not seeming to lose their heads.

Frequently I have been able to watch bears for some time while myself unobserved. With other game I have very often done this even when within close range, not wishing to kill creatures needlessly, or without a good object; but with bears, my experience has been that chances to secure them come so seldom as to make it very distinctly worth while improving any that do come, and I have not spent much time watching any bear unless he was in a place where I could not get at him, or else was so close at hand that I was not afraid of his getting away. On one occasion the bear was hard at work digging up squirrel or gopher catches on the side of a pine-clad hill. He looked rather like a big badger when so engaged. On two other occasions the bear was working around a carcass preparatory to burying it. On these occasions I was very close, and it was extremely interesting to note the grotesque, half human movements, and giant, awkward strength of the great beast. He would twist the carcass around with the utmost ease, sometimes taking it in his teeth and dragging it, at other times grasping it in his forepaws and half lifting, half shoving it. Once the bear lost his grip and rolled over during the course of some movement, and this made him angry, and he struck the carcass a savage whack, just as a pettish child will strike a table against which it has knocked itself.

At another time I watched a black bear some distance off getting his breakfast under stumps and stones. He was very active, turning the stone or log over, and then thrusting his muzzle into the empty space to gobble up the small creatures below before they recovered from the surprise and the sudden inflow of light. From under one log he put up a chipmunk, and danced hither and thither with even more agility than awkwardness, slapping at the chipmunk with his paw while it zigzagged about, until finally he scooped it into his mouth.

The Yellowstone Park now presents the best chance for observing the habits of bears that has ever been offered, for though they are wild in theory, yet in practice they have come to frequenting the hotels at dusk and after nightfall, as if they were half tame at least; and it is earnestly to be wished that some Boone and Crockett member who, unlike the present writer, does not belong to the laboring classes, would devote a month or two, or indeed a whole season, to the serious study of the life history of these bears. It would be time very well spent.

****

Like its predecessor piece, this selection comes from Trail and Camp-Fire: The Book of the Boone and Crockett Club *(New York: Forest and Stream Publishing 1897; pp. 204–220), edited by George Bird Grinnell and Theodore Roosevelt. TR's ranch was situated along the Little Missouri, so its environs provided the raw material for much of his work. In this piece, he covers hunting for antelopes in some detail and includes mention of the only other "wild beasts of any size" (coyotes and wolves) still found in the region. As his remarks here (and elsewhere) suggest, wolves held him in somewhat of the same thrall as bears.*

It is interesting to note that today, thanks to the sort of conservation efforts TR pioneered, both large and small game are abundant in his old haunts. Oddly enough, the wolves are gone, but some index of Roosevelt's farsightedness is provided by the fact that he points out that "game may . . . increase in certain districts where settlements are thin." The reverse now holds true, not only along the Little Missouri but in vast areas where wolves once roamed. They are creatures that do not interact well with humans.

ON THE LITTLE MISSOURI

Formerly the prong-horned antelope were very plentiful on the immense rolling prairies which stretch back of the Little Missouri, where my ranch house stands. In the old days they could often be procured by luring them with a red flag—for they are very inquisitive beasts. Now they have grown scarce and wary, and must usually either be stalked, which is difficult, owing to their extreme keenness of vision and the absence of cover on the prairies, or else must be ridden into. With first-class greyhounds and good horses they can often be run down in fair chase; without greyhounds the rider can hope for nothing more than to get within fair shooting-range, and this only by taking advantage of their peculiarity of running straight ahead in the direction in which they are pointed when once they have settled into their pace. Usually antelope, as soon as they see a hunter, run straight away from him; but sometimes they make their flight at an angle, and as they do not like to change their course when once started, it is occasionally possible to cut them off from the point toward which they are headed, and get a reasonably close shot.

In the fall of 1896 I spent a fortnight on the range with the ranch wagon. I was using for the first time one of the new small-calibre, smokeless-powder rifles, a 30-30-160 Winchester. I had a half-jacketed bullet, the butt being cased in hard metal, while the nose was of lead.

While traveling to and fro across the range we usually moved camp each day, not putting up the tent at all during the trip; but at one spot we spent three nights. It was in a creek bottom, bounded on either side by rows of grassy hills, beyond which stretched the rolling prairie. The creek bed, which at this season was of course dry in most places, wound in S-shaped curves, with here and there a pool and here and there a fringe of stunted wind-beaten timber. We were camped near a little grove of ash, box-elder, and willow, which gave us shade at noonday; and there were two or three pools of good water in the creek bed—one so deep that I made it my swimming-bath.

The first day that I was able to make a hunt I rode out with my foreman, Sylvane Ferris. I was mounted on Muley. Twelve years before, when Muley was my favorite cutting pony on the round-up, he never seemed to tire or lose his dash, but Muley was now sixteen years old, and on ordinary occasions he liked to go as soberly as possible; yet the good old pony still had the fire latent in his blood, and at the sight of game— or, indeed, of cattle or horses—he seemed to regain for the time being all the headlong courage of his vigorous and supple youth.

On the morning in question it was two or three hours before Sylvane and I saw any game. Our two ponies went steadily forward at a single foot or shack, as the cow-punchers term what Easterners call "a fox-trot." Most of the time we were passing over immense grassy flats, where the mat of short curled blades lay brown and parched under the bright sunlight. Occasionally we came to ranges of low barren hills, which sent off gently rounded spurs into the plain.

It was on one of these ranges that we first saw our game. As we were traveling along the divide we spied eight antelope far ahead of us. They saw us as soon as we saw them, and the chance of getting to them seemed small; but it was worth an effort, for by humoring them when they start to run, and galloping toward them at an angle oblique to their line of flight, there is always some little chance of getting a shot. Sylvane was on a light buckskin horse, and I left him on the ridge crest to occupy their attention while I cantered off to one side. The prong-horns became uneasy as I galloped away, and ran off the ridge crest in a line nearly parallel to mine. They did not go very fast, and I held in Muley, who was all on fire at the sight of the game. After crossing two or three spurs, the antelope going at half speed, they found I had come closer to them, and turning, they ran up one of the valleys between two spurs. Now was my chance, and wheeling at right angles to my former course, I galloped Muley as hard as I knew how up the valley nearest and parallel to where the antelope had gone. The good old fellow ran like a quarter-horse, and when we were almost at the main ridge crest I leaped off, and ran ahead with my rifle at the ready, crouching down as I came to the sky-line. Usually on such occasions I find that the antelope have gone on, and merely catch a glimpse of them half a mile distant, but on this occasion everything went right. The band had just reached the ridge crest about 220 yards from me across the head of the valley, and had halted for a moment to look around. They were starting as I raised my rifle, but the trajectory is very flat with these small-bore smokeless-powder weapons, and taking a coarse front sight I fired at a young buck which was broadside to me. There was no smoke, and as the band raced away I saw him sink backward, the ball having broken his hips.

We packed him bodily behind Sylvane on the buckskin and continued our ride, as there was no fresh meat in camp, and we wished to bring in a couple of bucks if possible. For two or three hours we saw nothing. The unshod feet of the horses made hardly any noise on the stretches of sun-cured grass, but now and then we passed through patches of thin weeds, their dry stalks rattling curiously, making a sound like that of a rattlesnake. At last, coming over a gentle rise of ground, we spied two more prong-bucks, half a mile ahead of us and to our right.

Again there seemed small chance of bagging our quarry, but again fortune favored us. I at once cantered Muley ahead, not toward them, but so as to pass them well on one side. After some hesitation they started, not straight away, but at an angle to my own course. For some moments I kept at a hand gallop, until they got thoroughly settled in their line of flight; then I touched Muley, and he went as hard as he knew how. Immediately the two panic-stricken and foolish beasts seemed to feel that I was cutting off their line of retreat, and raced forward at mad speed. They went much faster than I did, but I had the shorter course, and when they crossed me they were not fifty yards ahead—by which time I had come nearly a mile. At the pull of the rein of Muley stopped short, like the trained cow-pony he is; I leaped off, and held well ahead of the rearmost and largest buck. At the crack of the little rifle down he went with his neck broken. In a minute or two he was packed behind me on Muley, and we bent our steps toward camp.

During the remainder of my trip we were never out of fresh meat, for I shot three other bucks—one after a smart chase on horseback, and the other two after careful stalks; and I missed two running shots.

The game being both scarce and shy, I had to exercise much care, and after sighting a band I would sometimes have to wait and crawl round for two or three hours before they would get into a position where I had any chance of approaching. Even then they were more apt to see me and go off than I was to get near them.

Antelope are the only game that can be hunted as well at noonday as in the morning or evening, for their times for sleeping and feeding are irregular. They never seek shelter from the sun, and when they lie down for a noonday nap they are apt to choose a hollow, so as to be out of the wind; in consequence, if the band is seen at all at this time, it is easier to approach them than when they are up and feeding. They sometimes come down to water in the middle of the day, sometimes in the morning or evening. On this trip, I came across bands feeding and resting at almost every time of the day. They seemed usually to feed for a couple of hours, then begin feeding again.

The last shot I got was when I was out with Joe Ferris, in whose company I had killed my first buffalo, just thirteen years before, and not very far from this same spot. We had seen two or three bands that morning, and in each case, after a couple of hours of useless effort, I failed to get near enough. At last, toward mid-day, after riding and tramping over a vast extent of broken sun-scorched country, we got within range of a small band lying down in a little cup-shaped hollow in the middle of a great flat. I did not have a close shot, for they were running about 180 yards off. The buck was rearmost, and at him I aimed; the bullet struck him in the flank, coming out of the opposite shoulder, and he fell in his next bound. As we stood over him, Joe shook his head, and said, "I guess that little .30-.30 is the ace"; and I told him I guessed so to.

Beside antelope, the only wild beasts of any size which are still left on the plains anywhere near the Little Missouri are wolves and coyotes. Coyotes are more or less plentiful everywhere in thinly settled districts.

They are not dangerous to horses or cattle, but they will snap up lambs, young pigs, cats, and hens, and if very hungry several often combine to attack a young calf. In consequence, farmers and ranchers kill them whenever the chance offers; but they do no damage which is very appreciable when compared with the ravages of their grim big brother, the gray wolf, which in many sections of the West is now a veritable scourge of the stock-men.

The big wolves shrink back before the growth of the thickly settled districts, and in the Eastern States they often tend to disappear even from districts that are uninhabited, save by a few wilderness hunters. They have thus disappeared almost entirely from Maine, the Adirondacks, and the Alleghanies, although here and there they are said to be returning to their old haunts. Their disappearance is rather mysterious in some instances, for they are certainly not all killed off. The black bear is much easier killed, yet the black bear holds its own in many parts of the land from which the wolf has vanished. No animal is quite so difficult to kill as is the wolf, whether by poison or rifle or hound. Yet, after a comparatively few have been slain, the entire species will perhaps vanish from certain localities.

But with all wild animals, it is a noticeable fact that a course of contact with man continuing over many generations of animal life causes a species so to adapt itself to its new surroundings that it ceases to diminish in numbers. When white men take up a new country, the game, and especially the big game, being entirely unused to contend with the new foe, succumbs easily, and is almost completely killed out. If any individuals survive at all, however, the succeeding generations are far more difficult to exterminate than were their ancestors, and they cling much more tenaciously to their old homes. The game to be found in old and long-settled countries is much more wary and able to take care of itself than the game of an untrodden wilderness. It is a very difficult matter to kill a Swiss chamois; but it is a very easy matter to kill a white goat after a hunter has once penetrated among the almost unknown peaks of the mountains of British Columbia. When the ranchmen first drove their cattle to the Little Missouri they found the deer tame and easy to kill, but the deer of Maine and the Adirondacks test to the full the highest skill of the hunter.

In consequence, after a time, game may even increase in certain districts where settlements are thin. This has been true of the wolves throughout the northern cattle country in Montana, Wyoming, and the western ends of the Dakotas. In the old days wolves were very plentiful throughout this region, closely following the huge herds of buffaloes. The white men who followed these herds as professional buffalo-hunters were often accompanied by other men, known as wolfers, who poisoned these wolves for the sake of their furs. With the disappearance of the buffalo the wolves diminished in numbers so that they also seemed to disappear. During the last ten years their numbers have steadily increased, and now they seem to be as numerous as they ever were in the region in question, and they are infinitely more wary and more difficult to kill.

Along the Little Missouri their ravages have been so serious during the past four years as to cause heavy damage to the stock-men. Not only colts and calves, but young trail stock, and in midwinter even full-grown horses and steers, are continually slain; and in some seasons the losses have been so heavy as to more than eat up all the profits of the ranchman. The county authorities have put a bounty on wolf scalps of three dollars each, and in my own neighborhood the ranchmen have of their own accord put on a further bounty of five dollars. This makes eight dollars for every wolf, and as the skin is also worth something, the business of killing wolves is quite profitable.

Wolves are very shy, and show extraordinary cunning both in hiding themselves and in slinking out of the way of the hunter. They are rarely killed with the rifle. I have myself shot but one with the rifle, though I have several times taken part in the chase of a wolf with dogs, and have if necessary helped the pack finish the quarry. They are occasionally trapped, but after a very few have been procured in this way the survivors became so wary that it is almost impossible even for a master of the art to do much with them, while an ordinary man can never get one into a trap except by accident. More can be done with poison, but even in this case the animal speedily learns caution by experience. When poison is first used in a district wolves are very easily killed, and perhaps most of them will be slain, but nowadays it is difficult to catch any but young ones in this way. Occasionally an old one will succumb, but there are always some who cannot be persuaded to touch a bait. The old she-wolves teach their cubs, as soon as they are able to walk, to avoid man's trace in every way, and to look out for traps and poison.

In consequence, though most cow-punchers carry poison with them, and are continually laying out baits, and though some men devote most of their time to poisoning for the sake of the bounty and the fur, the results are not very remunerative. The most successful wolf-hunter on the Little Missouri for the past year was a man who did not rely on poison at all, but on dogs. He is a hunter named Massingale, and he always has a pack of at least twenty hounds. The number varies, for a wolf at bay is a terrible fighter, with jaws like that of a steel trap and teeth that cut like knives, so that the dogs are continually disabled and sometimes killed, and the hunter has always to be on the watch to add animals to his pack. It is not a pack that would appeal, as far as looks go, to an Old-World huntsman, but it is thoroughly fitted for its own work. Most of the dogs are grey-hounds, whether rough or smooth haired, but many of them are big mongrels, part greyhound and part some other breed, such as bull-dog, mastiff, Newfoundland, bloodhound, or collie. The only two requisites are that the dogs shall run fast and fight gamely; and in consequence they form as wicked, hard-biting a crew as ever ran down and throttled a wolf. They are usually taken out ten at a time, and by their aid Massingale killed two hundred wolves during the year. Of course there is no pretence of giving the game fair play. The wolves are killed as vermin, not for sport. The greatest havoc is in the spring-time, when the she-wolves are followed to their dens, which are sometimes holes in the earth and sometimes natural caves. There are from three to nine whelps in each litter. Some of the hounds are very fast, and they can usually overtake a young or weak wolf; but an old dog-wolf, with a good start, unless run into at once, will surely get away if he is in running trim. Frequently, however, he is caught when he is not in running trim, for the hunter is apt to find him when he has killed a calf or taken part in dragging down a horse or steer, and is gorged with meat. Under these circumstances he cannot run long before the pack.

If possible, as with all such packs, the hunter himself will get up in time to end the worry by a stab of his hunting-knife; but unless he is quick he will have nothing to do, for the pack is thoroughly competent to do its own killing. Grim fighter though a great dog-wolf is, he stands no show before the onslaught of ten such hounds, agile and powerful, who rush on their antagonist in a body. They possess great power in their jaws, and unless Massingale is up within two or three minutes after the wolf is taken, the dogs literally tear him to pieces, though one or more of their number may be killed or crippled in the fight.

Other hunters are now striving to get together packs thoroughly organized, and the wolves may soon be thinned out; but at present they are certainly altogether too plentiful. Last fall I saw a number myself, although I was not looking for them. I frequently came upon the remains of sheep and young stock which they had killed, and once, on the top of a small plateau, I found the body of a large steer, while the torn and trodden ground showed that he had fought hard for his life before succumbing. There were apparently two wolves engaged in the work, and the cunning beasts had evidently acted in concert. While one attracted the steer's attention, the other, according to the invariable wolf habit, attacked him from behind, hamstringing him and tearing out his flanks. His body was still warm when I came up, but his murderers had slunk off, either seeing or smelling me. Their handiwork was unmistakable, however, for, unlike bears and cougars, wolves invariably attack their victim at the hindquarters, and begin their feast on the hams or flanks if the animal is of any size.

It will be noticed that in some points my observations about wolves are in seeming conflict with those of Mr. Grinnell; but I think the conflict is more seeming than real; and in any event I have concluded to let the article stand just as it is. The great book of Nature contains many passages which are hard to read, and at times conscientious students may well draw up different interpretations of the obscurer and least known texts. It may not be that either observer is at fault; but what is true of an animal in one locality may not be true of the same animal in another, and even in the same locality two individuals of a species may widely differ in their habits. On the Little Missouri, for the last two or three years, as formerly on the Sun River, hunting with dogs has been found to be a far more successful method of getting rid of wolves than trapping. Doubtless there are places where this would not be true. I am inclined to think that wherever wolves have been chased in one manner for a long time, a new method will at first prove particularly efficacious. When they have become thoroughly used to poison, traps have a great success. If they are persistently trapped, then poisoning does well.

I am particularly interested in what Mr. Grinnell's informants have described as to the occasional tolerance, even by hungry wolves, of kit foxes; for frequently a wolf will snap up a fox as quickly as he would a fawn, and once, at least, I have known of a coyote being killed by a wolf for food.

PART III

A Sportsman in His Prime

Introductory Note

During the important career interludes centering on public service in New York and military endeavors in the Spanish-American War, once Roosevelt entered the political arena, he needed the respites and recreation provided by sport. He also found himself ideally placed to speak and act as a proponent of conservation on a number of fronts. In this arena, he served as progenitor of America's system of national parks, fostered a sensible approach to forestry and forest protection, and heightened national awareness of the importance of wildlife protection and preservation. Although he to some degree backed away from his work with the Boone and Crockett Club, this was only because he realized that the organization had been solidly established and was moving nicely along a course that continues even in the present.

Roosevelt also hunted and traveled to remote, wild areas whenever possible during his presidency. When affairs of state kept him in or near Washington, he soothed his longings for wilderness by reading, corresponding with fellow hunters and naturalists, and writing. Indeed, the first years of the twentieth century, when Roosevelt was president and when several of the following pieces were published, were the busiest ones of TR's life, although the years just before and after his residence in the White House saw greater literary production.

All of the twelve selections included here come from these frenzied years, and they offer abundant evidence of the remarkable mental powers and unmatched energy of the sportsman in his prime. Two of the pieces, "Small Country Neighbors" and "In the Louisiana Canebreaks," actually appeared in the enlarged edition of *Outdoor Pastimes of an American Hunter,* published in 1908. However, the version of that work that forms a part of the Theodore Roosevelt Classics Library does not contain these stories, thereby justifying their inclusion. They first appeared in magazines, as did some of the other selections.

The remainder appeared in a now largely overlooked and forgotten two-volume work, *The Encyclopaedia of Sport.* Edited by Hedley Peek, earl of Suffolk and Berkshire, and F. G. Aflalo and published in 1898, this compendium is typical of many similar works that appeared in the late Victorian and Edwardian eras. Among the most important of these were the various volumes in the Badminton Library; two massive four-volume series, *The Gun at Home and Abroad* and *British Sports and Sportsmen;* the three-volume *Harmsworth Natural History;* and the four-volume *Wonders of Natural History.* The selections from *The Encyclopaedia of Sport* are of particular importance for several reasons. In addition to being largely unknown to today's readers, they offer compelling evidence of the author's ability to write in lucid fashion on hunting and related subjects for a general audience, indicate that TR was held in high regard by his fellow naturalists, and in many instances show just how much the status of wildlife (and knowledge about wildlife) has changed in the course of a century.

Roosevelt knew most of the contributors to these collections, and had the collections appeared at some other time in his career, his writings would likely have made more frequent appearances in their pages. Also, had the publisher with which he worked most frequently, Scribner's, produced works of this kind, he might have been more actively involved. However, most of the aforementioned collections, along with many others of a similar nature, were printed by English publishing houses. (In fact, even though *The Encyclopaedia of Sport* did come from New York–based G. P. Putnam, the firm also had London offices at that time.)

****

Originally published in the May 6, 1903, issue of the New York Sun, *this is the text of an (uncharacteristically) brief speech Roosevelt made advocating leaving Arizona's Grand Canyon untouched. The speech is particularly interesting thanks to obvious links with the issue of wilderness status. The piece was previously reprinted in* Wilderness Writings *(1986), edited by Paul Schullery. TR's advocacy of wilderness preservation was a long-standing part of his persona. His comments in an 1892 letter written to the editor of* Forest and Stream *magazine speak eloquently in this regard:*

> *It is of the utmost importance that the Park [Yellowstone] shall be kept in its present form as a great forest preserve and a National pleasure ground, the like of which is not found on any other continent than ours; and all public-spirited Americans should join with* Forest and Stream *in the effort to prevent the greed of a little group of speculators, careless of everything save their own selfish interests, from doing the damage to the whole people of the United States by wrecking the Yellowstone National Park. So far from having this Park cut down it should be extended.*

GRAND CANYON SPEECH, 1903

I have come here to see the Grand Cañon of Arizona, because in that cañon Arizona has a natural wonder, which, so far as I know, is in its kind absolutely unparalleled throughout the rest of the word. I shall not attempt to describe it, because I cannot. I could not choose words that would convey or that could convey to any outsider what that cañon is. I want to ask you to do one thing in connection with it in your own interest, and in the interest of the country.

Keep this great wonder of nature as it now is.

I was delighted to learn of the wisdom of the Santa Fe Railroad in deciding not to build their hotel on the brink of the cañon. I hope you will not have a building of any kind, not a summer cottage, a hotel or anything else, to mar the wonderful grandeur, sublimity, the great loneliness and beauty of the cañon.

Leave it as it is. You cannot improve on it; not a bit. The ages have been at work on it, and man can only mar it. What you can do is to keep it for your children, your children's children and for all who come after you, as one of the great sights which every American, if he can travel at all, should see. Keep the Grand Cañon as it is.

****

After leaving the presidency, Roosevelt contributed regularly to the Outlook *for a number of years. His subject matter ranged widely, but one of his real strengths was the review essay. Here, in a piece that appeared in the November 30, 1912, issue of the magazine, he looks at three recent books on hunting and natural history, two of them with African settings. The coverage of J. Stevenson-Hamilton's* Animal Life in Africa *might seem a bit strange, given the fact that it featured a foreword by Roosevelt (a fact he fails to mention in his review), but there is no denying the book's importance. It is one of several works (the others include* South African Eden, Wild Life in South Africa, *and* The Low-Veld: Its Wild Life and Its People) *in which the founding warden of the famed Kruger National Park shared his experiences as a natural historian.*

The second Africa-related work, Stewart Edward White's The Land of Footprints, *is one of many from the pen of this prolific writer and accomplished sportsman. Among White's other volumes with African settings are* African Camp-Fires, The Leopard Woman,

Lions in the Path, *and* The Rediscovered Country. *Roosevelt likely knew White, who was an American, and certainly such was the case with Charles Sheldon, the author of the third book he reviews.*

Sheldon created an outstanding private library on sport and natural history that ultimately found a home at Yale University and was the basis for one of the most notable reference works in the field, John C. Phillips' A Bibliography of American Sporting Books *(1930). Sheldon's* The Wilderness of the North Pacific Coast Islands *is one of a trilogy of "wilderness" books he wrote. The others were* The Wilderness of Denali *(1930) and* The Wilderness of the Upper Yukon *(1911). The latter book, incidentally, describes a hunting trip taken with Fred Selous, a good friend of Roosevelt who played a key role in the planning of the ex-president's great African safari.*

The sentence with which TR concludes this essay, while describing the authors whose books he is considering, might well have been a self-description: "These are . . . books written by three men of the best outdoors type, three men who are hunters, who are naturalists, who are keen observers and excellent writers."

THREE CAPITAL BOOKS OF THE WILDERNESS

Major Stevenson-Hamilton, the warden of the Transvaal Government Game Reserves, has written an entirely new type of book.[1] It is the first time that full advantage has been taken of his opportunities by any competent observer and writer whose good fortune has put him in charge of one of the great sanctuaries for the wilder forms of life that have been created in both the Eastern and the Western hemispheres of recent years. There have been plenty of good books about African game, some by professional naturalists, some by men whose interests were primarily those of the hunter; and it is a mistake to suppose that there is not room for other good books of this type. But Major Stevenson-Hamilton's book is far more than any ordinary hunting book can be. He deals with African travel; he deals with hunting; but the great value of his book consists in the notes on the life histories of the big game, as well as of the crocodiles, poisonous snakes, and some of the birds and

---

[1]*Animal Life in Africa.* By Major J. Stevenson-Hamilton. William Heinemann, London.

insects, which give its peculiar character to the South African fauna. I know of no other book which contains as much and as valuable information on outdoor African natural history of an interesting kind. There are of course books by great hunters in which more information will be found upon some particular species of big game—lion, or elephant, or buffalo, or rhinoceros. But taking game in the aggregate, and other interesting animals as well, there is no other book I know which equals this. Take the account of the ratel or honey-badger, for instance, the most valiant and I am inclined to think the most interesting beast in Africa. Major Stevenson-Hamilton's work has been such as to enable him to make observations and investigations in a way that the big-game hunter pure and simple cannot possibly do, and in consequence he has added some really extraordinary bits of information to our knowledge of the ratel. Its partnership with the honey-bird is one of the noteworthy facts of natural history. Both the bird and the mammal have a peculiar and marked individuality in their make-up and habits; the whole life history of each is well worth studying, but their partnership in marauding against the bees is the most extraordinary of all. Normally the ratel feeds on vegetable matter, insects, and the like, yet Major Stevenson-Hamilton gives what seem to be unquestionable incidents of its attacking and killing adult males of the largest and most formidable antelopes. If attacked, it will fight to the death against any odds, and it is no easy work for even a lion or leopard to kill it.

Major Sevenson-Hamilton's position enabled him to note closely all kinds of incidents in the life of the great carnivores, the big cats, the hyenas, and those bush pirates the hunting-dogs. His running notes on natural history are enlivened by accounts of very interesting adventures—one or two of them in connection with lions were of a really extraordinary nature. Like every other competent observer—including the authors of both the other volumes here considered—he dwells on the extreme variability of character among the higher mammals. This is a factor always to be considered in speaking of dangerous game. There is a certain average difference in the danger of hunting lion, buffalo, elephant, and rhinoceros, but this average difference is less than the very wide differences among individuals of the same species. On the whole, lions charge more readily than any other species; yet some can hardly be bullied into making any kind of a fight.

The account of the tame eland makes one regret more than ever that some government does not somewhere undertake the task of taming this splendid animal. The eland is probably by nature much fitter for domestic uses than are cattle. Unfortunately, as with the American bison, it lived in regions where the natives never reached the stage of themselves taming species of wild animals. Accordingly in Africa, as in America, the tame animals that now flourish were taken over from races who had domesticated them through long ages, so that they had become entirely fitted for their work. At least two, and probably three, wild species of oxen proper were thus tamed, not to speak of the buffalo, the gaur, or gayal, and the yak, in Asia, from which region doubtless the cattle-owners spread into Europe and Africa many thousands of years ago, just as within the last few hundred years they have spread into the Americas and Australia. The bison could unquestionably have been domesticated at least as easily as the other species of cattle were domesticated in the long-buried past, and the eland probably much more easily, and certainly very much more easily than the reindeer. In the case of the eland it is not too late now, although the work would probably have to be done by a government rather than by a private individual.

Major Stevenson-Hamilton is not only a keen observer and good writer as well as a good hunter, but he is also admirably fitted to give advice on the whole subject of game reserves and of preserving the wonderful fauna of the wilderness without interfering with the legitimate demands of the settlers in wild places. His book should be in the library of every hunter, of every naturalist, of every man who cares for the life of the wilderness. Moreover, it should be in the hands of every man who is awake to the need of preserving at least a fragment of that extraordinary wild life which vanishes before civilization.

There are all kinds of problems connected with preserving wild creatures, by the way, and one of the most important of them, of a totally unexpected kind, has come to the front during the last decade in connection with the wapiti, the elk, of the Yellowstone Park. The Yellowstone Park was always a favorite summer range of the elk. Under protection they have increased enormously in numbers. They summer within the park; although some of them winter within it, especially near its northern border, the majority tend to go out, especially to the south. All wild birds and animals of course possess a fecundity such that where natural checks are removed they increase in geometrical ratio. This is true of them just as it is true of tame animals; let any kind-hearted lover of animals remove all checks on the increase of, say, the cats or rabbits on his place, and inside of a year he will find this truth illustrated by practical experiment. Almost any species, if freed from natural enemies, increases so fast as speedily to encroach on the possible limits of its food supply, and then either disease or starvation must come in to offset the fecundity. In European game reserves the shooting tends to keep down any abnormal increase—although even in these game reserves over-preservation often results in stunting the development of the animal or exposing it to disease. In America hitherto the success of the effort to preserve the different kinds of wild creatures has not been great enough to cause us any alarm as to their over-increase, with the single exception of the elk in the Yellowstone Park. But this is a very serious exception. Elk are hardy animals and prolific. It is probable that a herd under favorable conditions in its own habitat will double in numbers about every four years. There are now in the Yellowstone Park probably thirty thousand elk. A very few moments' thought ought to show any one that under these circumstances, if nothing interfered to check the increase, elk would be as plentiful as cattle throughout the whole United Sates inside of half a century. But their possible range is of course strictly limited, and as there are no foes to kill them down, the necessary death rate is kept up by nature in a far more cruel way—that is, by starvation in winter. The suffering and misery that this means is quite heartrending. Every winter the wapiti herds that go south of the Yellowstone Park lose thousands upon thousands of their numbers by the long-drawn agony of slow starvation. The loss falls especially, of course, on the calves of the year, and the cows in calf—the very animals that under any proper system of hunting suffer least. From time to time well-meaning people propose that the difficulty shall be met by feeding the elk hay in winter or by increasing the size of the winter grounds. Of course there are circumstances under which feeding hay is not only proper but necessary, and it may be that there can properly be made a slight enlargement of the summer range of the elk. But as a permanent way of meeting the difficulty neither enlarging the range not feeding with hay would be of the slightest use. All that either method could accomplish would be to remove the difficulty for two or three years until the elk had time to multiply once more to the danger-point. What is needed is recognition of the simple fact that the elk will always multiply beyond their means of subsistence, and that if their numbers are not reduced in some other way they will be reduced by starvation and disease. It would be infinitely better for the elk, infinitely less cruel, if some method could be devised by which hunting them should be permitted right up to the point of killing each year on an average what would amount to the whole annual increase. The herd must be kept stationary, and it should be kept stationary in some way that will work the least possible cruelty to the animals and will be of most use to the people of the country, especially of the States in which the park is situated. Of course the regulation should be so strict and intelligent as to enable all killing to be stopped the moment it was found to be in any way excessive or detrimental. There should be no profit hunting—that is, no sale of the meat or trophies.

Mr. Sheldon is an outdoor naturalist, a faunal naturalist, as well as a great hunter. His present volume[2] is one of a series he is writing dealing with the animals of Alaska and the northwest, a series which when finished will give us more information on the natural history of the most interesting animals of the Northwest than any or indeed all other volumes contain. Mr. Sheldon and Mr. White—whose book I shall next consider—are big-game hunters of the best type. They are not professionals, but in point of hardihood, of skill in their craft, of ability to fend for themselves, and of readiness to meet every emergency and every risk, it is not too much to say that they are fairly entitled to come in the line of descent straight down from the Boones and Crocketts, the Kit Carsons and Bridgers, of the old days. Each of them by preference hunts entirely alone. Each is as competent to care for himself as any Indian. The book is admirably written by a man who loves the mountains, the great woods, and the stormy seacoasts, and who describes with power and charm what he has seen. He is the direct reverse of a game butcher; he cares nothing for a "big bag." He kills only what must be killed. His book is of practical value to naturalists.

Mr. Sheldon's book is most interesting, as well. Its greatest value consists in the account of his hunting trip after the huge bear of Montague Island, a bear which Hart Merriam has made into a new species—"species" nowadays having no such significance as in former times, it being a mere term of convenience. His observations of the habits of the big bear have a particular value. It is evident that nowadays these bears are not dangerous game in the sense that various African animals are to be considered dangerous game. The book is illustrated by exceedingly good and well-chosen photographs, and also by certain pictures of Carl Rungius's, which make us realize vividly that even the best photograph in no shape or way replaces or comes anywhere near replacing a really good picture by an artist who is himself a first-class out-of-doors man.

Stewart Edward White's book[3] deals with hunting-grounds as unlike those of northwestern America as can well be imagined. He too has writ-

---

[2]*The Wilderness of the North Pacific Coast Islands.* By Charles Sheldon. Charles Scribner's Sons, New York.
[3]*The Land of Footprints.* By Stewart Edward White. Doubleday, Page & Co., New York.

ten a notable book, and has given a fresh proof, if one were necessary, that the fact that many first-class books about hunting in a given region already exist in no way means that there is not ample room for another first-class book. It is totally unlike Sheldon's, except in the sense that both men have a great love for wild natural scenery and good power of describing it, that each is an observer as well as a hunter, that both are thoroughly hardy men whose deeds in no way resemble those of the mere holiday hunter. I am not running down the holiday hunter at all, for he may do the best that his opportunities allow: I am only pointing out that he must not compare himself with the man who can push boldly into the unknown and do all his work for himself.

Mr. White was for part of the time while in Africa a companion of Mr. Cuninghame, a professional elephant hunter, who managed my safari during most of my own trip in Africa, and Cunimghame wrote me that White was the very best game-shot with a rifle he had ever seen in his life. The account of some of his adventures with lion and buffalo is thrilling, and, moreover, it is so written as to give a real and satisfactory idea of just what it was that happened, and, without either understatement or exaggeration, of what might have happened if the powder had not been straight. Moreover, his account of his gun-bearers, of the natives they met, of the vast, strange, barren country through which he traveled, and of the great beasts by which he was continually surrounded, is all most interesting. The chapter on the lion dance of the wild savages who were his porters is as vivid as anything of the kind in any book. And the following chapter, describing the precarious rise from the ranks of a porter with aspirations to become a gun-bearer, is not only very humorously told, but affords a practical illustration of some of the things which Mr. White does that make him a good hunter. Not the least interesting chapters are the two which describe the visit to Mr. McMillan's Juja Farm, where the fortunate visitor can relish, as probably nowhere else on earth, the experience of living in a house with every comfort and luxury, right in the middle of the teeming life of the African wilderness.

In the appendix Mr. White treats of rifles and equipment. In his protest against the needless luxury, in fact the cumbrous luxury, of present-day African hunting he is quite right. At the same time, in the outdoor sense of the word, Mr. White is a very "hard" man, and it would not be well for the average holiday sportsman to try to follow his example in cutting down the paraphernalia of African camping life, and more than in cutting down cartridges. Moreover, he is mistaken in thinking that all the men who use shorts and leggings, leaving their knees bare, do so for the sake of looks. Much the best hunter of my own party speedily adopted them, purely because he liked them; and he has used them since then, hunting sheep in the Mexican desert, and moose and caribou in the great northern forest. Personally, I cannot stand them; but that does not alter the fact that other people genuinely like them better than any other rig. It is rather gratifying to find that White used three rifles of the same kinds that I used—a Springfield, a 405 Winchester, and a double cordite Holland & Holland—and that he found that each of them did just what I found they did; that is, the Springfield was his ordinary weapon—his walking-cane, so to speak; the Winchester was his lion gun and the gun for the big antelope; while the Holland was for the few species of very heavy game. But I emphatically dissent from Mr. White's advice to take out only three cartridges for every head of game which it is expected to shoot. His own record was extraordinary, for he got about one animal for every two cartridges fired. I believe that the great majority of animals he killed cost him but one cartridge apiece. Moreover, the antelope of the plains were killed at an average of 245 yards, with a maximum of 638 yards. Now I am an ordinary shot, neither better nor worse than the average big-game hunter who has had some experience. But I could not begin to approach these figures. I did not ordinarily shoot at such long ranges, and yet I averaged about three times as many cartridges to a kill as did Mr. White. As a matter of fact, Mr. White at a hundred yards shoots about as well with a pistol as I do with a rifle. Unless the hunter going to Africa is a very unusually good man, I advise him to triple the number of cartridges which Mr. White thinks it necessary for him to take.

Mr. White hunts his lions in the most sportsmanlike style. I agree with him that rounding them up on horseback and following them on foot are the two most sportsmanlike ways. But when he speaks as he does about hunting them with dogs he should remember that it is an exceedingly difficult feat to train a lion (sic) pack with real efficiency, and that a pack not so trained is only a doubtful and occasional help. For a century hunters have employed dogs occasionally in chasing lions, and never with any marked success. It was not until Mr. Paul Rainey, an experienced bear hunter, introduced his pack of Mississippi bear hounds into East Africa that this method of hunting became a really startling success. Until Rainey brought his hounds to East Africa few people believed that anything could be done with hounds against lions. Then when Rainey had made his striking success most people jumped to the opposite extreme, and said that it was not a really sporting way in which to hunt lions. As a matter of fact Rainey's was a great feat—not quite as great as the feats of

Buffalo Jones and his associates in roping lions, rhinos, and giraffes, but still a great feat. Wherever settlers are found lions must be destroyed, and the very few hunters able to train a pack as Rainey trained his can do more for their destruction than any other man. Of course, where it is desired to preserve lions it is wise not to let such a man as Rainey with such a pack as Rainey's go after them!

These are three capital books, written by three men of the best outdoors type, three men who are hunters, who are naturalists, who are keen observers and excellent writers.

****

Originally published in the October 1907 issue of Scribner's Magazine *(pp. 385–395), this piece was previously reprinted in* Wilderness Writings *(1986), edited by Paul Schullery, and, as has already been noted, it was included in the enlarged edition of* Outdoor Pastimes of an American Hunter *(1908). Unlike the majority of the selections found in the present work, "Small Country Neighbors" touches less on hunting than on natural history. However, anyone who has observed the glorious comeback of America's big-game bird, the wild turkey, will find TR's coverage of a gobbler hunt of considerable interest. On the whole, though, what we see here is the product of keen and astute observation of the small birds and animals Roosevelt had the opportunity to encounter at Sagamore Hill, the White House, Mount Vernon, and elsewhere.*

SMALL COUNTRY NEIGHBORS

Small mammals, with the exception of squirrels, are so much less conspicuous than birds, and indeed usually pass their lives in such seclusion, that the ordinary observer is hardly aware of their presence. At Sagamore Hill, for instance, except at haying time, I rarely see the swarming meadow-mice, the much less plentiful pine-mice, or the little mole-shrews, alive, unless they happen to drop into a pit or sunken area which has been dug at one point to let light through a window into the cellar. The much more graceful and attractive white-footed mice and jumping mice are almost as rarely seen, though if one does come across a jumping mouse it at once attracts attention by its extraordinary leaps. The jumping mouse hibernates, like the woodchuck and chipmunk. The other little animals just mentioned are abroad all winter, the meadow-mice under the snow, the white-footed mice, and often the shrews, above the snow. The telltale snow, showing all the tracks, betrays the hitherto unsuspected existence of many little creatures; and the commonest marks upon it are those of the rabbit and especially of the white-footed mouse. The shrew walks or trots and makes alternate footsteps in the snow. Whitefoot, on the contrary, always jumps, whether going slow or fast, and his hind feet leave their prints side by side, often with the mark where the tail has dragged. I think whitefoot is the most plentiful of all our furred wild creatures, taken as a whole. He climbs trees well. I have found his nest in an old vireo's nest; but more often under stumps or boards. The meadow-mice often live in the marshes and are entirely at home in the water.

The shrew-mouse which I most often find is a short-tailed, rather thickset little creature, not wholly unlike his cousin the shrew-mole, and just as greedy and ferocious. When a boy I captured one of these mole-shrews and found to my astonishment that he was a blood-thirsty and formidable little beast of prey. He speedily killed and ate a partially grown white-footed mouse which I put in the same cage with him. (I think a full-grown mouse of this kind would be an overmatch for a shrew.) I then put a small snake in with him. The shrew was very active but seemed nearly blind, and as he ran to and fro he never seemed to be aware of the presence of anything living until he was close to it, when he would instantly spring on it like a tiger. On this occasion he attacked the little snake with great ferocity, and after an animated struggle in which the snake whipped and rolled all around the cage, throwing the shrew to and fro a dozen times, the latter killed and ate the snake in triumph. Larger snakes frequently eat shrews, by the way.

One of my boys—the special friend of Josiah the badger—once discovered a flying squirrel's nest, in connection with which a rather curious incident occurred. The little boy had climbed a tree which is hollow at the top; and in this hollow he discovered a flying-squirrel mother with six young ones. She seemed so tame and friendly that the little boy for a moment hardly realized that she was a wild thing, and called down that he had "found a guinea-pig up the tree." Finally the mother made up her mind to remove her family. She took each one in turn in her mouth and flew or sailed down from the top of the tree to the foot of another tree near by; ran up this, holding the little squirrel in her mouth; and again sailed down to the foot of another tree some distance off. Here she deposited her young one on the grass, and then, reversing the process, climbed and sailed back to the tree where the nest was; then she took out another young one and returned with it, in exactly the same fashion as with the first. She repeated this until all six of the young ones were laid on the bank, side by side in a row, all with their heads the same way. Finding that she was not molested she ultimately took all six of the little fellows back to her nest, where she reared her brood undisturbed.

Among the small mammals at Sagamore Hill the chipmunks are the most familiar and the most in evidence; for they readily become tame and confiding. For three or four years a chipmunk—I suppose the same chipmunk—has lived near the tennis-court; and it has developed the rather puzzling custom of sometimes scampering across the court while we are in the middle of a game. This has happened two or three times every year, and is rather difficult to explain, for the chipmunk could just as well go round the court, and there seems no possible reason why he should suddenly run out on it while the game is in full swing. If he is seen, every one stops to watch him, and then he may himself stop and sit up to look about; but we may not see him until just as he is finishing a frantic scurry across, in imminent danger of being stepped on.

Usually birds are very regular in their habits, so that not only the same species but the same individuals breed in the same places year after year. In spite of their wings they are almost as local as mammals, and the same pair will usually keep to the same immediate neighborhood, where they can always be looked for in their season. There are wooded or brush-grown swampy places not far from the White House where in the spring or summer I can count with certainty upon seeing wrens, chats, and the ground-loving Kentucky warbler; an attractive little bird, which, by the way, itself looks much like a miniature chat. There are other places, in the neighborhood of Rock Creek, where I can be almost certain of finding the blue-gray gnat-catcher, which ranks just next to the humming-bird itself in exquisite daintiness and delicacy. The few pairs of mocking-birds around Washington have just as sharply defined haunts.

Nevertheless, it is never possible to tell when one may run across a rare bird, and even birds that are not rare now and then show marked individual idiosyncrasy in turning up, or even breeding, in unexpected places. At Sagamore Hill, for instance, I never knew a purple finch to breed until the summer of 1906. Then two pairs nested with us, one right by the house and the other near the stable. My attention was drawn to them by the bold, cheerful singing of the males, who were spurred to rivalry by one another's voices. In September of the same year, while sitting in a rocking-chair on the broad veranda and looking out over the Sound, I heard the unmistakable "ank-ank" of nuthatches from a young elm at one corner of the house. I strolled over, expecting to find the white-bellied nuthatch, which is rather common on Long Island. But instead there were a couple of red-bellied nuthatches, birds familiar to me in the northern woods, but which I had never before seen at Sagamore Hill. They were tame and fearless, running swiftly up and down the tree-trunk and around the limbs while I stood and looked at them not ten feet away. The two younger boys ran out to see them; and then we hunted up their picture in Wilson. I find, by the way, that Audubon's and Wilson's are still the most satisfactory large ornithologies, at least for nature-lovers who are not specialists; but of course any attempt at serious study of our birds means recourse to the numerous and excellent books and pamphlets by recent observers.

In May, 1907, two pairs of robins built their substantial nests, and raised their broods, on the piazza at Sagamore Hill; one over the transom of the north hall door and one over the transom of the south hall door. Only one pair of purple finches returned to us this year; and for the first time in many years no Baltimore orioles built in the elm by the corner of the house; they began their nest, but for some reason left it unfinished. The red-winged blackbirds, however, were more plentiful than for years previously, and two pairs made their nests near the old barn, where the grass stood lush and tall; this was the first time they had ever built nearer than the wood-pile pond, and I believe it was owing to the season being so cold and wet. It was perhaps due to the same cause that so many black-throated green warblers spent June and July in the woods on our place; they must have been breeding, though I only noticed the males. Each kept to his own special tract of woodland, among the tops of the tall trees, seeming to prefer the locusts, and throughout June each sang all day long—a drawling, cadenced little warble of five or six notes, usually uttered at intervals of a few seconds; sometimes while the little bird was perched motionless, sometimes as it flitted and crawled actively among the branches. With the resident of one particular grove I became well acquainted, as I was chopping a path through the grove. Every day the little warbler was singing away in the grove when I reached it, one locust-tree being his favorite perch. He paid not the slightest attention to my chopping; whereas a pair of downy woodpeckers, and a pair of great crested flycatchers, both of which, evidently, were likewise nesting near by, were much put out by my presence. While listening to my little black-throated friend I would continually hear the songs of his cousins, the prairie-warbler, the redstart, the black-and-white creeper, and the Maryland yellow throat, not to speak of other birds, towhees, oven-birds, thrashers, vireos, and the beautiful, golden-voiced wood-thrushes.

The black-throated green warbler has seemingly become a regular summer resident of Long Island, for after discovering them on my place I found that two or three bird-loving neighbors were already familiar with them, and I heard them on several different occasions as I rode through the country round about. I already knew as summer residents in my neighborhood the following representatives of the warbler family: The ovenbird, chat, black-and-white creeper, Maryland yellowthroat, summer yellowbird, prairie-warbler, pine-warbler, blue-winged warbler, golden-winged warbler (very rare), blue yellow-backed warbler, and redstart.

The black-throated green warbler as a breeder and summer resident is a newcomer who has extended his range southward. But this same summer I found one warbler, the presence of which, if more than accidental, means that a southern form is extending its range northward. This was the Dominican or yellow-throated warbler. Two of my bird-loving friends are Mrs. E. H. Swan, Jr., and Miss Alice Weeks. On July 4 Mrs. Swan told me that a new warbler, the yellow-throated, was living near their house, and that she and her husband had seen him on several occasions. I was rather skeptical and told her I thought that it must be a Maryland yellowthroat. Mrs. Swan meekly acquiesced in the theory that she might have been mistaken; but two or three days afterward she sent me word that she and Miss Weeks had seen the bird again, had examined it thoroughly through their glasses, and were sure it was a yellow-throated warbler. Accordingly, on the morning of the 8th, I walked down and met them both near Mrs. Swan's house, about a mile from Sagamore Hill. We did not have to wait long before we heard an unmistakably new warbler song— loud, ringing, sharply accented, just as the yellowthroat's song is described in Chapman's book. At first the little bird kept high in the tops of the pines, but after a while he came to the lower branches and we were able to see him distinctly. Only a glance was needed to show that my two friends were quite right in their identification, and that the bird was undoubtedly the Dominican or yellow-throated warbler. Its bill was as long as that of a black-and-white creeper, in sharp contrast to the bills of the other true wood-warblers, and the olive-gray back, yellow throat and breast, streaked sides, white belly, black cheek and forehead, and white line above eye and spot on the side of the neck, could all be plainly made out. The bird kept continually uttering its loud, sharply modulated and attractive warble. It never left the pines, and though continually on the move, it yet moved with a certain deliberation, like a pine-warbler, and not with the fussy agility of most of its kinsfolk. Occasionally it would catch some insect on the wing, but most of the time kept hopping about among the pine-needles at the ends of the twig clusters, or moving along the larger branches, stopping from time to time to sing. Now and then it would sit still on one twig for several minutes, singing at short intervals and preening its feathers.

In one apple-tree we find a flicker's nest every year; the young make a queer, hissing, bubbling sound, a little like the boiling of a pot. This year one of the young ones fell out; I popped it back into the hole, whereupon its brothers and sisters "boiled" for several minutes, sounding like the caldron of a small and friendly witch. John Burroughs, and a Long Island neighbor, John Lewis Childs, came to see me one day, in June, 1907; and I was able to show them the various birds of most interest—the purple finch, the black-throated green warbler, the redwings in their unexpected nesting-place by the old barn, and the orchard-orioles and yellow-billed cuckoos in the garden.

At the White House we are apt to stroll around the grounds for a few minutes after breakfast; and during the migrations, especially in spring, I often take a pair of field-glasses so as to examine any bird as to the identity of which I am doubtful. From the end of April the warblers pass in troops—myrtle, magnolia, chestnut-sided, bay-breasted, blackburnian, black-throated blue, Canadian, and many others, with at the very end of the season the blackpolls; exquisite little birds, but not conspicuous as a rule, except perhaps the blackburnian, whose brilliant orange throat and breast flame when they catch the sunlight as he flits among the trees. The males in their dress of courtship are easily recognized by any one who has Chapman's book on the warblers. On May 4, 1906, I saw a Cape May warbler, the first I had ever seen. It was in a small pine. It was fearless, allowing a close approach, and as it was a male in high plumage, it was unmistakable.

In 1907, after a very hot week in early March, we had an exceedingly cold and late spring. The first bird I heard sing in the White House grounds was a white-throated sparrow on March 1, a song-sparrow speedily following. The whitethroats stayed with us until the middle of May, overlapping the arrival of the indigo-buntings; but during the last week in April and first week in May their singing was drowned by the music of the purple finches, which I never before saw in such numbers around the White House. When we sat by the south fountain, under an apple-tree then blossoming, sometimes three or four purple finches would be singing in the fragrant bloom overhead. In June a pair of wood-thrushes and a pair of black-and-white creepers made their homes in the White House grounds, in addition to our ordinary home-makers, the flickers, redheads, robins, catbirds, song-sparrows, chippies, summer yellowbirds, grackles, and I am sorry to say, crows. A handsome sapsucker spent a week with us. In this same year five night-herons spent January and February in a swampy tract by the Potomac, half a mile or so from the White House.

At Mount Vernon there are of course more birds than there are around the White House, for it is in the country. At present but one mocking-bird sings around the house itself, and in the gardens, and the woods of the immediate neighborhood. Phœbe-birds nest at the heads of the columns under the front portico; and a pair—or rather, doubtless, a succession of pairs—has nested in Washington's tomb itself, for the twenty years since I have known it. The cardinals, beautiful in plumage, and with clear ringing voices, are characteristic of the place. I am glad to say that the woods still hold many gray—not red—foxes, the descendants of those which Washington so perseveringly hunted.

At Oyster Bay on a desolate winter afternoon many years ago I shot an Ipswich sparrow on a strip of ice-rimmed beach, where the long course grass waved in front of a growth of blueberries, beach-plums, and stunted pines. I think it was the same winter that we were visited not only by flocks of crossbills, pine-linnets, redpolls, and pine-grosbeaks, but by a number of snowy owls, which flitted to and fro in ghostlike fashion across the wintry landscape and showed themselves far more diurnal in their habits than our native owls. One fall about the same time a pair of duck-hawks appeared off the bay. It was early, before many ducks had come, and they caused havoc among the night-herons, which were then very numerous in the marshes around Lloyd's Neck, there being a big heronry in the woods near by. Once I saw a duck-hawk come around the bend of the shore, and dart into a loose gang of young night-herons, still in the brown plumage, which had jumped from the marsh at my approach. The pirate struck down three herons in succession and sailed swiftly on without so much as looking back at his victims. The herons, which are usually rather dull birds, showed every sign of terror whenever the duck-hawk appeared in the distance; whereas, they paid no heed to the fish-hawks as they sailed overhead. The little fish-crows are not rare around Washington, though not so common as the ordinary crows; once I shot one at Oyster Bay. They are not so wary as their larger kinsfolk. The soaring turkey-buzzards, so beautiful on the wing and so loathsome near by, are seen everywhere around the Capital.

In Albemarle County, Virginia, we have a little place called Pine Knot, where we sometimes go, taking some or all of the children for a three or four days' outing. It is a mile from the big stock farm "Plain Dealing," belonging to an old friend, Mr. Joseph Wilmer. The trees and flowers are like those of Washington, but their general close resemblance to those of Long Island is set off by certain exceptions. There are osage-orange hedges, and in spring many of the roads are bordered with bands of the brilliant yellow blossoms of the flowering broom, introduced by Jefferson. There are great willow-oaks here and there in the woods or pastures, and occasional groves of noble tulip-trees in the many stretches of forest; these trees growing to a much larger size than on Long Island. As at Washington, among the most plentiful flowers are the demure little Quaker ladies, which are not found at Sagamore Hill—where we also miss such northern forms as the wake-robin and the other trilliums, which used to be among the characteristic marks of springtime at Albany. At Pine Knot the redbud, dogwood, and laurel are plentiful; though in the case of the last two no more so than at Sagamore Hill. The azalea—its Knickerbocker name in New York was pinkster—grows and flowers far more luxuriantly than on Long Island. The moccasin-flower and the china-blue Virginia cowslip with its pale-pink buds, the blood-red Indian pink, the painted columbine, and many, many other flowers somewhat less showy, carpet the woods. The birds are, of course, for the most part the same as on Long Island, but with some differences. These differences are, in part, due to the more southern locality; but in part I cannot explain them, for birds will often be absent from one place seemingly without any real reason. Thus around us in Albemarle County song-sparrows are certainly rare and I have not seen Savannah sparrows at all; but the other common sparrows, such as the chippy, field-sparrow, vesper-sparrow, and grasshopper-sparrow, abound; and in an open field, where bindweed, morning-glories, and evening primroses grew among the broom-sedge, I found some small grass-dwelling sparrows, which with the exercise of some little patience I was able to study at close quarters with the glasses; as I had no gun I could not be positive about their identification, though I was inclined to believe that they were Henslow's sparrows. Of birds of brilliant color there are six species—the cardinal, the summer redbird, and the scarlet tanager, in red; and the bluebird, indigo-bunting, and blue gros-beak, in blue. I saw but one pair of blue grosbeaks; but the little indigo-buntings abound, and bluebirds are exceedingly common, breeding in numbers. It has always been a puzzle to me why they do not breed around us at Sagamore Hill, where I only see them during the migrations. Neither the rosy summer redbirds nor the cardinals are quite as brilliant as the scarlet tanagers, which fairly burn like live flames; but the tanager is much less common than either of the others in Albemarle County, and it is much less common than it is at Sagamore Hill. Among the singers the wood-thrush is not common, but the meadow-lark abounds. The yellow-breasted chat is everywhere and in the spring its clucking, whistling, whooping, and calling seem never to stop for a minute. The white-eyed vireo is found in the same thick undergrowth as the chat, and among the smaller birds it is one of those most in evidence to the ear. In one or two places I came across parties of the long-tailed Bewick's wren, as familiar as the house-wren but with a very different song. There are gentle mourning-doves; and black-billed cuckoos seem more common than the yellowbills. The mocking-birds are, as always, most interesting. I was much amused to see one of them following two crows; when they lit in a ploughed field the mocking-bird paraded alongside of them six feet off, and then fluttered around to the attack. The crows, however, were evidently less bothered by it than they would have been by a king-bird. At Plain Dealing many birds nest within a stone's throw of the rambling, attractive house, with its numerous outbuildings, old garden, orchard, and venerable locusts and catalpas. Among them were Baltimore and orchard orioles, purple grackles, flickers, and red-headed woodpeckers, bluebirds, robins, king-birds, and indigo-buntings. One observation which I made was of real interest. On May 18, 1907, I saw a small party of a dozen or so passenger-pigeons, birds I had not seen for a quarter of a century and never expected to see again. I saw them two or three times flying hither and thither with great rapidity, and once they perched in a tall dead pine on the edge of an old field. They were unmistakable; yet the sight was so unexpected that I almost doubted my eyes, and I welcomed a bit of corroborative evidence coming from Dick, the colored foreman at Plain Dealing. Dick is a frequent companion of mine in rambles around the country, and he is an unusually close and accurate observer of birds, and of wild things generally. Dick had mentioned to me having seen some "wild carrier-pigeons," as he called them; and thinking over this remark of his, after I had returned to Washington, I began to wonder whether he too might not have seen passenger-pigeons. Accordingly, I wrote to Mr. Wilmer, asking him to question Dick and find out what the "carrier-pigeons" looked like. His answering letter runs in part as follows:

"On May 12th last Dick saw a flock of about thirty wild pigeons, followed at a short distance by about half as many, flying in a circle very rapidly, between the Plain Dealing house and the woods, where they disappeared. They had pointed tails and resembled somewhat large doves—the breast and sides rather a brownish red. He had seen them before, but many years ago. I think it is unquestionable the passenger pigeon—

ectopistes migratoria—described on page 25 of the fifth volume of Audubon. I remember the pigeon roosts as he describes them, on a smaller scale, but large flocks have not been seen in this part of Virginia for many years."

The house at Pine Knot consists of one long room, with a broad piazza, below, and three small bedrooms above. It is made of wood, with big outside chimneys at each end. Wood-rats and white-footed mice visit it; once a weasel came in after them; now a flying squirrel has made his home among the rafters. On one side the pines and on the other side the oaks come up to the walls; in front the broom-sedge grows almost to the piazza, and above the line of its waving plumes we look across the beautiful rolling Virginia farm country to the foot-hills of the Blue Ridge. At night whipporwills call incessantly around us. In the late spring or early summer we usually take breakfast and dinner on the veranda, listening to mocking-bird, cardinal, and Carolina wren, as well as to many more common singers. In the winter the little house can only be kept warm by roaring fires in the great open fireplaces, for there is no plaster on the walls, nothing but the bare wood. Then the table is set near the blazing logs at one end of the long room which makes up the lower part of the house, and at the other end the colored cook—Jim Crack by name—prepares the delicious Virginia dinner; while around him cluster the little darkies, who go on errands, bring in wood, or fetch water from the spring, to put in the bucket which stands below where the gourd hangs on the wall. Outside the wind moans or the still cold bites if the night is quiet; but inside there is warmth and light and cheer.

There are plenty of quail and rabbits in the fields and woods near by, so we live partly on what our guns bring in; and there are also wild turkeys. I spent the first three days of November, 1906, in a finally successful effort to kill a wild turkey. Each morning I left the house between three and five o'clock, under a cold, brilliant moon. The frost was heavy; and my horse shuffled over the frozen ruts as I rode after Dick. I was on the turkey grounds before the faintest streak of dawn had appeared in the east; and I worked as long as daylight lasted. It was interesting and attractive in spite of the cold. In the night we heard the quavering screech-owls; and occasionally the hooting of one of their bigger brothers. At dawn we listened to the lusty hammering of the big log-cocks, or to the curious coughing or croaking sound of a hawk before it left its roost. Now and then loose flocks of small birds straggled by us as we sat in the blinds or rested to eat our lunch; chickadees, tufted tits, golden-crested kinglets, creepers, cardinals, various sparrows, and small woodpeckers. Once we saw a shrike pounce on a field-mouse by a haystack; once we came on a ruffed grouse sitting motionless in the road.

The last day I had with me Jim Bishop, a man who had hunted turkeys by profession, a hard-working farmer, whose ancestors have for generations been farmers and woodsmen; an excellent hunter, tireless, resourceful, with an eye that nothing escaped; just the kind of man one likes to regard as typical of what is best in American life. Until this day, and indeed until the very end of this day, chance did not favor us. We tried to get up to the turkeys on the roosts before daybreak; but they roosted in pines, and, night though it was, they were evidently on the lookout, for they always saw us long before we could make them out, and then we could hear them fly out of the tree-tops. Turkeys are quite as wary as deer, and we never got a sight of them while we were walking through the woods; but two or three times we flushed gangs, and my companion then at once built a little blind of pine boughs, in which we sat while he tried to call the scattered birds up to us by imitating, with marvelous fidelity, their yelping. Twice a turkey started toward us, but on each occasion the old hen began calling some distance off and all the scattered birds at once went toward her. At other times I would slip around to one side of a wood while my companion walked through it; but either there were no turkeys or they went out somewhere far away from us.

On the last day I was out thirteen hours. Finally, late in the afternoon, Jim Bishop marked a turkey into a point of pines which stretched from a line of wooded hills down into a narrow open valley on the other side of which again rose wooded hills. I ran down to the end of the point and stood behind a small oak, while Bishop and Dick walked down through the trees to drive the turkeys toward me. This time everything went well; the turkey came out of the cover not too far off and sprang into the air, heading across the valley and offering me a side shot at forty yards as he sailed by. It was just the distance for the close-shooting ten-bore duck gun I carried; and at the report down came the turkey in a heap, not so much as a leg or wing moving. It was an easy shot. But we had hunted hard for three days; and the turkey is the king of American game-birds; and besides I knew he would be very good eating indeed when we brought him home; so I was as pleased as possible when Dick lifted the fine young gobbler, his bronze plumage iridescent in the light of the westering sun.

Formerly we could ride across country in any direction around Washington; and almost as soon as we left the beautiful, tree-shaded streets of the city we were in the real country. But as Washington grows, it naturally—and to me most regrettably—becomes less and less like its former, glorified-village, self; and wire fencing has destroyed our old cross-country rides. Fortunately there are now many delightful bridle trails in Rock Creek Park; and we have fixed up a number of good jumps at suitable places—a stone wall, a water jump, a bank with a ditch, two or three post-and-rails, about four feet high, and some stiff brush-hurdles, one of five feet seven inches. The last, which is the only formidable jump, was put up to please two sporting members of the administration, Bacon and Meyer. Both of them school their horses over it; and my two elder boys, and Fitzhugh Lee, my cavalry aide, also school my horses over it. On one of my horses, Roswell, I have gone over it myself; and as I weigh two hundred pounds without my saddle I think that the jump, with such a weight, in cold blood, should be credited to Roswell for righteousness. Roswell is a bay gelding; Audrey a black mare; they are Virginia horses. In the spring of 1907 I had photographs taken of them going over the various jumps. Roswell is a fine jumper, and usually goes at his jumps in a spirit of matter-of-fact enjoyment. But he now and then shows queer kinks in his temper. On one of these occasions he began by wishing to rush his jumps, and by trying to go over the wings instead of the jumps themselves. He fought hard for his head; and as it happened that the best picture we got of him in the air was at this particular time, it gives a wrong idea of his ordinary behavior, and also, I sincerely trust, a wrong idea of my hands. Generally he takes his jumps like a gentleman.

****

This story of a bear hunt that took place during Roosevelt's second term as president first appeared in the January 1908 edition of Scribner's Magazine *(pp. 47–60). It also appears in the revised and expanded version of* Outdoor Pastimes of an American Hunter *(1908) and in* Wilderness Writings *(1986), edited by Paul Schullery. TR had carefully studied the exploits of old-time bear hunters such as Wade Hampton III, John "Grizzly" Adams, and Davy Crockett, and in time he became an accomplished bear hunter in his own right. (For a detailed account of his forays into this aspect of sport, see the chapter on Roosevelt in* The Bear Hunter's Century: Profiles from the Golden Age of Bear Hunting *[Harrisburg, PA: Stackpole Books, 1988; pp. 131–156], by Paul Schullery). Furthermore, he was so enamored of the sport and its history that noted historian Paul Schullery rightly commented, in the work just mentioned, "Roosevelt studied no one animal more than he did the bear."*

On this particular hunt, TR was joined by a contemporary who also ranks as one of America's great bear hunters, Ben Lilly (misspelled "Lilley" in this selection).

Roosevelt was anxious to pursue black bears in the traditional way, using hounds (it is still a sport that approaches a religion in the Great Smokies of North Carolina, where I grew up). He took a reasonably large bruin (just over 200 pounds) in front of the dogs, and his account is redolent of the flavor and flair of traditional Southern hunts. This immensely readable piece is Roosevelt the storyteller at his best, for he takes the reader vicariously to camp and bear stands in the Louisiana woods in a fashion that almost leaves the armchair adventurer with the hallelujah chorus of the hounds, their throaty music making the bayous ring.

IN THE LOUISIANA CANEBREAKS*

In October, 1907, I spent a fortnight in the canebrakes of northern Louisiana, my hosts being Messrs. John M. Parker and John A. McIlhenny. Surgeon-General Rixey, of the United States Navy, and Dr. Alexander Lambert were with me. I was especially anxious to kill a bear in these canebrakes after the fashion of the old southern planters, who for a century past have followed the bear with horse and hound and horn in Louisiana, Mississippi, and Arkansas.

Our first camp was on Tensas Bayou. This is in the heart of the great alluvial bottom-land created during the countless ages through which the mighty Mississippi has poured out of the heart of the continent. It is in the black belt of the South, in which the negroes outnumber the whites four or five to one, the disproportion in the region in which I was actually hunting being far greater. There is no richer soil in all the earth; and when, as will soon be the case, the chances of disaster from flood are over, I believe the whole land will be cultivated and densely peopled. At present the possibility of such flood is a terrible deterrent to settlement, for when the Father of Waters breaks his boundaries he turns the country for a breadth of eighty miles into one broad river, the plantations throughout all this vast extent being from five to twenty feet under water. Cotton

---

*Editor's Note: You'll note a discrepancy in the spelling of "canebreaks" in the title and text of the essay. This mistake is in the original essay. The correct spelling is "canebrakes".

is the staple industry, corn also being grown, while there are a few rice fields and occasional small patches of sugar cane. The plantations are for the most part of large size and tilled by negro tenants for the white owners. Conditions are still in some respects like those of pioneer days. The magnificent forest growth which covers the land is of little value because of the difficulty in getting the trees to market, and the land is actually worth more after the timber has been removed than before. In consequence, the larger trees are often killed by girdling, where the work of felling them would entail disproportionate cost and labor. At dusk, with the sunset glimmering in the west, or in the brilliant moonlight when the moon is full, the cottonfields have a strange spectral look, with the dead trees raising aloft their naked branches. The cottonfields themselves, when the bolls burst open, seem almost as if whitened by snow; and the red and white flowers, interspersed among the burst-open pods, make the whole field beautiful. The rambling one-story houses, surrounded by outbuildings, have a picturesqueness all their own; their very looks betoken the lavish, whole-hearted, generous hospitality of the planters who dwell therein.

Beyond the end of cultivation towers the great forest. Wherever the water stands in pools, and by the edges of the lakes and bayous, the giant cypress loom aloft, rivalled in size by some of the red gums and white oaks. In stature, in towering majesty, they are unsurpassed by any trees of our eastern forests; lordlier kings of the green-leaved world are not to be found until we reach the sequoias and redwoods of the Sierras. Among them grow many other trees—hackberry, thorn, honey locust, tupelo, pecan and ash. In the cypress sloughs the singular knees of the trees stand two or three feet above the black ooze. Palmettos grow thickly in places. The canebrakes stretch along the slight rises of ground, often extending for miles, forming one of the most striking and interesting features of the country. They choke out other growths, the feathery, graceful canes standing in ranks, tall, slender, serried, each but a few inches from his brother, and springing to a height of fifteen or twenty feet. They look like bamboos; they are well-nigh impenetrable to a man on horseback; even on foot they make difficult walking unless free use is made of the heavy bush-knife. It is impossible to see through them for more than fifteen or twenty paces, and often for not half that distance. Bears make their lairs in them, and they are the refuge for hunted things. Outside of them, in the swamp, bushes of many kinds grow thick among the tall trees, and vines and creepers climb the trunks and hang in trailing festoons from the branches. Here, likewise, the bush-knife is in constant play, as the skilled horsemen thread their way, often at a gallop in and out among the great tree trunks, and through the dense, tangled, thorny undergrowth.

In the lakes and larger bayous we saw alligators and garfish; and monstrous snapping turtles, fearsome brutes of the slime, as heavy as a man, and with huge horny beaks that with a single snap could take off a man's hand or foot. One of the planters with us had lost part of his hand by the bite of an alligator; and had seen a companion seized by the foot by a huge garfish from which he was rescued with the utmost difficulty by his fellow swimmers. There were black bass in the waters, too, and they gave us many a good meal. Thick-bodied water moccasins, foul and dangerous, kept near the water; and farther back in the swamp we found and killed rattlesnakes and copperheads.

Coon and 'possum were very plentiful and in the streams there were minks and a few otters. Black squirrels barked in the tops of the tall trees or descended to the ground to gather nuts or gnaw the shed deer antlers— the latter a habit they shared with the wood rats. To me the most interesting of the smaller mammals, however, were the swamp rabbits, which are thoroughly amphibious in their habits, not only swimming but diving, and taking to the water almost as freely as if they were muskrats. They lived in the depths of the woods and beside the lonely bayous.

Birds were plentiful. Mocking-birds abounded in the clearings, where, among many sparrows of more common kind, I saw the painted finch, the gaudily colored brother of our little indigo bunting, though at this season his plumage was faded and dim. In the thick woods where we hunted there were many cardinal birds and winter wrens, both in full song. Thrashers were even more common; but so cautious that it was rather difficult to see them, in spite of their incessant clucking and calling and their occasional bursts of song. There were crowds of warblers and vireos of many different kinds, evidently migrants from the North, and generally silent. The most characteristic birds, however, were the woodpeckers, of which there were seven or eight species, the commonest around our camp being the handsome red-bellied, the brother of the redhead which we saw in the clearings. The most notable birds and those which most interested me were the great ivory-billed woodpeckers. Of these I saw three, all of them in groves of giant cypress; their brilliant white bills contrasted finely with the black of their general plumage. They were noisy but wary, and they seemed to me to set off the wildness of the swamp as much as any of the beasts of the chase. Among the birds of prey the commonest were the barred owls, which I have never seen elsewhere found so plentiful. Their hooting and yelling were heard all around us throughout the night, and once one of them hooted at intervals for several minutes at mid-day. One of these owls had caught and was devouring a snake in the late afternoon, while it was still daylight. In the dark nights and still mornings and evenings their cries seemed strange and unearthly, the long hoots varied by screeches, and by all kinds of uncanny noises.

At our first camp our tents were pitched by the bayou. For four days the weather was hot, with steaming rains; after that it grew cool and clear. Huge biting flies, bigger than bees, attacked our horses; but the insect plagues, so veritable a scourge in this country during the months of warm weather, had well-nigh vanished in the first few weeks of the fall.

The morning after we reached camp we were joined by Ben Lilly, the hunter, a spare, full-bearded man, with wild, gentle, blue eyes and a frame of steel and whipcord. I never met any other man so indifferent to fatigue and hardship. He equaled Cooper's Deerslayer in woodcraft, in hardihood, in simplicity—and also in loquacity. The morning he joined us in camp, he had come on foot through the thick woods, followed by his two dogs, and had neither eaten nor drunk for twenty-four hours; for he did not like to drink the swamp water. It had rained hard throughout the night and he had no shelter, no rubber coat, nothing but the clothes he was wearing, and the ground was too wet for him to lie on; so he perched in a crooked tree in the beating rain, much as if he had been a wild turkey. But he was not in the least tired when he struck camp; and, though he slept an hour after breakfast, it was chiefly because he had nothing else to do, inasmuch as it was Sunday, on which day he never hunted nor labored. He could run through the woods like a buck, was far more enduring, and quite as indifferent to weather, though he was over fifty years old. He had trapped and hunted throughout almost all the half century of his life, and on trail of game he was as sure as his own hounds. His observations on wild creatures were singularly close and accurate. He was particularly fond of the chase of the bear, which he followed by himself, with one or two dogs; often he would be on the trail of his quarry for days at a time, lying down to sleep wherever night overtook him; and he had killed over a hundred and twenty bears.

Late in the evening of the same day we were joined by two gentlemen, to whom we owed the success of our hunt. They were Messrs. Clive and Harley Metcalf, planters from Mississippi, men in the prime of life, thorough woodsmen and hunters, skilled marksmen, and utterly fearless horsemen. For a quarter of a century they had hunted bear and deer with horse and hound, and were masters of the art. They brought with them their pack of bear hounds, only one, however, being a thoroughly staunch and seasoned veteran. The pack was under the immediate control of a negro hunter, Holt Collier, in his own way as remarkable a character as Ben Lilley. He was a man of sixty and could neither read nor write, but he had all the dignity of an African chief, and for half a century he had been a bear hunter, having killed or assisted in killing over three thousand bears. He had been born a slave on the Hinds plantation, his father, an old man when he was born, having been the body-servant and cook of "old General Hinds," as he called him, when the latter fought under Jackson at New Orleans. When ten years old Holt had been taken on the horse behind his young master, the Hinds of that day, on a bear hunt, when he killed his first bear. In the Civil War he had not only followed his master to battle as his body-servant, but had acted under him as sharpshooter against the Union soldiers. After the war he continued to stay with his master until the latter died, and had then been adopted by the Metcalfs; and he felt that he had brought them up, and treated them with that mixture of affection and grumbling respect which an old nurse shows toward the lad who has ceased being a child. The two Metcalfs and Holt understood one another thoroughly, and understood their hounds and the game their hounds followed almost as thoroughly.

They had killed many deer and wildcat, and now and then a panther; but their favorite game was the black bear, which, until within a very few years, was extraordinarily plentiful in the swamps and canebrakes on both sides of the lower Mississippi, and which is still found here and there, although in greatly diminished numbers. In Louisiana and Mississippi the bears go into their dens toward the end of January, usually in hollow trees, often very high up in living trees, but often also in great logs that lie rotting on the ground. They come forth toward the end of April, the cubs having been born in the interval. At this time the bears are nearly as fat, so my informants said, as when they enter their dens in January; but they lose their fat very rapidly. On first coming out in the spring they usually eat ash buds and tender young cane called mutton cane, and at that season they generally refuse to eat the acorns even when they are plentiful. According to my informants it is at this season that they are most apt to take to killing stock, almost always the hogs which run wild or semi-wild in the woods. They are very individual in their habits, however; many of them never touch stock, while others, usually old he-bears, may kill numbers of hogs; in one case an old he-bear began this hog killing just as soon as he left his den. In the summer months they find but little to eat, and it is at this season that they are most industrious in hunting for grubs, insects, frogs and small mammals. In some neighborhoods they do not eat fish, while in other places, perhaps not far away, they not only greedily eat dead fish, but will themselves kill fish if they can find them in shallow pools left by the receding waters. As soon as the mast is on the ground they begin to feed upon it, and when the acorns and pecans are plentiful they eat nothing else, though at first berries of all kinds and grapes are eaten also. When in November they have begun only to eat the acorns they put on fat as no other wild animal does, and by the end of December a full-grown bear may weigh at least twice as much as it does in August, the difference being as great as between a very fat and a lean hog. Old he-bears which in August weigh three hundred pounds and upwards will, toward the end of December, weigh six hundred pounds, and even more in exceptional cases.

Bears vary greatly in their habits in different localities, in addition to the individual variation among those of the same neighborhood. Around Avery Island, John McIlhenny's plantation, the bears only appear from June to November; there they never kill hogs, but feed at first on corn and then on sugar-cane, doing immense damage in the fields, quite as much as hogs would do. But when we were on the Tensas we visited a family of settlers who lived right in the midst of the forest ten miles from any neighbors; and although bears were plentiful around them they never molested their corn-fields—in which the coons, however, did great damage.

A big bear is cunning, and is a dangerous fighter to the dogs. It is only in exceptional cases, however, that these black bears, even when wounded and at bay, are dangerous to men, in spite of their formidable strength. Each of the hunters with whom I was camped had been charged by one or two among the scores or hundreds of bears he had slain, but no one of them had ever been injured, although they knew other men who had been injured. Their immunity was due to their own skill and coolness; for when the dogs were around the bear the hunter invariably ran close in so as to kill the bear at once and save the pack. Each of the Metcalfs had on one occasion killed a large bear with a knife, when the hounds had seized it and the men dared not fire for fear of shooting one of them. They had in their younger days hunted with a General Hamberlin, a Mississippi planter whom they well knew, who was then already an old man. He was passionately addicted to the chase of the bear, not only because of the sport it afforded, but also in a certain way as a matter of vengeance; for his father, also a keen bear-hunter, had been killed by a bear. It was an old he, which he had wounded and which had been bayed by the dogs; it attacked him, throwing him down and biting him so severely that he died a couple of days later. This was in 1847. Mr. W.H. Lambeth sends the following account of the fatal encounter:

"I send you an extract from the 'Brother Jonathon,' published in New York in 1847:

"Dr. Monroe Hamberlin, Robert Wilson, Joe Brazeil, and others left Satartia, Miss., and in going up Big Sunflower River, met Mr. Leiser and his party of hunters returning to Vicksburg. Mr. Leiser told Dr. Hamberlin that he saw the largest bear track at the big Mound on Lake George that he ever saw, and was afraid to tackle him. Dr. Hamberlin said, "I never saw one that I was afraid to tackle." Dr. Hamberlin landed his skiff at the Mound and his dogs soon bayed the bear. Dr. Hamberlin fired and the ball glanced on the bear's head. The bear caught him by the right thigh and tore all the flesh off. He drew his knife and the bear crushed his right arm. He cheered the dogs and they pulled the bear off. The bear whipped the dogs and attacked him the third time, biting him in the hollow back of his neck. Mr. Wilson came up and shot the bear dead on Dr. Hamberlin. The party returned to Satartia, but Dr. Hamberlin told them to put the bear in the skiff, that he would not leave without his antagonist. The bear weighed 640 pounds.'

"Dr. Hamberlin lived three days. I knew all the parties. His son John and myself hunted with them in 1843 and 1844, when we were too small to carry a gun."

A large bear is not afraid of dogs, and an old he, or a she with cubs, is always on the lookout for a chance to catch and kill any dog that comes near enough. While lean and in good running condition it is not an easy matter to bring a bear to bay; but as they grow fat they become steadily less able to run, and the young ones, and even occasionally a full-grown she, will then readily tree. If a man is not near by, a big bear that has become tired will treat the pack with whimsical indifference. The Metcalfs recounted to me how they had once seen a bear, which had been chased quite a time, evidently make up its mind that it needed a rest and could afford to take it without much regard for the hounds. The bear accordingly selected a small opening and lay flat on its back with its nose and all its four legs extended. The dogs surrounded it in frantic excitement, barking and baying, and gradually coming in a ring very close up. The bear was watching, however, and suddenly sat up with a jerk, frightening the dogs nearly into fits. Half of them turned back-somersaults in their panic, and all promptly gave the bear ample room. The bear having looked about, lay flat on its back again, and the pack gradually regaining courage once more closed in. At first the bear, which was evidently reluctant to arise, kept them at a distance by now and then thrusting an unexpected paw toward them; and when they became too bold it sat up with a jump and once more put them all to flight.

For several days we hunted perseveringly around this camp on the Tensas Bayou, but without success. Deer abounded, but we could find no bear; and of the deer we killed only what we actually needed for use in camp. I killed one myself by a good shot, in which, however, I fear that the element of luck played a considerable part. We had started as usual by sunrise, to be gone all day; for we never counted upon returning to camp before sunset. For an hour or two we threaded our way, first along an indistinct trail, and then on an old disused road, the hardy woods-horses keeping on a running walk without much regard to the difficulties of the ground. The disused road lay right across a great canebrake, and while some of the party went around the cane with the dogs, the rest of us strung out along the road so as to get a shot at any bear that might come across it. I was following Harley Metcalf, with John McIlhenny and Dr. Rixey behind on the way to their posts, when we heard in the far-off distance two of the younger hounds, evidently on the trail of a deer. Almost immediately afterward a crash in the bushes at our right hand and behind us made me turn around, and I saw a deer running across the few feet of open space; and as I leaped from my horse it disappeared in the cane. I am a rather deliberate shot, and under any circumstances a rifle is not the best weapon for snap shooting, while there is no kind of shooting more difficult than on running game in a canebrake. Luck favored me in this instance, however, for there was a spot a little ahead of where the deer entered in which the cane was thinner, and I kept my rifle on its indistinct, shadowy outline until it reached this spot; it then ran quartering away from me, which made my shot much easier, although I could only catch its general outline through the cane. But the 45-70 which I was using is a powerful gun and shoots right through cane or bushes; and as soon as I pulled the trigger the deer, with a bleat, turned a tremendous somersault and was dead when we reached it. I was not a little pleased that my bullet should have sped so true when I was making my first shot in company with my hard-riding straight-shooting planter friends.

But no bear were to be found. We waited long hours on likely stands. We rode around the canebrakes through the swampy jungle, or threaded our way across them on trails cut by the heavy wood-knives of my companions; but we found nothing. Until the trails were cut the canebrakes were impenetrable to a horse and were difficult enough to a man on foot. On going through them it seemed as if we must be in the tropics; the silence, the stillness, the heat, and the obscurity, all combining to give a certain eeriness to the task, as we chopped our winding way slowly through the dense mass of close-growing, feather-fronded stalks. Each of the hunters prided himself on his skill with the horn, which was an essential adjunct of the hunt, used both to summon and control the hounds, and for signaling among the hunters themselves. The tones of many of the horns were full and musical; and it was pleasant to hear them as they wailed to one another, backwards and forwards, across the great stretches of lonely swamp and forest.

A few days convinced us that it was a waste of time to stay longer where we were. Accordingly, early one morning we hunters started for a new camp fifteen or twenty miles to the southward, on Bear Lake. We took the hounds with us, and each man carried what he chose or could in his saddle-pockets, while his slicker was on his horse's back behind him. Otherwise we took absolutely nothing in the way of supplies, and the negroes with the tends and camp equipage were three days before they overtook us. On our way down we were joined by Major Amacker and Dr. Miller, with a small pack of cat hounds. These were good deer dogs, and they ran down and killed on the ground a good-sized bob-cat—a wild-cat, as it is called in the South. It was a male and weighed twenty-three and a half pounds. It had just killed and eaten a large rabbit. The stomachs of the deer we killed, by the way, contained acorns and leaves.

Our new camp was beautifully situated on the bold, steep bank of Bear Lake—a tranquil stretch of water, part of an old river-bed, a couple of hundred yards broad, with a winding length of several miles. Giant cypress grew at the edge of the water; the singular cypress knees rising in every direction round about, while at the bottoms of the trunks themselves were often cavernous hollows opening beneath the surface of water, some the them serving as dens for alligators. There was a waxing moon, so that the nights were as beautiful as the days.

From our new camp we hunted as steadily as from the old. We saw bear sign, but not much of it, and only one or two fresh tracks. One day the hounds jumped a bear, probably a yearling from the way it ran; for at this season a yearling or a two-year-old will run almost like a deer, keeping to the thick cane as long as it can and then bolting across through the bushes of the ordinary swamp land until it can reach another canebrake. After a three hours' run this particular animal managed to get clear away without one of the hunters ever seeing it, and it ran until all the dogs were tired out. A day or two afterwards one of the other members of the party shot a small yearling—that is, a bear which would have been two years old in the following February. It was very lean, weighing but fifty-five pounds. The finely-chewed acorns in its stomach showed that it was already beginning to find mast.

We had seen the tracks of an old she in the neighborhood, and the next morning we started to hunt her out. I went with Clive Metcalf. We had been joined overnight by Mr. Ichabod Osborn and his son Tom, two Louisiana planters, with six or eight hounds—or rather bear dogs, for in these packs most of the animals are of mixed blood, and, as with all packs that are used in the genuine hunting of the wilderness, pedigree counts for nothing as compared with steadiness, courage and intelligence. There were only two of the new dogs that were really staunch bear dogs. The father of Ichabod Osborn had taken up the plantation upon which they were living in 1811, only a few years after Louisiana became part of the United States, and young Osborn was now the third in line from father to son who had steadily hunted bears in this immediate neighborhood.

On reaching the cypress slough near which the tracks of the old she had been seen the day before, Clive Metcalf and I separated from the others and rode off at a lively pace between two of the canebrakes. After an hour or two's wait we heard, very far off, the notes of one of the loudest-mouthed hounds, and instantly rode toward it, until we could make out the babel of the pack. Some hard galloping brought us opposite the point toward which they were heading—for experienced hunters can often tell the probable line of a bear's flight, and the spots at which it will break cover. But on this occasion the bear shied off from leaving the thick cane and doubled back; and soon the hounds were once more out of hearing, while we galloped desperately around the edge of the cane. The tough woods-horses kept their feet like cats as they leaped logs, plunged through bushes, and dodged in and out among the tree trunks; and we had all we could do to prevent the vines from lifting us out of the saddle, while the thorns tore our hands and faces. Hither and thither we went, now at a trot, now at a run, now stopping to listen for the pack. Occasionally we could hear the hounds, and then off we would go racing through the forest toward the point for which we thought they were heading. Finally, after a couple of hours of this, we came up on one side of a canebrake on the other side of which we could hear, not only the pack, but the yelling and cheering of Harley Metcalf and Tom Osborn and one or two of the negro hunters, all of whom were trying to keep the dogs up to their work in the thick cane. Again we rode ahead, and now in a few minutes were reward-ed by hearing the leading dogs come to bay in the thickest of the cover. Having galloped as near to the spot as we could we threw ourselves off the horses and plunged into the cane, trying to cause as little disturbance as possible, but of course utterly unable to avoid making some noise. Before we were within gunshot, however, we could tell by the sounds that the bear had once again started, making what is called a "walking bay." Clive Metcalf, a finished bear-hunter, was speedily able to determine what the bear's probable course would be, and we stole through the cane until we came to a spot near which he thought the quarry would pass. Then we crouched down, I with my rifle at the ready. Nor did we have long to wait. Peering through the thick-growing stalks I suddenly made out the dim outline of the bear coming straight toward us; and noiselessly I cocked and half-raised my rifle, waiting for a clearer chance. In a few seconds it came; the bear turned almost broadside to me, and walked forward very stiff-legged, almost as if on tiptoe, now and then looking back at the nearest dogs. These were two in number—Rowdy, a very deep-voiced hound, in the lead, and Queen, a shrill-tongued brindled bitch, a little behind. Once or twice the bear paused as she looked back at them, evidently hoping that they would come so near that by a sudden race she could catch one of them. But they were too wary.

All of this took but a few moments, and as I saw the bear quite distinctly some twenty yards off, I fired for behind the shoulder. Although I could see her outline, yet the cane was so thick that my sight was on it and not on the bear itself. But I knew my bullet would go true; and, sure enough, at the crack of the rifle the bear stumbled and fell forward, the bullet having passed through both lungs and out at the opposite side. Immediately the dogs came running forward at full speed, and we raced forward likewise lest the pack should receive damage. The bear had but a minute or two to live, yet even in that time more than one valuable hound might lose its life; so when within half a dozen steps of the black, angered beast, I fired again, breaking the spine at the root of the neck; and down went the bear stark dead, slain in the canebrake in true hunter fashion. One by one the hounds struggled up and fell on their dead quarry, the noise of the worry filling the air. Then we dragged the bear out to the edge of the cane, and my companion wound his horn to summon the other hunters.

This was a big she-bear, very lean, and weighing two hundred and two pounds. In her stomach were palmetto berries, beetles and a little mutton cane, but chiefly acorns chewed up in a fine brown mass.

John McIlhenny had killed a she-bear about the size of this on his plantation at Avery's Island the previous June. Several bear had been raiding his corn-fields, and one evening he determined to try to waylay them. After dinner he left the ladies of his party on the gallery of his house while he rode down in a hollow and concealed himself on the lower side of the corn-field. Before he had waited ten minutes a she-bear and her cub came into the field. There she rose on her hind legs, tearing down an armful of ears of corn which she seemingly gave to the cub, and then rose for another armful. McIlhenny shot her; tried in vain to catch the cub; and rejoined the party on the veranda, having been absent but one hour.

After the death of my bear I had only a couple of days left. We spent them a long distance from camp, having to cross two bayous before we got to the hunting grounds. I missed a shot at a deer, seeing little more than the flicker of its white tail through the dense bushes; and the pack caught and killed a very lean two-year-old bear weighing eighty pounds. Near a beautiful pond called Panther Lake we found a deer-lick, the ground not merely bare, but furrowed into hollows by the tongues of countless generations of deer that had frequented the place. We also passed a huge mound, the only hillock in the entire district; it was the work of man, for it had been built in the unknown past by those unknown people whom we call mound-builders. On the trip, all told, we killed and brought into camp three bear, six deer, a wildcat, a turkey, a possum and a dozen squirrels; and we ate everything except the wildcat.

In the evenings we sat around the blazing campfires, and, as always on such occasions, each hunter told tales of his adventures and of the strange feats and habits of the beasts of the wilderness. There had been beaver all through this delta in the old days, and a very few are still left in out-of-the-way places. One Sunday morning we saw two wolves, I think young of the year, appear for a moment on the opposite side of the bayou, but they vanished before we could shoot. All of our party had had a good deal of experience with wolves. The Metcalfs had had many sheep killed by them, the method of killing being invariably by a single bite which tore open the throat while the wolf ran beside his victim. The wolves also killed young hogs, but were very cautious about meddling with an old sow; while one of the big half-wild boars that ranged free through the woods had no fear of any number of wolves. Their endurance and the extremely difficult nature of the country made it difficult to hunt them, and the hunters all bore them a grudge, because if a hound got lost in a region where wolves were at all plentiful they were almost sure to find and kill him before he got home. They were fond of preying on dogs, and at times would boldly kill the hounds right ahead of the hunters. In one instance, while the dogs were following a bear and were but a couple of hundred yards in front of the horsemen, a small party of wolves got in on them and killed two. One of the Osborns, having a valuable hound which was addicted to wandering in the woods, saved him from the wolves by putting a bell on him. The wolves evidently suspected a trap and would never go near the dog. On one occasion another of his hounds got loose with a chain on, and they found him a day or two afterwards unharmed, his chain having become entangled in the branches of a bush. One or two wolves had evidently walked around and around the imprisoned dog, but the chain had awakened their suspicions and they had not pounced on him. They had killed a yearling heifer a short time before, on Osborn's plantation, biting her in the hams. It has been my experience that fox hounds as a rule are afraid of attacking a wolf; but all of my friends assured me that their dogs, if a sufficient number of them were together, would tackle a wolf without hesitation; the packs, however, were always composed, to the extent of at least half, of dogs which, though part hound, were part shepherd or bull or some other breed. Dr. Miller had hunted in Arkansas with a pack specially trained after the wolf. There were twenty-eight of them all told, and on this hunt they ran down and killed unassisted four full-grown wolves, although some of the hounds were badly cut. None of my companions had ever known of wolves actually molesting men, but Mr. Ichabod Osborn's son-in-law had a queer adventure with wolves while riding alone through the woods one late afternoon. His horse acting nervously, he looked about and saw that five wolves were coming towards him. One was a bitch, the other four were males. They seemed to pay little heed to him, and he shot one of the males, which crawled off. The next minute the bitch ran straight toward him and was almost at his stirrup when he killed her. The other three wolves, instead of running away, jumped to and fro growling, with their hair bristling, and he killed two of them; whereupon the survivor at last made off. He brought the scalps of the three dead wolves home with him.

Near our first camp was the carcass of a deer, a yearling buck, which had been killed by a cougar. When first found, the wounds on the carcass showed that the deer had been killed by a bite in the neck at the back of the head; but there were scratches on the rump as if the panther had landed on its back. One of the negro hunters, Brutus Jackson, evidently a trustworthy man, told me that he had twice seen cougars, each time under unexpected conditions.

Once he saw a bobcat race up a tree, and riding toward it saw a panther reared up against the trunk. The panther looked around at him quite calmly, and then retired in leisurely fashion. Jackson went off to get some hounds, and when he returned two hours afterwards the bobcat was still up the tree, evidently so badly scared that he did not wish to come down. The hounds were unable to follow the cougar. On another occasion he heard a tremendous scuffle and immediately afterwards saw a big doe racing along with a small cougar literally riding it. The cougar was biting the neck, but low down near the shoulders; he was hanging on with his front paws, but was tearing away with his hind claws, so that the deer's hair appeared to fill the air. As soon as Jackson appeared the panther left the deer. He shot it, and the doe galloped off, apparently without serious injury.

****

Originally published in volume 2 of The Encyclopaedia of Sport *(New York: G. P. Putnam, 1898; pp. 540–541), edited by Hedley Peek, earl of Suffolk and Berkshire, and F. G. Aflalo, this piece should not be confused with one of the same title that forms chapter 3 of* Outdoor Pastimes of an American Hunter *(1908). The latter describes specific hunting experiences and includes significant coverage of coyotes as well as wolves, while this piece is an overview of precisely the sort one would expect to find in an encyclopedia. It makes clear the fact that TR had not only participated in the sport but had read extensively about its origins and traditions. This is one of eight selections taken from* The Encyclopaedia of Sport. *All are little known; they receive no mention in John Hall Wheelock's* A Bibliography of Theodore Roosevelt *(1920).*

WOLF-COURSING

The wolf has always been recognised as the inveterate foe of man, and especially of domestic beasts; moreover, his fur is quite valuable. Wherever he is found, therefore, men wage merciless war upon him with guns, traps, and poison. He is very wary and cunning, however, and is well able to take care of his skin, so that every means must be taken to outwit him and every ally enlisted against him. Accordingly, from the earliest times, man in chasing the wolf has made use of the wolf's close kinsman and hated foe, the dog. Most domestic dogs loathe and fear the wolf more than any other beast; and a hungry wolf will snap up one of them as readily as he will snap up a sheep. Only a few breeds can be brought to face the wolf, and these must be specially trained. The huge shaggy dogs used in different pastoral countries to guard the sheep or cattle often have to encounter wolves. The big smooth-haired dogs, certain varieties of which were especially trained in the Middle Ages to assist in the death-grapple with dangerous beasts of the chase, can also be used against wolves. Hounds proper will only run a wolf if specially trained, and they are too weak to assail him singly or in small parties; but for centuries the great sportsmen of Continental Europe have hunted the wolf with specially trained packs, and a few of these are still kept up and trained for this purpose. But the true dog to use in the chase of the wolf is what was anciently called the "long dog", the gaze-hound, now called the greyhound. The Irish wolf-dog was simply a giant, rough-haired greyhound, and the quaint old sporting books of three centuries back show how frequently powerful greyhounds were used to overtake and tackle wolves, which the ordinary track-hounds had roused from their lairs.

The ordinary greyhound used for the chase of the hare is too light for rough work against dangerous prey, and in most countries the few remaining wolves have retired into wooded and rocky fastnesses where greyhounds are of no use; but where wolves are found on great open plains, like those of Russia and Siberia, and parts of western North America, greyhounds are specially adapted for their chase. At present there is a good deal of wolf-coursing done both in America and in Russia, though the conditions of the sport are widely different in the two places; for in Russia it is regarded as a sport pure and simple, to be followed only by a few of the great nobles; while in America, aside from an occasional army officer or ranchman, it is followed as a business by men who wish to exterminate the wolves, either for the bounty or to protect the cattle heads. Moreover, as in America the settlements continually increase, the wolves continually decrease, and the sport is so much more evanescent that it has never had the opportunity to assume any fixity of type.

In both places special types of dog have been bred for the purpose. In Russia these are the so-called borzois, or long-haired greyhounds, a type which has been in existence for centuries. In America a few men, during the last thirty or forty years, have bred big greyhounds, both smooth- and rough-coated, producing a type which shows signs of reversion to the old Irish wolfhound; dogs weighing something like 100 pounds, of remarkable power and of reckless and savage temper. The professional hunters, however, draft into their packs any animal which can run fast and fight hard, and their so-called greyhounds are often of mongrel breed.

In Russia the sport is a science. The princes and great landowners who take part in it have their hunting equipages perfected to the smallest detail. Not only do they follow wolves in the open, but they capture them and let them out before the dogs, as hares are let out at ordinary coursing matches. The huntsman follows his hounds on horseback. Two, three, or four dogs usually run together, and they are not expected to kill the wolf, but merely to hold him; and as soon as possible after he is thrown the huntsman leaps to the ground, forces the short handle of his riding-whip between the beast's jaws, and then binds them tightly together with the long thong. Great skill and coolness is needed, both on the part of dogs and men. The borzois can readily overtake and master partly-grown wolves, but a full-grown dog-wolf, in good trim, will usually gallop away from them, and will outfight any reasonable number. A good many borzois have been imported into America, but when tried against our wolves they have not, as a rule, done as well as the best home-bred dogs.

In America, the only place where I have had a chance to take part in the sport, it is of course conducted in a much more rough-and-ready manner. For fifty years the officers of the United States army on the great plains have used greyhounds to chase jackrabbits, foxes, coyotes, and occasionally antelopes. Now and then those dogs which had been entered on coyotes were used against the big wolves; but it was only during the last few decades that the sport became at all common. There are now, however, a good many men who follow it in Montana, Wyoming, and here and there in Colorado and western North Dakota. There is a pack near my ranch on the Little Missouri which has a record of several hundred wolves to its credit. The owner is a professional wolfer, and his dogs represent every kind of pure blood and half-blood greyhound; but they are a wicked, hard-biting crew, and as they are usually hunted eight or ten together, they will, unlike the borzois, tear even the biggest wolf literally to pieces, without assistance from the hunter. Numerous casualties of course occur in the pack, for a wolf is a desperate fighter, and the sound and sight of the worry is fairly blood-curdling. The Sun River, in Western Montana, was at one time a famous place for its wolfhounds, and there was another celebrated pack near Fort Benton; but it is eight years since I was in either neighbourhood, and time marches fast in the Far West. My own experiences have usually been with scratch packs, to which I have occasionally contributed a dog or two myself. Ordinarily these packs contained nothing but greyhounds, either smooth- or rough-coated, but in one of them there were two huge fighting dogs of mixed ancestry, which could not keep up with the greyhounds, but did most of the killing when their lighter-footed friends had succeeded in stopping the quarry. The greyhounds with which we usually hunted had not been specially trained to the work, and were not bred for the purpose, having simply served an apprenticeship as coyote hunters. In consequence they were not capable of killing the wolf without assistance. They usually stopped him by snapping at his hams, and would then form a ring through which he could not break; or if he did break they would overhaul him shortly, and once more bring him to a standstill. The hunters either shot him or roped him.

I doubt if the sport, even when carried on in a more legitimate manner, could afford more fun than these helter-skelter skurries over the plains gave us. We generally started for the hunting-grounds very early riding across the country in a widely spread line of dogs and men, and if we put up a wolf we simply went at him as hard as we knew how. Young wolves or those that had not attained their full strength, were readily overtaken, and the pack would handle a small she-wolf quite readily. A big dog-wolf, or even a full-grown and powerful bitch-wolf, offered an altogether different problem. Frequently we came upon them after they had gorged themselves on a colt or calf. Under such conditions, if the dogs had a good start, they ran into the wolf and held him; but if a big wolf in good running trim was able to keep ahead of them for half a mile or so, his superior strength and endurance told, and he gradually drew away.

Of course the packs composed of nothing but specially trained and specially bred greyhounds of great size and power made a better showing. Under favourable circumstances three or four of these dogs readily overtook and killed the largest wolf, rushing in together and invariably seizing by the throat. The risk to the pack was so great, however, and dogs were so frequently killed or crippled in the worry, that the hunter always endeavoured to keep as close as possible, and on his arrival he put an immediate end to the contest by a knife-thrust. In running, the dogs usually had an advantage, because they were so apt to find the wolf near a carcase (sic) from which it had just made a hearty meal; and, moreover, the dogs, when possible, were taken on a wagon to the field of their exploits. Their dashing courage and ferocious fighting capacity were marvellous, and in this respect I was never able to see much difference between the smooth-haired and the wire-haired, or Scotch deer-hound, types, while the smooth-haired were generally faster.

****

Wild turkeys were already becoming scarce during Roosevelt's heyday, and they would become increasingly more so in ensuing decades. Only after biologists discovered that the birds could be effectively restocked through use of live trapping and transfer techniques did the saga of the turkey's comeback, one of America's greatest wildlife conservation stories, begin. In this piece from vol-

ume 2 of The Encyclopedia of Sport *(New York: G. P. Putnam, 1898;*
pp. 501–502), edited by Hedley Peek, earl of Suffolk and Berkshire,
and F. G. Aflalo, we find out just how much the sport has altered over
the course of a century.

Several of the practices Roosevelt describes — roost shooting,
coursing with greyhounds, and driving — are now either illegal or
considered unethical. Similarly, his comment that "the most sports-
manlike way of killing turkeys . . . is by fair still-hunting with a small
calibre rifle" would likely raise eyebrows in many turkey hunting
circles today. Many states, in fact, allow shotgun hunting only,
although others continue to permit the use of rifles. Even more strik-
ing is the scant attention that TR devotes to the most widely accept-
ed modern method of hunting, the use of calling techniques to draw
the bird to the hunter.

This reveals some uncharacteristic ignorance on his part, because
well before this piece was written, C. L. Jordan was writing on the
use of yelpers made of cane or of turkey wing bones, and Henry L.
Gibson had already patented his box call. Furthermore, hunting with
the use of calls was commonplace over much of the wild turkey's
range, most notably in the South. Accordingly, this little essay is of
interest primarily for its quaintness and as an example of how much
things can change in a hundred years. The article was reprinted
under the title "Turkey Hunting a Century Ago," with introductory
commentary by the present writer, in the March/April 2000 issue of
Turkey Call.

TURKEY

The wild turkey is the king of the game birds of North America. It was formerly very abundant throughout most portions of the United States, but it is almost as eagerly followed as the deer, and is less well able to protect itself, so that it has now been practically exterminated from most of the Northern States. In the Southern States, however, there are still plenty of places where excellent wild turkey shooting can be obtained. The sport is carried on in several different ways. Sometimes the shot-gun is used, and sometimes the rifle. The birds are sometimes baited, corn being scattered about in some place until they get into the habit of going there, and the shooter then lies in wait for them. More often they are called, a peculiar little whistle being used, and the hunter lying concealed while he imitates the notes either of the gobblers or of the hens. In its essence this is a repetition of moose calling on a small scale, and almost as much skill is necessary, for the wild turkey is an extremely wary bird, and only an expert can call an old gobbler up to a blind.

In the wildest regions it is still possible to enjoy the fun of shooting turkeys on their roosts. Frequently large flocks will make an habit of going to one place to roost, and the hunter can, by taking proper precautions, lie hidden there until they have settled down and night has fallen. The turkeys are then very loth (sic) to leave, and frequently a goodly number can be shot, especially if those lowest on the branches are selected, before the others will take flight.

The most sportsmanlike way of killing turkeys, however, is by fair still-hunting with a small calibre rifle. Turkeys are quite noisy, especially in the early morning, and if the still-hunter is out early enough, he can hear them as they fly off from their roosting trees or settle on their feeding grounds. Extreme caution is necessary, for the turkeys are very wary, and the man must be both a good and a quick shot with the rifle.

An even more sporting way of chasing wild turkey is with greyhounds. This is of course only possible in country which is open, interspersed here and there with groves, or gullies filled with brushwood; and of course turkeys are much more quickly killed off in such places than in regions of dense forests, so the sport is necessarily evanescent. It was at one time followed a good deal by the Army officers, and some of the ranchmen, in Texas. The method was to start out quite early in the morning to some ground where the birds were known to be feeding away from thick timber, and to get between them and the cover. Then all possible care was used to bring the dogs near the birds as possible before the latter took alarm. As the turkey sprang into the air the greyhounds raced after him, for they speedily grew to understand their work, and kept an eye on the bird in front of them.

If the turkey managed in his first flight to get to cover, or if he crossed such difficult country that the greyhounds were thrown out, the hunt was over; but if the ground was open and fairly level, and the dogs good, they kept him in sight until he lit. The heavy bodied, short winged turkey is not a bird of strong flight; it gets very tired after going about a mile, and lights. If the greyhounds had been favoured by fortune they were near enough to see the bird as it lit. The turkey then began to run along the ground, but in a minute or so the greyhounds were on him and put him up again.

His second flight was always much shorter and slower than the first, for he was now tired. Probably, however, he still kept ahead of the dogs. If he did not distance them at the outset they gained on him towards the end of his flight as he came toward the ground, and ran underneath, making wonderful springs at the spent bird as he sailed along fifteen or twenty feet above their heads. Sooner or later, as the bird became exhausted and sank nearer the ground, one of these springs would be successful, the sharp teeth would close on the old gobbler, and the chase would be at an end. Even if the turkey distanced his pursuers the second time, they would be on him again very soon, and the third flight was so weak that only the close proximity of cover gave the quarry any show at all. It was usually too exhausted to try a fourth flight.

In some old European hunting book I have read of taking the great bustard with greyhounds, and I have elsewhere seen it stated that this was an impossibility, as the bustard was a bird that flew well; but on reading Mr. Abel Chapman's very interesting book on Wild Spain, I was struck by his account of his experience with bustards, and how he followed them on horseback, with the result of finding that after one or two flights the usually wary birds would lie close to the ground and seek to escape observation instead of trusting again to their wings. Under such circumstances it is evident that good greyhounds might take them just as they take wild turkeys.

****

Roosevelt had some familiarity with elk (or wapiti) as a hunter, and one of his lasting legacies, Yellowstone Park, has become vital habitat for the massive animals. He worried about the fate of the elk, which had become extinct east of the Mississippi River, and he would be delighted to learn that today some restoration efforts are under way (in West Virginia, Kentucky, and Arkansas, with the Great Smoky Mountains National Park being considered as a site as well). He would also give a nod of approval to the Rocky Mountain Elk Foundation, whose efforts underlie most of the restoration work, and he would be pleased that their national headquarters is in the same city (Missoula, Montana) as those of his beloved Boone and Crockett Club. This piece comes from volume 2 of The Encyclopaedia of Sport *(New York: G. P. Putnam, 1898; pp. 528–530), edited by Hedley Peek, earl of Suffolk and Berkshire, and F. G. Aflalo.*

WAPITI

The wapiti (*Cervus canadensis*) is the lordliest of all the true deer; and among all the beasts of the chase there is none more stately or more beautiful, and none which yields a finer trophy to the hunter. It is essentially a gigantic Scotch stag, or rather, the stag and the wapiti are the extreme forms of several races of the red deer type, which succeed one another in tolerably regular gradation as we pass from west to east through temperate portions of Europe, Asia, and North America.

Habitat—The white hunters throughout its range invariably call the wapiti "elk," because this was the name given to it by the settlers, who first encountered it near the Atlantic coast a couple of centuries ago. Formerly no game animal of North America, except the common or white-tailed deer, was so widely distributed as the wapiti; for though its habitat was, generally speaking, the same as that of the bison, it extended further west and further east. It abounded throughout the Alleghany ranges in the middle of the eighteenth century, and was very plentiful between them and the Mississippi as late as the Revolutionary War. Like other large game, however, it vanished with melancholy rapidity before the oncoming of the rifle-bearing settler.

By the beginning of the present century it had become practically extinct in most regions east of the Mississippi, except in some spots just south of the Great Lakes and in a small stretch of the Pennsylvania mountains, where the last individuals lingered until after the close of the Civil War. During the first half of the present century, wapiti abounded on the great plains; and all the earlier explorers bore witness to the abundance of the great herds, though they were not found in such incredible myriads as were the bison. Being conspicuous animals, which could often be run down with a good horse, they were killed off much sooner than deer or antelope. Like the bison, they were practically exterminated from the plains early in the eighties, excepting in an isolated tract here and there. They are now limited to the wooded mountains of the Rockies and the Cascades, where they are in places still very abundant. Indeed, there are parts of western Wyoming, Montana, Colorado, and Washington where they are almost as plentiful as ever.

Characteristics—The wapiti is highly polygamous, and during the rut the master bulls gather great harems about them, and do fierce battle with one another, while the weaker bulls are driven off by themselves. At this time the bulls are comparatively easy to approach, because they are very noisy, incessantly challenging one another by night and day. Settlers and hunters usually speak of their challenge as "whistling," but this is a very inadequate description. The challenge consists of several notes, first rising and then falling. Heard near by, especially amid unattractive surroundings, it is not particularly impressive, varying in tone from a squeal to a roar, and ending with grunts; but at a little distance it is one of the most musical sounds in nature, sounding like some beautiful wind instrument. Nothing makes the heart of a hunter leap and thrill like the challenge of a wapiti bull, as it comes pealing down under the great archways of the mountain pines through the still, frosty, fall weather; all the more if it be at night, under the full moon, and if there is light snow on the ground.

Methods of Pursuit—Doubtless the most exciting way to follow the wapiti was on horseback in the old days. Then the mounted hunter pursued him either with dogs or without, and in the latter case trusted to get alongside and kill him with a revolver-shot. The great size of the quarry was such that only the largest and most powerful dogs could in any way interfere with its flight.

Nowadays, however, wapiti must be generally killed by still-hunting, and the rifle has of need supplanted horse and hound. To me, still-hunting the wapiti has always been amongst the most attractive of sports. It cannot be said to be as difficult as the chase of the big horn, and it is free from the almost intolerable fatigue attendant upon clambering over mountain-tops after the white goat; but there is plenty of exercise about it if one hunts faithfully. Usually the scenery is very grand, for the wapiti are found scattered through the glade-broken forests which clothe the rolling mountain sides, and they have a habit of occasionally standing and even lying on bare, jutting look-out points on the edges of cliffs, from which one can see, as far as the eye can reach, nothing but vast stretches of lake-dotted, wooded wilderness. Often when I have killed a wapiti bull early in the morning, or at least with plenty of daylight ahead, so that there was no hurry about reaching camp, I have sat down by the dressed carcass, and literally for hours have gazed across deep valleys and at giant mountains, whose wild and savage beauty was unmarred by the least trace of man; then, with the tongue at my belt, I would start off to camp, timing myself so as to get there just as dusk came on and the blaze of the pitchy pine stumps shot upward through the darkness.

In the old days I not infrequently killed wapiti near my ranch on the Little Missouri. Even when I first went there, however, in the early eighties, wapiti had become scarce, while the black-tail deer still swarmed. I do not think I ever got a wapiti in one day's hunt from the ranch house. We always went with a wagon to some likely spot and began the hunt early the following morning. At the ranch house we depended for our fresh meat exclusively on our rifles; and on these occasions I was usually hunting for the table. I never got a wapiti head of any size on the Little Missouri.

My chief hunting after wapiti has been done in north-western Wyoming and western Montana, and there I got many splendid trophies. The largest head I ever killed had antlers fifty-six inches in length, and this is well above the ordinary size; nevertheless, in wholly exceptional cases they grow eight or ten inches and even a foot longer. Nothing can exceed the splendid massive symmetry of such a head.

On a trip in the mountains after elk it is usual to go with a pack train, for the country is too rough for wagons, and yet not so utterly impractica-ble as to forbid the use of horses, which is often the case in the haunts of sheep, goat, and caribou. With a pack train many comforts can be carried along, such as tents, and an ample supply of bedding, and of small luxu-ries for the table. In consequence it is far pleasanter, especially on a long trip, to have a pack train, for although any good hunter will always rough it as much as is necessary to get the game, still it is a pleasant thing to be comfortable when the chance offers. In fine weather a man can lie out in the open with impunity, and indeed I personally much prefer it to lying in a tent; but in the rain a man who has to lie out in the open is sure to have a rather dismal time. In the plains country, long-continued rains are rare, and, with a stout tarpaulin in which to wrap the bedding, a man can afford to disregard the chances of bad weather; but sometimes in the mountains it will rain every day for a considerable time, and then the discomfort of coming back to camp at night to pass a wretched hour standing up in a downpour, or couching under a leaking brush lean-to, with the certainty of damp blankets for the night, takes away a good deal of the fun of hunting. On the other hand, with a comfortable tent, a great deal of the fun of the hunting trip is after nightfall. To come back from a long all-day's walk, thoroughly tired, yet not so done up as to be unable to appreciate rest and a hot supper, to sit around the blazing pine logs after the meal of elk veni-son, grouse, trout, and flap-jacks, and to turn into one's warm sleeping bag as the ice begins to skim the water in the buckets, make up, in the aggre-gate, as much real comfort as often comes to any man.

From the point where one meets the pack train it is now usually sever-al days' journey into good elk country, for the skin- and meat-hunters butcher all game, the haunts of which are accessible from railroads. Once on the hunting grounds, it is easy to determine what are the chances for elk. If they are at all numerous, their trails will be seen everywhere, making well-beaten paths through the forests, while the edges of the streams and marshy hollows will be trodden up by the great round foot-prints, like those of two-year-old cattle. If it is during the rut, bulls are certain to be heard challenging one another. Later in the season, when there is apt to be snow on the ground, the trails are of course more distinct than ever.

In fairly wild country, there is less need in the case of wapiti than in the case of deer for being abroad early in the day. Although fond of taking siestas, they feed irregularly throughout the day; and during the rut the bulls are rarely still for any length of time, either by night or by day. In wild weather the herds are particularly active, although they are also then rather more difficult to get at, seeming to be more on the alert than when the weather is still and warm.

In hunting wapiti, some use can be made of glasses, but not nearly as much as in the case of sheep or goats, for there is too much forest. If it is rutting time, the bull can usually be placed by the sound of his challenge; otherwise his tracks must be diligently searched for, or else the hunter simply works his way cautiously through and across likely places until he comes upon some sign of his quarry. It is always necessary to go across or up wind, the nose of the wapiti being very sharp; but his eyesight is not particularly good—hardly as good as that of a deer, and not to be compared to that of a prong buck or mountain sheep. In very wild places wapiti bulls, especially during the rut, are so bold and self-confident that it is easy to stalk and kill them; but where they have been much hunted they become as wary as a deer, and it is then only their superior size, and the greater eagerness with which hunters follow them, that places them at a disadvantage in the struggle for life when compared with their smaller kinsfolk. Owing to its bulk, the wapiti is much more easily seen, and the hunter will of course follow it under circumstances in which he would abandon the chase of a deer, because the trophy is so much more valuable. Moreover, the wapiti lives in ground that favours the still hunter. The moose and the white-tail deer dwell in forests so dense that the difficulty of approaching them is very great; for it is almost impossible for any white man not to make some noise in slipping through the bushes and over the dead sticks and dried leaves. The sheep and goat are protected by the inaccessible nature of the lofty cliffs in which they delight. But the wapiti, like the black-tail deer, is not a beast of the high crags, nor, by preference, of the dense woods. The ground in which he delights is the broken rolling hill country, where groves and glades alternate, just as the black-tail loves the open hillsides, riven by gorges clad with ash and cedar. In consequence the wapiti and black-tail can be readily seen at quite a distance; whereas the moose and white-tail live in cover where it is hard to catch a glimpse of anything thirty yards off; and, moreover, when once seen, the wapiti and black-tail can generally be stalked without much difficulty, for there is always cover on rough hillsides and among patches of scattered timber. Under like conditions, however, I do not think that there is very much difference in point of wariness and keenness of sense among these four different beasts. Undoubtedly the moose and the white-tail are a little more clever, and the white-tail especially is the most cunning of all; but those wapiti and black-tail which do haunt the deep woods are nearly as hard to get at as their two slier relatives; at any rate, the difference is not great enough to warrant the hunter in taking liberties. Of course, in places which hunters have not yet penetrated—and there are a very few such in out-of-the-way mountain regions even nowadays—all four beasts are absurdly tame; but they never show the stupid self-confidence of the white goat.

Though the wapiti is so large and powerful, it is not a very tough beast, and succumbs to a bullet as readily as a deer or antelope. In shooting it I have usually carried a 45·75 or a 45·90 Winchester; but the new small calibre smokeless powder cartridges, using a bullet with the nose of naked lead, will probably become more and more in use among the hunters who follow them.

The flesh of the wapiti is to my taste more delicious than that of almost any other wild game; though it must be eaten hot, as the fat tends to form tallow as soon as cool. The wapiti is easily domesticated, at least to the extent of being hardy and breeding well when kept in parks; but as soon as the bulls lose the dread of man which they have when wild, they become very dangerous in the rutting season.

There are several aberrant forms of wapiti, including one that dwells in the great Tule swamps of California. There is also an entirely distinct species with its centre of abundance in the Olympic mountains of Washington and in Vancouver Island. This species, which Dr. Hart Merriam has recently done the present writer the honour of naming after him (*Cervus roosevelti*), is larger than the common form, with the head in winter black instead of dark brown; and the antlers have a straight beam, ending in a cluster of erect points instead of the long terminal prong with backward sweep, so characteristic of the ordinary form. The ordinary wapiti in the north reaches west to the Rocky Mountains. There then comes a great space where no wapiti are found at all until the coast ranges of the Pacific are reached, and the recently described species appears. From the days of Lewis and Clark these wapiti of the Pacific coast have been known, but they have always been confounded with the ordinary form, from which they are as distinct as is the Columbia black-tail deer from the ordinary black-tail or mule deer of the Rockies and the great plains.

****

Roosevelt was fascinated by the story of America's achievement of its manifest destiny, expansion across the continent from the Atlantic to the Pacific. We see concrete evidence of this in his widely acclaimed four-volume history, The Winning of the West *(1889–1896), and throughout his writings. He recognized that the bison played an important, even pivotal, role in his country's inexorable progress toward greener fields in the West. The meat fed mountain men and the hides drew hunters. The animal figured prominently in the traditions of Native American. The story of the Great Plains revolved in large measure around the vast herds. Roosevelt rightly bemoans the fate of the bison, saying that with its demise "there passed away what was perhaps the most imposing feature of American wilderness life." Unlike the sagas of the wild turkey, the white-tailed deer, and the elk, that of the bison has not been one marked by a significant comeback. The animal hangs on in protected areas in the wild and inside fences in the domesticated state, but it seems unlikely that the days when they could be hunted in fair chase will ever return. This piece comes from volume 1 of* The Encyclopaedia of Sport *(New York: G. P. Putnam, 1898; pp. 116–118), edited by Hedley Peek, earl of Suffolk and Berkshire, and F. G. Aflalo.*

BISON

The American Bison (*Bos americanus*), like its European congener, is on the verge of extinction, and as a beast of the chase it has already practically vanished, though a dwindling remnant of the northern form may still occasionally yield a trophy to the sportsman hardy enough to brave the wintry desolation of Athabaska. A very few head are left in the Yellowstone National Park, but are being killed out by poachers. There are several small tame herds here and there; and there are one or two spots in the Rocky Mountains, and possible one on the Mexican border, where two or three individuals still linger in a wild state. These are all.

Yet, fifteen years ago this was the characteristic animal of the plains, and still swarmed in the Upper Missouri Basin. It was hunted in two ways: by running it down on horseback, in which form of chase the heavy revolver was the weapon usually preferred, and by still-hunting, or stalking, on foot. The last was the method by which the great slaughter of the herds was accomplished. The hunters used long-range rifles, Sharps being probably the favourite weapon. These rifles were usually of .40 or .45 calibre, with a long heavy bullet, backed by about 100 grams of powder; they were very accurate long-range weapons, and as the buffalo (as the bison were always miscalled) were slow and stupid animals, a good marksman and skillful hunter could often slaughter twenty or thirty at a "stand," as it was termed.

I never came in contact with buffalo myself until at the very end of its existence as a species, and shot only two; one an unusually large solitary bull on the Little Missouri in 1883, and the other a very fine herd bull in Southwestern Montana in 1889. The first I stumbled across, and slew out of hand, with one of the ordinary buffalo rifles. The second was procured only after very careful tracking through a mountain forest and was killed with a single bullet from my Winchester.

My brother was in at the death of the southern buffalo herds early in 1877 in Northwestern Texas. He had full experience of both kinds of chase. Running buffalo on horseback was by far the most exciting method of killing them. The secret of success consisted in racing at full speed from the very outset, since the buffalo, though not very fleet, possessed marvellous endurance; and in riding up almost within arm's length of the brute before firing. It is a very difficult thing to shoot with any accuracy from a horse running at full speed, and especially at another object going at a somewhat different rate of speed. If the shots are fired from any distance, they are apt to miss or only would. The true method was to push right alongside and fire with the muzzle of the weapon but a couple of feet from the animal's back. It was important that the horse should be trained to sheer off as soon as the shot was fired, as the buffalo sometimes turned and charged with great fury. On a well-trained hunting pony there was little danger, for the buffalo had neither the pace not agility of the horse. An untrained horse, however, was generally afraid to come to close quarters, and moreover turned clumsily. I know of one instance where riding a large untrained Eastern horse caused a hunter to lose his life, the buffalo making good his charge and inflicting fatal injuries on both horse and rider. Even in this branch of the sport, however, accidents to life and limb from the quarry were not common, though there was no little risk from the falls naturally incident to riding at full speed over rough and broken country. It was a splendid sport, full of excitement, and it is melancholy to think that it is gone for ever.

Still-hunting the buffalo did not differ materially from still-hunting any other kind of game, except that it was rather easier when once the haunts of the bison were reached. Most game animals are adept at concealing themselves, but the buffalo never sought concealment, and its huge black body could be seen against the yellow prairie as far as the eye could reach; its sense of smell was very acute, but its eyesight was poor, and so stalking was easy. Occasionally the beast charged, but against heavy rifles in skillful hands his prowess availed nothing, and the danger was so inconsiderable, that with anything like proper caution it could be disregarded.

Pursuit by sportsmen had practically nothing to do with the extermination of the bison. It was killed by the hide hunters, red, white, and halfbreed. The railways, as they were built, hastened its destruction, for they gave means for transporting the heavy robes to market; but it would have been killed out anyhow, even were there no railroads in existence, and, once the demand for the robe became known to the Indians, they were certain to exterminate it in time, even had the white hunter refrained. Not even in South Africa has there been an instance where so many large game beasts of one species have been slain within so short a time. Originally the bison ranged between the Rocky Mountains and the Alleghanies and from Mexico to the Peace River; but its centre of abundance was the vast stretch of grass land reaching from the Saskatchewan to the Rio Grande. All the earlier explorers who crossed these great plains, from Lewis and Clark and Pike onward, dwelt upon the astounding multitudes of the bison, who furnished the entire means of subsistence for the tribes of Horse Indians. The herds were pressed steadily back, but the period of greatest slaughter did not begin until after the Civil War; then the commercial value of the robes became fully recognised, and the Trans-Continental Railways rendered the hunting-grounds more accessible. The slaughter was almost incredible, for the buffalo were slain literally by millions every year. They were exterminated first from Canada and from the Southern plains; it was not until 1883 that the last herd was killed form the Great Northwestern plains; and when the fierce greed of the skin hunter and skin buyer had exterminated the last of these great herds, there passed away what was perhaps the most imposing feature of American wilderness life.

****

Even species he did not have extensive opportunities to hunt, and this included caribou, were studied by Roosevelt in his uniquely intense fashion. It was his attention to detail and an insatiable quest for solid knowledge that placed him at the forefront of naturalists of his time. In this brief selection, taken from volume 1 of The Encyclopaedia of Sport *(New York: G. P. Putnam, 1898; pp. 180–181), edited by Hedley Peek, earl of Suffolk and Berkshire, and F. G. Aflalo, he gives a useful, informed view of the status of two species of caribou just before the turn of the century.*

CARIBOU

Owing to the inaccessible nature of its haunts, the life history of the Caribou is involved in some obscurity, and it is not quite certain whether there are two species, the Woodland and the Barren Ground, (C. tarandus and C. tarandus arcticus), or whether they are not both merely varieties of the European and Asiatic Reindeer. The forms certainly seem to intergrade, so as to make it difficult to draw any specific line; but the extreme varieties have very different habits.

The *Barren Ground Caribou* wanders far beyond the Arctic Circle, into those desolate regions which it shares with the Musk Ox, and it indulges in very curious and extensive migrations in the spring and fall; these migrations being in some respects different for the two sexes. When migrating, the herds assemble in enormous numbers, as the Bison used of old on the great plains of the West, and the Spring Buck in South Africa. In fact, this is the only American mammal which can still, at certain times and places, be found in the same incredible numbers as of old; for it is protected, as Bison, Elk, Deer, and Antelope are not, by the remoteness and frozen desolation of the wastes where it dwells.

The *Woodland Caribou*, on the other hand, is a beast of the dense Northern forests; in most localities it does not possess any very marked habit of annual migration, though at all times a restless, wandering beast; and it is usually found in small parties, and never in immense herds. The Woodland Caribou is found here and there in the forests of Canada, from the Atlantic to the Pacific, and in two or three places penetrates across the border of the United States.

Like all other large game, it retreats before man, but nevertheless it holds its own against him better than most of its congeners. Caribou are more plentiful in Maine at present than they were thirty years ago. They have one very great advantage in the struggle for life over their giant cousin, the Moose, who so often dwells in the same forest with them. The Moose's long legs and vast power enable him in winter to go through snows where an ordinary deer flounders helplessly; but, when the snows are very deep and a crust forms, he can be run down and killed, with no difficulty beyond the severe toil involved, by any hardy man who is an expert snow-shoer. In many localities, in consequence, the settlers have completely killed out the Moose by this villainous habit of "crusting."

The Caribou, however, is not, like the Moose, forced to plunge his legs through the snow to hard ground; he possesses huge splay hoofs and very limber joints, so that he himself has snow-shoes, as it were, and only under very peculiar conditions of crust is it possible for any man to get near him. When plunging at a gallop through the snow, the tracks he makes are not unlike those of a gigantic Rabbit; for the limber hind legs take his weight almost up to the hock. I have seen a Caribou run right away from a party of expert snow-shoers without showing any distress, though in snow where a Moose would have been overtaken in half a mile. This capacity tells immensely in his favour, and more than offsets the fact that under ordinary circumstances he is less wary and more stupid than the Moose.

The best time for hunting the Caribou is when there has been a light fall of snow, and he can be tracked while the footfall of the still-hunter is muffled. But in good ground he is not a very difficult beast to kill earlier in the season. He is very fond of lurking about the barrens and cranberry bogs which dot the Northern forests, and, if the hunter can see him here, there is always a good chance to creep up on him. In thick timber, where the trees are close together and there is much brush, with crisp, dry leaves on the ground, it is exceedingly difficult for anyone but an Indian to get up to the Caribou, or indeed any other kind of game. In open forests of large conifers, however, I have found it easy to track and still-hunt Caribou, whether they were feeding or lying down. If one is close on the game, they will often be so panic-struck by the first shot that it is an easy matter to kill several if there is need of the meat. I have had a young bull, whose companion I had just shot, stand looking at me fully half a minute in paralysed terror before it made up its mind to run off unmolested, as I did not want to kill it.

The sight of a Caribou seems scarcely as quick as that of the ordinary Deer, nor are its other senses so sharp, though like all game it has a good nose. It is not so wary as the Moose; but I may remark in passing that my own experience has been that under like conditions the common American or White Tail Deer is the most difficult game on the continent to circumvent; doubtless it is for this reason that it holds its own in the land better than other beasts of the chase.

Caribou are great swimmers, and it is a very common thing to kill them in the water. Of course, however, no man would kill game swimming for sport, although, when exploring and travelling in the wilderness, any man must kill the animals he needs for food, just as he happens to come upon them. It must be remembered that the wilderness hunter, the man who roams through far-off wilds in chase of big game, cannot afford to give law to the beasts of the chase, as can his brother of civilized regions, who does not depend for his dinner, and perhaps for his life, upon the result of a single shot. Where parties of sportsmen merely take a three weeks' trip into the woods for Caribou, they of course kill only the bulls, and these only in legitimate fashion; but a man who travels for three months without seeing a single white face, or who spends his winter alone 500 miles from the nearest human habitation, cannot afford to take chances. If he finds a favourite pass in a lake, across which Caribou swim, he will kill them at this pass; and if, during the time of short rations in midwinter, the conditions of the snow enable him to run up to a herd on snow-shoes, he takes all possible advantage of the opportunity.

****

Hunting America's big cats, variously known as cougars, pumas, and panthers, held considerable interest for Roosevelt. He enjoyed the thrill of the chase and the fact that the hunt involved canine companions. In this piece, he suggests that the animal is cowardly and that instances of attacks on humans are "wholly exceptional." However, today, in areas where cougar hunting has been outlawed, occurrences of this sort have become all too common. Nonetheless, TR exhibits his keen analytical powers when he notes that the puma and wolf fare less well under hunting pressure than the bear, even though the latter is easier to hunt with success. This selection comes from volume 2 of The Encyclopaedia of Sport *(New York: G. P. Putnam, 1898; pp. 154–155), edited by Hedley Peek, earl of Suffolk and Berkshire, and F. G. Aflalo.*

PUMA

The puma (*Felis concolor*) or cougar, also known as panther or painter, and as mountain lion and Mexican lion, is found from Patagonia to southern Canada. It is now very rare in most places north of Mexico, except in the Rocky Mountains and coast ranges, where it is locally not uncommon. It was formerly very plentiful in the Southern States; but, for some unexplained reason, neither the puma nor the wolf hold their ground in the presence of man so well as the black bear, which nevertheless seems an easier animal to kill than either of them.

Like all cats, the puma is not difficult to trap. It is, however, extremely difficult to kill according to the ordinary methods of the still hunter. The rifleman who trusts merely to his own skill hardly ever runs across the puma except by accident. In all my hunting I have come across but two, both by chance; and of these one escaped. If dogs are used, however, the puma is by no means a difficult quarry. In the wilder portions of the Southern States, the puma was often killed in olden times by the packs with which the planters hunted the deer and the grey fox; hounds readily run the trail of the puma, showing none of the fear and disgust which they are apt to betray at the scent of the wolf. These packs rarely did more than bay the puma, which was then shot by the hunters. Occasionally the pack was specially trained to rush in and take hold, and the hunter ended the battle by a thrust with his knife.

In the Rocky Mountains, of recent years, the practice has grown up in several localities of following the puma on foot with packs of dogs specially trained for the purpose. Such packs usually contain both the ordinary hound generally used in the chase of the deer and the fox, and large, active, hard-biting dogs, by preference collies. The puma will sometimes make a long and hard run, especially in difficult ground. At other times it will come to bay very speedily; or, what is more common, climb a tree. The puma is perhaps the least formidable of all the large cats, in spite of its extreme agility, for it is cowardly, and its head and jaws are small compared to those of the jaguar. There are on record authentic instances of its attacking man, but these are wholly exceptional. Even when at bay it can usually be killed without much danger; but it is never safe to take liberties with it, for exceptional individuals display the utmost ferocity, and I have known of several instances of men being maimed, and even killed in such contests. If the dogs are well trained, however, they usually occupy the puma's attention to the exclusion of everything else; and five or six of them, even ordinary hounds and collies, if thoroughly entered to their work, can themselves kill a puma. Such a fighting pack performs the work in the most business-like manner, each dog having its own favourite hold, and each being confident in the support of its fellows. If a wolf is throttled by a powerful dog, it can inflict little damage; but if the puma is throttled it may rip open the dog with its hind claws. A trained pack will, therefore, rush in together and spread-eagle the puma, which is then soon worried to death. Accidents to the pack, of course, frequently happen.

****

Roosevelt took particular delight in any type of sport that demanded great physical exertion or posed exceptional difficulties. Thanks to the nature of its preferred habitat — TR said that "there is no game animal in America the pursuit of which entails such severe toil" — he had a special affinity for an animal that in truth is a member of the antelope family rather than a goat. Little has changed in the century since this piece first appeared in volume 1 of The Encyclopaedia of Sport *(New York: G. P. Putnam, 1898; pp. 455–456), edited by Hedley Peek, earl of Suffolk and Berkshire, and F. G. Aflalo. The animal still exists in huntable numbers in remote Rocky Mountain ranges, and its inaccessibility, along with careful protection that includes limited-draw hunts, promises to ensure such will continue to be the case.*

ROCKY MOUNTAIN GOAT

The white or Rocky Mountain (*Haploceros montanus*) goat is not a goat at all, but a very peculiar mountain antelope, its nearest relatives being certain of the Himalayan antelopes. The fact that we call our only antelope a goat may, I suppose, be taken as an offset to the other fact that the prongbuck, which is universally called antelope by American hunters, is not one at all, standing among ruminants in a position as unique as that of the giraffe.

The white goat has certain peculiarities which mark it off from all other mountain game. It occasionally sits up on its haunches like a dog to look at something which strikes it as suspicious. It is extraordinarily tame or stupid, showing a bold self-confidence which no other animal of its size displays. Moreover, though it dwells by choice among appalling precipices, and is a marvellous climber, it utterly lacks the bounding agility, not only of the chamois, but even of such heavy beasts as the mountain sheep. It generally climbs with a sort of sturdy deliberation, and often lifts itself on a ledge by spreading its elbows apart and drawing the body up much as a man would. It is singularly intolerant of heat, and even on rather cold days will retire to a cave, with the temperature freezing, in order to get out of the sunlight.

There is a muskpod between the horn and ear which makes the flesh of all but young animals uneatable. The needle-pointed horns are from eight to ten inches long, and so do not offer much of a trophy. The pure white robe, which is very thick, long and woolly in winter, and which contrasts so vividly with the black hoofs, horns and muzzle, has some commercial value, but at present not very much. In consequence the beast is not much followed by the professional hunters, who can find more valuable game in less inaccessible places; for the chief protection of the white goat is the extraordinary roughness of its haunts.

Sportsmen have, within the last dozen years, begun to follow the white goat quite eagerly; but game is really never thinned out by true sportsmen, and the queer, musky self-confident beasts offer a striking contrast to other American game in the fact that they have hitherto decreased very little in numbers.

There is no game animal in America the pursuit of which entails such severe toil. In places where the mountains run down into little-frequented fiords, or great lonely lakes, it is possible to go right into the haunts of the white goat by canoe, and occasionally to surprise one near the water; but ordinarily the animals are to be found only after heart-breaking climbing. To get into the region where they are found it is sometimes possible to take a packtrain, and at other times a canoe. Often, however, the journey must be performed on foot from the beginning; and this is almost always the case when the edges of the hunting grounds themselves are reached, and it is desired to camp within reasonable distance of the range of the game. Only the barest necessities can be carried on a man's back. In my own experience I have usually gone after white goats with but one companion, some old mountaineer who knew the ranges; though in one instance I also took an Indian with me. The wooded lower slopes of the mountains throughout most of the white goats' range are so broken, and covered with such a tangled mass of forest and undergrowth, that the walking is difficult beyond belief. Every step is severe exertion. A walk is one perpetual scramble over fallen timber, through deep gullies, across boulder-strewn points up sheer cliff walls, through masses of twisted bushes, over windfalls where the down timber, amid the wildest confusion, lies sometimes thirty feet from the ground, with young spruce growing thickly between the logs—an added touch of discomfort being given where the country is burnt. After an hour's scramble over country like this a man will be so drenched with sweat that he will look as if he had fallen into water. His fare is of course but meagre, unless he can manage to shoot something, and this is very difficult in such a forest, because it is out of the question not to make a noise.

Camp is usually made in some glade by a stream, as near the upper edge of the timber as possible, for ordinarily the goats are found far above timer land. They can best be hunted in the evening and morning, although they feed at intervals all through the day. The start has to be made very early, because there is sure to be several hours' climbing before one finds the animal. They are by no means difficult to see, their white bodies being very conspicuous, and once seen the stalk itself is comparatively easy. All that is necessary is to get above them, for they seem to suspect danger only from below, and if surprised will almost always run up-hill. They are bold, pugnacious and stupid, and are so accustomed to the noise of falling rocks that they are not readily alarmed by a slip or a misstep on the part of the hunter. In consequence, there is little need to display the hunting craft absolutely necessary in the chase of the big horn, the moose and the wapiti. The qualities called for in the hunter are ability to endure the prolonged and extreme fatigue of climbing among the stupendous rock walls where the goat antelope dwells, and the nerve to cross the occasional bits of dangerous ground encountered. In other words, the demand is made upon the qualities called for in mountaineering rather than in ordinary hunting. Nevertheless, as the test of the highest sport is the display of manliness and hardihood, the chase of the white goat deserves fair rank; for the white goat hunter must be hardy and persevering, and must have a good head, good lungs, and good muscles.

****

Taken from volume 2 of The Encyclopaedia of Sport *(New York: G. P. Putnam, 1898; pp. 131–132), edited by Hedley Peek, earl of Suffolk and Berkshire, and F. G. Aflalo, this selection rightly suggests that Roosevelt's interests as a naturalist were by no means limited to big game. Indeed, birds had formed the primary basis for his fledgling studies in natural history and for the "Roosevelt Museum of Natural History" that had its beginnings in his boyhood bedroom. Here he looks at both true prairie chickens and sharp-tailed grouse, with characteristic comments on how to hunt them and the sport they offer.*

PRAIRIE CHICKEN

Of all American grouse, the species of ground grouse, found as a rule away from woodland, and commonly called "prairie chicken," yield most sport; though the ruffed-grouse, a dweller in the woods, is a well-known and highly appreciated game bird whenever it is found. The big sage fowl, also a grouse of the open country, the largest of all, exists so far from water that it is ordinarily not much sought after by the men who use setters and pointers. The blue-grouse, spruce-grouse, and ptarmigan are as yet chiefly killed for the pot by men who are on trips after big game. The ptarmigan, except in the extreme north, is only found high up on the mountains, and the blue-grouse and spruce-grouse in thick timber, where they are frequently killed with the rifle, their heads being shot off as they sit on trees.

There are two entirely distinct birds known as prairie chickens. The true prairie chicken, or pinnated-grouse (*Cupidonia cupido;* there are several geographical varieties or sub-species), which was formerly, in one of its forms, a common bird east to the Atlantic coast, has now vanished from practically all the eastern part of its range, and has been sadly thinned out even in Illinois and Wisconsin. In Iowa and Minnesota it is still abundant, and it works its way westward with the cultivation of the land. The ordinary way to shoot the birds is to take two or three dogs for each sportsman, and a wagon to carry the entire party. The distances are so great that the dogs must travel well and range far. Men on foot could hardly cover enough ground, as it will often be necessary to pass over a mile or two of country which is not worth beating. In all likely spots the wagon is left, and the sportsmen follow their dogs, just as was done in England before the days of "battues." The birds are sometimes found in the stubble fields, and sometimes out on the prairie. Early in the season they are easy to kill. By October they are very strong and wild, and then need straight powder. They are most delicious eating.

The other kind of prairie fowl is the sharp-tailed grouse (*Pediœcetes phasianellus;* likewise with several geographical sub-species), a more northern and western bird. The limits of the two species overlap; and in the Dakotas the pinnated grouse has been extending its range westwards, the sharp-tail seeming to recede before it. As the sharp-tail is especially the grouse of the cattle country, it is much followed by all sport-loving ranchmen; but as it inhabits a drier country than the pinnated-grouse, it offers a rather more difficult problem for dogs. Early in the season, sharp-tails are shot precisely as ordinary prairie chickens are shot. As cold weather comes on, they assemble on the river bottoms and take to perching on the trees. They then become very wild and shy, and do not offer much sport.

The first sparse settlement of the land does not in any way interfere with the increase of these grouse. On the contrary, the ranchmen, by the war they wage on the wolves and coyotes, help the grouse in their struggle for existence. In the purely pastoral parts of Montana and the Dakotas, these birds are probably more plentiful now than they were fifty years ago. But they disappear as the settlements become dense. This seems to be true of all the game of the plains, whether furred or feathered. The beasts and birds of the deep woods hold their own, as those of the plains cannot. There is no likelihood of the extinction of the ruffed-grouse; it is still found in places from which the pinnated-grouse has absolutely disappeared, though once the latter outnumbered it fifty to one. But both species of prairie chicken are steadily diminishing in numbers. The efforts of the game associations and sportsmen's clubs to have the game laws properly enforced have done much to arrest this diminution, and here and there to stop it; but the communities as a whole will have to see more clearly than they now do the effects of wasteful slaughter of game birds and game beasts before these birds and beasts can be effectually preserved.

PART IV

Sporting Ways in Later Days

Introductory Note

Long before he became an internationally renowned figure, Roosevelt had established extensive connections with individuals both in the United States and abroad who shared his interest in sport and natural history. However, that circle of contacts and correspondents broadened even more once he was in the White House, and during his presidential years TR's interests in the outdoors showed no sign of waning. He entertained the great English hunter-explorer Fred Selous in Washington, and the man whom he described as "the greatest of the world's big-game hunters" would figure prominently in the preparations underlying Roosevelt's African adventure. TR's tribute to him, reprinted here, is a eulogistic masterpiece.

In addition to Selous, TR regularly invited individuals such as John Burroughs and John Muir to dinner or other social functions. He also established an acquaintance with Sir Harry Johnston, the discoverer of the okapi and the first European to reach the snow line on Mount Kilimanjaro, and he wrote literally scores of letters every week. Roosevelt had long dreamed of hunting abroad, and the conclusion of his second term as president gave him that opportunity. His African safari was in many senses the highlight of his sporting career, and the subsequent trip to Brazil, though it took a devastating physical toll, afforded great pleasure as well. There were other outings that, while not so lengthy or exotic, brought real fulfillment. Descriptions of two of them — a cougar hunt in the West and an unusual trip after rays (devilfish) — appear here.

****

One of the great friendships of Roosevelt's life, even though the pair came in personal contact on only a handful of occasions, was with the English hunter Fred Selous. A man who has often been credited with being the inspiration for H. Rider Haggard's fictional character Alan Quatermain, Selous epitomized the virtues that Roosevelt cherished. He was a first-rate amateur naturalist, a consummate master of woodcraft, courageous to a fault, and an accomplished author. He also lived (to a far greater degree than Roosevelt) the "strenuous life," or, as TR so aptly put it, "a singularly adventurous and fascinating life."

Roosevelt's papers reveal an extensive correspondence with this kindred soul, and in the midst of his second term as president, TR found time to write a lengthy foreword to what many consider the best of Selous's books, African Nature Notes and Reminiscences *(1908). Selous was killed by a sniper's bullet in the East African theater during World War I, after having moved heaven and earth to secure a place in the British military (he was in his sixties when the Great War began). This overlooked tribute, which appeared on pages 410–411 of the March 7, 1917, edition of the* Outlook, *reads almost like a catalog of the characteristics Roosevelt considered important in a man. It is included in the second volume of my two-volume collection of forgotten Selous writings,* Selous: An African Legend *(2000), under the Safari Press imprint.*

****

FREDERICK COURTENEY SELOUS

Last December, just before reaching the age of sixty-five years, Selous, the great hunter-naturalist and explorer, was killed in action against the Germans in East Africa. In the brief press dispatches it is stated that he was shot and mortally wounded, but continued to urge forward his men until he was hit a second time and killed. It was a fit and gallant end to a gallant and useful life. In John Guille Millais's delightful "Breath from the Veldt" the frontispiece, by Sir John E. Millais, shows the "Last Trek" of a hunter, dying beside his wagon in the wilderness. The hunter in this picture is drawn from Selous. Many of us used to think that it was the death he ought to die. But the death he actually met was better still.

Selous was born on the last day of the year 1851. Before he was twenty years old he went to South Africa, and a year or two later he embarked on the career of a professional elephant hunter; a career incredibly wearing and exhausting, in which mortal risk was a daily incident. For a quarter of a century he was a leading figure among the hard-bit men who pushed ever northward the frontier of civilization. His life was one of hazard, hardship, and daring adventure, and was as full of romantic interest and excitement as that of a Viking of the tenth century. He hunted the lion and the elephant, the buffalo and the rhinoceros. He knew the extremes of fatigue in following the heavy game, and of thirst when lost in the desert wilderness. He was racked by fever. Strange and evil accidents befell him. He faced death habitually from hostile savages and from the grim quarry he hunted; again and again he escaped by a hair's breadth, thanks only to his cool head and steady hand. Far and wide he wandered through unknown lands, on foot or on horseback, his rifle never out of his grasp, only his black followers bearing him company. Sometimes his outfit was carried in a huge white-topped wagon drawn by sixteen oxen, while he rode in advance on a tough, shabby horse; sometimes he walked at the head of a line of savage burden-bearers. He camped under the stars, in the vast wastes, with the ominous cries of questing beasts rising from the darkness round about. It was a wild and dangerous life, and could have been led only by a man with a heart of steel and a frame of iron.

There were other men, Dutch and English, who led the same hard life of peril and adventure. Selous was their match in daring and endurance. But, in addition, he was a highly intelligent civilized man, with phenomenal powers of observation and of narration. There is no more foolish cant than to praise the man of action on the ground that he will not or cannot tell of his feats. Of course loquacious boastfulness renders any human being an intolerable nuisance. But, except among the very foremost (and sometimes among these also, as witness innumerable men from Cæsar to Marco Polo and Livingstone) the men of action who can tell truthfully, and with power and charm, what they have seen and done add infinitely more to the sum of worthy achievement than do the inarticulate ones, whose deeds are often of value only to themselves. Selous when only thirty published his "Hunter's Wanderings in Africa," than which no better book of the kind has ever been written. It at once put him in the first rank of the men who can both do things worth doing and write of them books worth reading. He had the gift of seeing with extraordinary truthfulness, so that his first-hand observations—as in the case of the "species" of black rhinoceros—are of prime scientific value. He also had the gift of relating in vivid detail his adventures; in speaking he was even better than in writing, for he entered with voice and gesture so thoroughly into the part that he became alternately the hunter and the lion or buffalo with which he battled.

Elephant hunting in South Africa as a profitable profession became a thing of the past. But Selous worked for various museums as a field collector of the great game; and as the pioneers began to strive northward, he broke the trail for them into Mashonaland, doing the work of the road-maker, the bridge-builder, the leader of men through the untrodden wilderness; and he continued his hunting and exploration. His next book, "Travel and Adventure in Southeast Africa," was as good as his first. He now stood at the zenith of his fame as the foremost of all hunter naturalists.

Soon after this he left South Africa and returned to live in England. But he was not really in place as a permanent dweller in civilization. He longed overmuch for the lonely wilderness. At home he delivered lectures, rode to hounds, studied birds, and lived in a beautiful part of Sussex. Whenever he got the chance he again took up the life of a roaming hunter. He made trip after trip to Asia Minor, to East Africa, to Newfoundland and the Rockies, to the White Nile. He wrote various books about these trips. One, "African Nature Notes," is of first-class importance, being his most considerable contribution to field science—a branch of scientific work to the importance of which, in contradistinction to purely closet science we are only just beginning to awake.

The eighteen or twenty years he passed in this manner would of themselves have made a varied and satisfactory career for any ordinary man. But he was not wholly satisfied with them, because he compared them with the life of his greater fame and service in the vanguard of the South African movement. Speaking of the fact that his "Nature Notes" sold only fairly well, he remarked one day, "You see, all the young men think I am dead—at any rate, they think I ought to be dead!" He read much, but only along certain lines. I was much interested, on one occasion, to find him fairly enthralled by the ballad of "Twa Corbies." He himself possessed all the best characteristics of simplicity, directness, and strength which marked the old ballads and ballad heroes.

Then the great war came, and for months he ate his heart out while trying in vain to get to the front. The English did far better than we would have done. But they blundered in various ways—Ireland offers the most melancholy example. The cast-iron quality of the official mind was shown by the rigid application of certain rules which in time of stress becomes damaging unless made flexible. The War Office at first refused to use Selous—just as they kept another big-game hunter, Stigand, up the White Nile doing work that many an elderly sportsman could have done, instead of utilizing him in the East African fighting. Selous was as hardy as an old wolf; and, for all his gentleness, as formidable to his foes. He was much stronger and more enduring than the average man of half his age. But with a wooden dullness which reminded me of some of the antics of our own political bureaucracy, the War Office refused him permission to fight and sent him out to East Africa in the transport service—his letters on some of the things that occurred in East Africa were illuminating. However, he speedily pushed his way into the fighting line, and fought so well that the home authorities grudgingly accepted the accomplished fact, and made him a lieutenant. He won his captaincy and the

Distinguished Service Order before he died.

It was my good fortune to know Selous fairly well. He spent several days with me at the White House; he got me most of my outfit for my African hunt. He went to Africa on the same boat, and I came across him out there on two or three occasions. I also saw him in his attractive Sussex home, where he had a special building for his extraordinary collection of game trophies. He was exactly what the man of the open, the outdoors man of adventurous life, who is also a cultivated man, should be. He was very quiet and considerate, and without the smallest touch of the braggart or brawler; but he was utterly fearless and self-reliant and able to grapple with any emergency or danger. All men of the open took to him at once; with the Boers he was on terms of close friendship. Indeed, I think that any man of the right type would have found him sympathetic. His keenness of observation made him a delightful companion. He never drank spirits; indeed, his favorite beverage at all times was tea.

It is well for any country to produce men of such a type; and if there are enough of them the nation need fear no decadence. He led a singularly adventurous and fascinating life, with just the right alternations between the wilderness and civilization. He helped spread the borders of his people's land. He added much to the sum of human knowledge and interest. He closed his life exactly as such a life ought to be closed, by dying in battle for his country while rendering her valiant and effective service. Who could wish a better life, or a better death, or desire to leave a more honorable heritage to his family and his nation?

****

In this important article, which originally appeared by invitation in the American Museum Journal *(vol. 18, no. 5 [1918]: 321–330) as an essay liberally supported with photographs, Roosevelt provides an overview of his endeavors as a natural historian. Although he states, in a somewhat uncharacteristic self-effacing fashion, that his "experience as an amateur naturalist" has been "very limited," such decidedly was not the case. Those familiar with his work will find that this is in large measure a compendium of bits and pieces of material that previously appeared in print, but the overall result is a useful look at the high points of his forays afield, with natural history, as opposed to sport, being foremost in mind. As Roosevelt rightly indicates, his work as a naturalist "added immeasurably to my sum of enjoyment in life."*

MY LIFE AS A NATURALIST

I am asked to give an account of my interest in natural history, and my experience as an amateur naturalist. The former has always been very real; and the latter, unfortunately, very limited.

I don't suppose that most men can tell why their minds are attracted to certain studies any more than why their tastes are attracted by certain fruits. Certainly, I can no more explain why I like "natural history" than why I like California canned peaches; nor why I do not care for that enormous brand of natural history which deals with invertebrates any more than why I do not care for brandied peaches. All I can say is that almost as soon as I began to read at all I began to like to read about the natural history of beasts and birds and the more formidable or interesting reptiles and fishes.

The fact that I speak of "natural history" instead of "biology," and use the former expression in a restricted sense, will show that I am a belated member of the generation that regarded Audubon with veneration, that accepted Waterton—Audubon's violent critic—as the ideal of the wandering naturalist, and that looked upon Brehm as a delightful but rather awesomely erudite example of advanced scientific thought. In the broader field, thank Heaven, I sat at the feet of Darwin and Huxley; and studied the large volumes in which Marsh's and Leidy's palæontological studies were embalmed, with a devotion that was usually attended by a dreary lack of reward—what would I not have given fifty years ago for a writer like Henry Fairfield Osborn, for some scientist who realized that intelligent laymen need a guide capable of building before their eyes the life that was, instead of merely cataloguing the fragments of the death that is.

I was a very nearsighted small boy, and did not even know that my eyes were not normal until I was fourteen; and so my field studies up to that period were even more worthless than those of the average boy who "collects" natural history specimens as he collects stamps. I studied books industriously but nature only so far as could be compassed by a molelike vision; my triumphs consisted in such things as bringing home and raising—by the aid of milk and a syringe—a family of very young gray squirrels, in fruitlessly endeavoring to tame an excessively unamiable woodchuck, and in making friends with a gentle, pretty, trustful white-footed mouse which reared her family in an empty flower pot. In order to attract my attention birds had to be as conspicuous as bobolinks or else had to perform feats such as I remember the barn swallows of my neighborhood once performed, when they assembled for the migration alongside our house and because of some freak of bewilderment swarmed in through the windows and clung helplessly to the curtains, the furniture, and even to our clothes.

Just before my fourteenth birthday my father—then a trustee of the American Museum of Natural History—started me on my rather moth-like career as a naturalist by giving me a pair of spectacles, a French pin-fire double-barreled shotgun—and lessons in stuffing birds. The spectacles literally opened a new world to me. The mechanism of the pin-fire gun was without springs and therefore could not get out of order—an important point, as my mechanical ability was nil. The lessons in stuffing and mounting birds were given me by Mr. John G. Bell, a professional taxidermist and collector who had accompanied Audubon on his trip to the then "Far West." Mr. Bell was a very interesting man, an American of the before-the-war type. He was tall, straight as an Indian, with white hair and smooth-shaven clear-cut face; a dignified figure, always in a black frock coat. He had no scientific knowledge of birds or mammals; his interest lay merely in collecting and preparing them. He taught me as much as my limitations would allow of the art of preparing specimens for scientific use and of mounting them. Some examples of my wooden methods of mounting birds are now in the American Museum: three different species of Egyptian plover, a snowy owl, and a couple of spruce grouse mounted on a shield with a passenger pigeon—the three latter killed in Maine during my college vacations.

With my spectacles, my pin-fire gun, and my clumsy industry in skinning "specimens," I passed the winter of '72-'73 in Egypt and Palestine, being then fourteen years old. My collections showed nothing but enthusiasm on my part. I got no bird of any unusual scientific value. My observations were as valueless as my collections save on one small point; and this point is of interest only as showing, not my own power of observation, but the ability of good men to fail to observe or record the seemingly self-evident.

On the Nile the only book dealing with Egyptian birds which I had with me was one by an English clergyman, a Mr. Smith, who at the end of his second volume gave a short list of the species he had shot, with some comments on their habits but without descriptions. On my way home through Europe I secured a good book of Egyptian ornithology by a Captian Shelley. Both books enumerated and commented on several species of chats—the Old World chats, of course, which have nothing in common with our queer warbler of the same name. Two of these chats were common along the edges of the desert. One species was a boldly pied black and white bird, the other was colored above much like the desert sand, so that when it crouched it was hard to see. I found that the strikingly conspicuous chat never tried to hide, was very much on the alert, and was sure to attract attention when a long way off; whereas the chat whose upper color harmonized with its surroundings usually sought to escape observation by crouching motionless. These facts were obvious even to a dull-sighted, not particularly observant boy; they were essential features in the comparison between and in the study of the life histories of the two birds. Yet neither of the two books in my possession so much as hinted at them.

I think it was my observation of these, and a few similar facts, which prevented my yielding to the craze that fifteen or twenty years ago became an obsession with certain otherwise good men—the belief that all animals were protectively colored when in their natural surroundings. That this simply wasn't true was shown by a moment's thought of these two chats; no rational man could doubt that one was revealingly and the other concealingly colored; and each was an example of what was true in thousands of other cases. Moreover, the incident showed the only, and very mild, merit which I ever developed as a "faunal naturalist." I never grew to have keen powers of observation. But whatever I did see I saw truly, and I was fairly apt to understand what it meant. In other words, I saw what was sufficiently obvious, and in such case did not usually misinterpret what I had seen. Certainly this does not entitle me to any particular credit, but the outstanding thing is that it does entitle me to some, even although of a negative kind; for the great majority of observers seem quite unable to see, to record, or to understand facts so obvious that they leap to the eye. My two ornithologists offered a case in point as regards the chats; and I shall shortly speak of one or two other cases, as, for example, the cougar and the saddle-backed lechwi.

After returning to this country and until I was halfway through college, I continued to observe and collect in the fashion of the ordinary boy who is interested in natural history. I made copious and valueless notes. As I said above, I did not see and observe very keenly; later it interested and rather chagrined me to find out how much more C. Hart Merriam and John Burroughs saw when I went out with them near Washington or in the Yellowstone Park; or how much more George K. Cherrie and Leo E. Miller and Edmund Heller and Edgar A. Mearns and my own son Kermit saw in Africa and South America, on the trips I took to the Nyanza lakes and across the Brazilian hinterland.

During the years when as a boy I "collected specimens" at Oyster Bay or in the north woods, my contributions to original research were of minimum worth—they were limited to occasional records of such birds as the dominica warbler at Oyster Bay, or to seeing a duck hawk work havoc in a loose gang of night herons, or to noting the blood-thirsty conduct of a captive mole shrew—I think I sent an account of the last incident to C. Hart Merriam. I occasionally sent to some small ornithological publication a local list of Adirondack birds or something of the sort; and then proudly kept reprinted copies of the list on my desk until they grew dog-eared and then disappeared. I lived in a region zoölogically so well known that the obvious facts had all been set forth already, and as I lacked the power to find out the things that were not obvious, my work merely paralleled the similar work of hundreds of other young collectors who had a very good time but who made no particular addition to the sum of human knowledge.

Among my boy friends who cared for ornithology was a fine and manly young fellow, Fred Osborn, the brother of Henry Fairfield Osborn. He was drowned, in his gallant youth, forty years ago; but he comes as vividly before my eyes now as if he were still alive. One cold and snowy winter I spent a day with him at his father's house at Garrison-on-the-Hudson. Numerous northern birds, which in our eyes were notable rarities, had come down with the hard weather. I spied a flock of crossbills in a pine, fired, and excitedly rushed forward. A twig caught my spectacles and snapped them I knew not where. But dim though my vision was, I could still make out the red birds lying on the snow; and to me they were treasures of such importance that I abandoned all thought of my glasses and began a nearsighted hunt for my quarry. By the time I had picked up the last crossbill I found that I had lost all trace of my glasses; my day's sport—or scientific endeavor, whatever you choose to call it—came to an abrupt end; and as a result of the lesson I never again in my life went out shooting, whether after sparrows or elephants, without a spare pair of spectacles in my pocket. After some ranch experiences I had my spectacle cases made of steel; and it was one of these steel spectacle cases which saved my life in after years when a man shot into me in Milwaukee.

While in Harvard I was among those who joined in forming the Nuttall Club, which I believe afterward became one of the parent sources of the American Ornithologists' Union.

The Harvard of that day was passing through a phase of biological study which was shaped by the belief that German university methods were the only ones worthy of copy, and also by the proper admiration for the younger Agassiz, whose interest was mainly in the lower forms of marine life. Accordingly it was the accepted doctrine that a biologist—

the word "naturalist" was eschewed as archaic—was to work toward the ideal of becoming a section-cutter of tissue, who spent his time studying this tissue, and low marine organisms, under the microscope. Such work was excellent; but it covered a very small part of the biological field; and not only was there no encouragement for the work of the field naturalist, the faunal naturalist, but this work was positively discouraged, and was treated as of negligible value. The effect of this attitude, common at that time to all our colleges, was detrimental to one very important side of natural history research. The admirable work of the microscopist had no attraction for me, nor was I fitted for it; I grew even more interested in other forms of work than in the work of a faunal naturalist; and I abandoned all thought of making the study of my science my life interest.

But I never lost a real interest in natural history; and I very keenly regret that at certain times I did not display this interest in more practical fashion. Thus, for the dozen years beginning with 1883, I spent much of my time on the Little Missouri, where big game was then plentiful. Most big game hunters never learn anything about the game except how to kill it; and most naturalists never observe it at all. Therefore a large amount of important and rather obvious facts remains unobserved or inaccurately observed until the species becomes extinct. What is most needed is not the ability to see what very few people can see, but to see what almost anybody can see, but nobody takes the trouble to look at. But I vaguely supposed that the obvious facts were known; and I let most of the opportunities pass by. Even so, many of my observations on the life histories of the bighorns, white goats, prong-bucks, deer, and wapiti, and occasional observations on some of the other beasts, such as black-footed ferrets, were of value; indeed as regards some of the big game beasts, the accounts in *Hunting Trips of a Ranchman*, *Ranch Life and the Hunting Trail*, and *The Wilderness Hunter* gave a good deal of information which, as far as I know, is not to be found elsewhere.

To illustrate what I mean as "obvious" facts which nevertheless are of real value I shall instance the cougar. In the winter of 1910 I made a cougar hunt with hounds, spending about five weeks in the mountains of northwestern Colorado. At that time the cougar had been seemingly well known to hunters, settlers, naturalists, and novelists for more than a century; and yet it was actually impossible to get trustworthy testimony on such elementary points as, for instance, whether the male and female mated permanently, or at least until the young were reared (like foxes and wolves), and whether the animal caught its prey by rambling and stalking or, as was frequently asserted, by lying in wait on the branches of the tree.

The facts I saw and observed during our five weeks' hunt in the snow were obvious; they needed only the simplest powers of observation and of deduction from observation. But nobody had hitherto shown or exercised these simple powers! My narrative in the volume *Outdoor Pastimes of an American Hunter* gave the first reasonably full and trustworthy life history of the cougar as regards its most essential details—for Merriam's capital Adirondack study had dealt with the species when it was too near the vanishing point and therefore when the conditions were too abnormal for some of these essential details to be observed.

In South America I made observations of a certain value on some of the strange creatures we met, and these are to be found in the volume *Through the Brazilian Wilderness;* but the trip was primarily one of exploration. In Africa, however, we really did some good work in natural history. Many of my observations were set forth in my book *African Game Trails;* and I have always felt that the book which Edmund Heller and I jointly wrote, the *Life Histories of African Game Animals*, was a serious and worthwhile contribution to science. Here again, this contribution, so far as I was concerned, consisted chiefly in seeing, recording, and interpreting facts which were really obvious, but to which observers hitherto had been blind, or which they had misinterpreted partly because sportsmen seemed incapable of seeing anything except as a trophy, partly because stay-at-home systematists never saw anything at all except skins and skulls which enabled them to give Latin names to new "species" or "subspecies," partly because collectors had collected birds and beasts in precisely the spirit in which other collectors assembled postage stamps.

I shall give a few instances. In mid-Africa we came across a peculiar bat, with a greenish body and slate blue wings. Specimens of this bat had often been collected. But I could find no record of its really interesting habits. It was not nocturnal; it was hardly even crepuscular. It hung from the twigs of trees during the day and its activities began rather early in the afternoon. It did not fly continuously in swallow fashion, according to the usual bat custom. It behaved like a phœbe or other flycatcher. It hung from a twig until it saw an insect, then swooped down, caught the insect, and at once returned to the same or another twig—just as a phœbe or pee-wee or kingbird returns to its perch after a similar flight.

On the White Nile I hunted a kind of handsome river antelope, the white-withered or saddle-backed lechwi. It had been known for fifty years to trophy-seeking sportsmen, and to closet naturalists, some of whom had called it a kob and others a water buck. Its nearest kinsman was in reality the ordinary lechwi, which dwelt far off to the south, along the Zambezi. But during that half century no hunter or closet naturalist had grasped this obvious fact. I had never seen the Zambezi lechwi, but I had carefully read the account of its habits by Selous—a real hunter-naturalist, faunal naturalist. As soon as I came across the White Nile river bucks, and observed their habits, I said to my companions that they were undoubtedly lechwis; I wrote this to Selous, and to another English hunter-naturalist, Migand; and even a slight examination of the heads and skins when compared with those of the other lechwi and of the kobs and water bucks proved that I was right.

A larger, but equally obvious group of facts was that connected with concealing and revealing coloration. As eminent a naturalist as Wallace, and innumerable men of less note, had indulged in every conceivable vagary of speculative theory on the subject, largely based on supposed correlation between the habits and the shape or color patterns of big animals which, as a matter of fact, they had never seen in a state of nature. While in Africa I studied the question in the field, observing countless individuals of big beasts and birds, and comparing the results with what I had observed of the big game and the birds of North America (the result being borne out by what I later observed in South America). In a special chapter of the *Life Histories of African Game Animals*, as well as in a special number of the *American Museum Bulletin*, I set forth the facts thus observed and the conclusions inevitably to be deduced from them. All that I thus set forth, and all the conclusions I deduced, belonged to the obvious; but that there was need of thus setting forth the obvious was sufficiently shown by the simple fact that large numbers of persons refused to accept it even when set forth.

I do not think there is much else for me to say about my anything but important work as a naturalist. But perhaps I may say further that while my interest in natural history has added very little to my sum of achievement, it has added immeasurably to my sum of enjoyment of life.

****

In 1913, Roosevelt made a trip to the Grand Canyon in Arizona, shortly after the state had joined the Union. This sojourn inspired him with the rugged beauty and remoteness of place he encountered. Earlier we saw how he advocated protecting the region in perpetuity, and here he describes the sort of exacting, slightly risky sport that always titillated him. Cougar hunting can be extremely demanding from a physical perspective, inasmuch as the big cats invariably

take to rough terrain when pursued by hounds. Moreover, they some-
times run for miles before treeing. Roosevelt found the entire experi-
ence invigorating, and it is perhaps worthy of note that another
renowned American writer, Zane Grey, felt the same. Grey's Roping
Lions in the Grand Canyon *(1922) offers a different view on the sport*
in the same geographical region. The current piece comes from the
Outlook *(vol. 105 [1913]: 259–266).*

A COUGAR HUNT ON THE RIM
OF THE GRAND CANYON

On July 14, 1913, our party gathered at the comfortable El Tovar Hotel, on the edge of the Grand Canyon of the Colorado, and therefore overlooking the most wonderful scenery in the world. The moon was full. Dim, vast, mysterious, the canyon lay in the shimmering radiance. To all else that is strange and beautiful in nature the canyon stands as Karnak and Baalbec, seen by moonlight, stand to all other ruined temples and palaces of the bygone ages.

With me were my two younger sons, aged nineteen and fifteen respectively, and a cousin of theirs aged twenty. The cousin had driven our horses, and what outfit we did not ourselves carry, from southern Arizona to the north side of the canyon, and had then crossed the canyon to meet us. The youngest one of the three had not before been on such a trip as that we intended to take; but the two elder boys, for their good fortune, had formerly been at the Evans School in Mesa, Arizona, and among the by-products of their education was a practical and working familiarity with ranch life and with traveling through the desert and on the mountains. Jesse Cummings, of Mesa, was along to act as cook, packer, and horse-wrangler, helped in all three branches by the two elder boys; he was a Kentuckian by birth, and a better man for our trip and a stancher friend could not have been found.

On the 15th we went down to the bottom of the canyon. There we were to have been met by our outfit with two men whom we had engaged; but they never turned up, and we should have been in a bad way had not Mr. Stevenson, of the Bar Z Cattle Company, come down the trail behind us, while the foreman of the Bar Z, Mr. Mansfield, appeared to meet him, on the opposite side of the rushing, muddy torrent of the Colorado. Mansfield worked us across on the trolley which spans the river; and then we joined in and worked Stevenson, and some friends he had with him, across. Among us all we had food enough for dinner and for a light break-fast, and we had our bedding. With characteristic cattleman's generosity, our new friends turned over to us two pack-mules, which could carry our bedding and the like, and two spare saddle-horses—both the mules and the spare saddle-horses having been brought down by Mansfield because of a lucky mistake as to the number of men he was to meet.

Mansfield was a representative of the best type of old-style ranch fore-man. It is a hard climb out of the canyon on the north side, and Mansfield was bound that we should have an early start. He was up at half-past one in the morning; we breakfasted on a few spoonfuls of mush; packed the mules and saddled the horses; and then in the sultry darkness, which in spite of the moon filled the bottom of the stupendous gorge, we started up the Bright Angel trail. Cummings and the two elder boys walked; the rest of us were on horseback. The trail crossed and recrossed the rapid brook, and for rods at a time went up its boulder-filled bed; groping and stum-bling, we made our blind way along it; and over an hour passed before the first grayness of the dawn faintly lighted our footsteps.

At last we left the stream bed, and the trail climbed the sheer slopes and zigzagged upwards through the breaks in the cliff walls. At one place the Bar Z men showed us where one of their pack animals had lost his foot-ing and fallen down the mountain side a year previously. It was eight hours before we topped the rim and came out on the high, wooded, bro-ken plateau which at this part of its course forms the northern barrier of the deep-sunk Colorado River. Three or four miles farther on we found the men who were to have met us; they were two days behindhand, so we told them we would not need them, and reclaimed what horses, provi-sions, and other outfit were ours. With Cummings and the two elder boys we were quite competent to take care of ourselves under all circum-stances, and extra men, tents, and provisions merely represented a slight and dispensable, increase in convenience and comfort.

As it turned out, there was no loss even of comfort. We went straight to the cabin of the game warden, Uncle Jim Owens; and he instantly accepted us as his guests, treated us as such, and accompanied us through-out our fortnight's stay north of the river. A kinder host and better com-panion in a wild country could not be found. Through him we hired a very good fellow, a mining prospector, who stayed with us until we crossed the Colorado at Lee's Ferry. He was originally a New York State man, who had grown up in Montana, and had prospected through the mountains from the Athabaska River to the Mexican boundary. Uncle Jim was a Texan, born at San Antonio, and raised in the Panhandle, on the

Goodnight ranch. In his youth he had seen the thronging myriads of bison, and taken part in the rough life of the border, the life of the cowmen, the buffalo hunters, and the Indian fighters. He was by instinct a man of the right kind in all relations; and he early hailed with delight the growth of the movement among our people to put a stop to the senseless and wanton destruction of our wild life. Together with his—and my— friend Buffalo Jones, he had worked for the preservation of the scattered bands of bison; he was keenly interested not only in the preservation of the forests but in the preservation of the game. He had been two years buffalo warden in the Yellowstone National Park. Then he had come to the Colorado National Forest Reserve and the Game Reserve, where he had been game warden for over six years at the time of our trip. He has given a zealous and efficient service to the people as a whole; for which, by the way, his salary has been an inadequate return. One important feature of his work is to keep down the larger beasts and birds of prey, the arch-enemies of the deer, mountain sheep, and grouse; and the most formidable among these foes of the harmless wild life are the cougars. At the time of our visit he owned five hounds, which he had trained especially, as far as his manifold duties gave him the time, to the chase of cougars and bobcats. Coyotes were plentiful, and he shot these wherever the chance offered; but coyotes are best kept down by poison, and poison cannot be used where any man is keeping the hounds with which alone it is possible effectively to handle the cougars.

At this point the Colorado, in its deep gulf, bends south, then west, then north, and incloses on three sides the high plateau which is the heart of the forest and game reserve. It was on this plateau, locally known as Buckskin Mountain, that we spent the next fortnight. The altitude is from eight thousand to nearly ten thousand feet, and the climate is that of the far north. Spring does not come until June; the snow lies deep for seven months. We were there in midsummer, but the thermometer went down at night to 36, 34, and once to 33 degrees Fahrenheit; there was hoarfrost in the mornings. Sound was our sleep under our blankets, in the open, or under a shelf of rock, or beneath a tent, or most often under a thickly leaved tree. Throughout the day the air was cool and bracing.

Although we reached the plateau in mid-July, the spring was but just coming to an end. Silver-voiced Rocky Mountain hermit thrushes chanted divinely from the deep woods. There were multitudes of flowers, of which, alas! I know only a very few, and these by their vernacular names; for as yet there is no such handbook for the flowers of the southern Rocky Mountains as, thanks to Mrs. Frances Dana, we have for those of the

Eastern States, and, thanks to Miss Mary Elizabeth Parsons, for those of California. The sego lilies, looking like very handsome Eastern trilliums, were as plentiful as they were beautiful; and there were the striking Indian paintbrushes, fragrant purple locust blooms, the blossoms of that strange bush the plumed acacia, delicately beautiful white columbines, bluebells, great sheets of blue lupin, and the tall, crowed spikes of the brilliant red bell—and innumerable others. The rainfall is light and the ground porous; springs are few, and brooks wanting; but the trees are handsome. In a few places the forest is dense; in most places it is sufficiently open to allow a mountain horse to twist in and out among the tree-trunks at a smart canter. The tall yellow pines are everywhere; the erect spires of the mountain spruce and of the blue-tipped Western balsam shoot up around their taller cousins, and the quaking asps, the aspens with their ever-quivering leaves and glimmering white boles, are scattered among and beneath the conifers, or stand in groves by themselves. Blue grouse were plentiful—having increased greatly, partly because of the war waged by Uncle Jim against their foes the great horned owls; and among the numerous birds were long-crested dark blue jays, pinyon jays, doves, band-tailed pigeons, golden-winged flickers, chickadees, juncos, mountain bluebirds, thistle finches, and Louisiana tanagers. A very handsome cock tanager, the orange yellow of its plumage dashed with red on the head and throat, flew familiarly round Uncle Jim's cabin, and spent most of its time foraging in the grass. Once three birds flew by which I am convinced were the strange and interesting evening grosbeaks. Chipmunks and white-footed mice lived in the cabin, the former very bold and friendly; in fact, the chipmunks, of several species, were everywhere; and there were gophers or rock squirrels, and small tree squirrels, like the Eastern chickarees, and big tree squirrels—the handsomest squirrels I have ever seen—with black bodies and bushy white tails. These last lived in the pines, were diurnal in their habits, and often foraged among the fallen cones on the ground; and they were strikingly conspicuous.

We met, and were most favorably impressed by, the forest supervisor, Mr. Pelton, and some of his rangers. The forest and game reserve is thrown open to grazing, as with all similar reserves. Among the real settlers, the homemakers, of sense and farsightedness, there is a growing belief in the wisdom of the policy of the preservation of the National resources by the National Government. On small, permanent farms, the owner, if reasonably intelligent, will himself preserve his own patrimony; but everywhere the uncontrolled use in common of the public domain has meant reckless, and usually wanton, destruction. All the public domain that is used should be used under strictly supervised governmental lease; that is, the lease system should be applied everywhere substantially as it is now applied in the forest. In every case the small neighboring settlers, the actual homemakers, should be given priority of chance to lease the land in reasonably sized tracts (on the Colorado reserve, I may say as an aside to the experts, this should mean that as, owing to the lack of water, there are very few settlers of "Class A" type, the "Class B" settlers are given priority). Continual efforts are made by demagogues and by unscrupulous agitators to excite hostility to the forest policy of the Government; and needy men who are short-sighted and unscrupulous join in the cry, and play into the hands of the corrupt politicians who do the bidding of the big and selfish exploiters of the public domain. One device of these politicians is through their representatives in Congress to cut down the appropriation for the forest service; and in consequence the administrative heads of the service, in the effort to be economical, are sometimes driven to the expedient of trying to replace the permanently employed experts by short-term men, picked up at haphazard, and hired only for the summer season. This is all wrong; first, because the men thus hired give very inferior service; and, second, because the Government should be a model employer, and should not set a vicious example in hiring men under conditions that tend to create a shifting class of laborers who suffer from all the evils of unsteady employment, varied by long seasons of idleness. At this time the best and most thoughtful farmers are endeavoring to devise means for doing away with the system of employing farm hands in mass for a few months and then discharging them; and the Government should not itself have recourse to this thoroughly pernicious system.

The preservation of game and of wild life generally—aside from the noxious species—on these reserves is of incalculable benefit to the people as a whole. As the game increases in these National refuges and nurseries it overflows into the surrounding country. Very wealthy men can have private game preserves of their own. But the average man of small or moderate means can enjoy the vigorous pastime of the chase, and indeed can enjoy the vigorous pastime of the chase, and indeed can enjoy wild nature, only if there are good general laws, properly enforced, for the preservation of the game and wild life, and if, furthermore, there are big parks or reserves provided for the use of all our people, like those of the Yellowstone, the Yosemite, and the Colorado.

A small herd of bison has been brought to the reserve; it is slowly increasing. It is privately owned, one-third of the ownership being in

Uncle Jim, who handles the herd. The Government should immediately buy this herd. Everything should be done to increase the number of bison on the public reservations.

The chief game animal of the Colorado Canyon reserve is the Rocky Mountain blacktail, or mule deer. The deer have increased greatly in numbers since the reserve was created, partly because of the stopping of hunting by men, and even more because of the killing off of the cougars. The high plateau is their summer range; in the winter the bitter cold and driving snow send them and the cattle, as well as the bands of wild horses, to the lower desert country. For some cause, perhaps the limestone soil, their antlers are unusually stout and large. We found the deer tame and plentiful, and as we rode or walked through the forest we continually came across them—now a doe with her fawn, now a party of does and fawns, or a single buck, or a party of bucks. The antlers were still in the velvet. Does would stand and watch us go by within fifty or a hundred yards, their big ears thrown forward; while the fawns stayed hid near by. Sometimes we roused the pretty spotted fawns, and watched them dart away, the embodiments of delicate grace. One buck, when a hound chased it, refused to run and promptly stood at bay; another buck jumped and capered, and also refused to run, as we passed at but a few yards' distance. One of the most beautiful sights I ever saw was on this trip. We were slowly riding through the open pine forest when we came on a party of seven bucks. Four were yearlings or two-year-olds; but three were mighty master bucks, and their velvet-clad antlers made them look as if they had rocking-chairs on their heads. Stately of port and bearing, they walked a few steps at a time, or stood at gaze on the carpet of brown needles strewn with cones; on their red coats the flecked and broken sun rays played; and as we watched them, down the aisles of tall tree-trunks the odorous breath of the pines blew in our faces.

The deadly enemies of the deer are the cougars. They had been very plentiful all over the tableland until Uncle Jim thinned them out, killing between two and three hundred. Usually their lairs are made in the will-nigh inaccessible ruggedness of the canyon itself. Those which dwelt in the open forest were soon killed off. Along the part of the canyon where we hunted there was usually an upper wall of sheer white cliffs; then came a very steep slope covered by a thick scrub of dwarf oak and locust, with an occasional pinyon or pine; and then another and deeper wall of vermilion cliffs. It was along this intermediate slope that the cougars usually passed the day. At night they came up through some gorge or break in the cliff and rambled through the forests and along the rim after the deer.

They are the most successful of all still-hunters, killing deer much more easily than a wolf can; and those we killed were very fat.

Cougars are strange and interesting creatures. They are among the most successful and to their prey the most formidable beast of rapine in the world. Yet when themselves attacked they are the least dangerous of all beasts of prey, except hyenas. Their every movement is so lithe and stealthy, they move with such sinuous and noiseless caution, and are such past-masters in the art of concealment, that they are hardly ever seen unless roused by dogs. In the wilds they occasionally kill wapiti, and often bighorn sheep and white goats; but their favorite prey is the deer.

Among domestic animals, while they at times kill all, including, occasionally, horned cattle, they are especially destructive to horses. Among the first bands of horses brought to this plateau there were some of which the cougars killed every foal. The big males attacked full-grown horses. Uncle Jim had killed one big male which had killed a large draught-horse, and another which had killed two saddle-horses and a pack-mule, although the mule had a bell on its neck, which it was mistakenly supposed would keep the cougar away. We saw the skeleton of one of the saddle-horses. It was killed when snow was on the ground, and when Uncle Jim first saw the carcass the marks of the struggle were plain. The cougar sprang on its neck, holding the face with the claws of one paw while his fangs tore at the back of the neck, just at the base of the skull; the other fore paw was on the other side of the neck, and the hind claws tore the withers and one shoulder and flank. The horse struggled thirty yards or so before he fell, and never rose again. The draught-horse was seized in similar fashion. It went but twenty yards before falling; then in the snow could be seen the marks where it had struggled madly on its side, plunging in a circle, and the marks of the hind feet of the cougar in an outside circle, while the fangs and fore talons of the great cat never ceased tearing the prey. In this case the fore claws so ripped and tore the neck and throat that it was doubtful whether they, and not the teeth, had not given the fatal wounds.

We came across the bodies of a number of deer that had been killed by cougars. Generally the remains were in such condition that we could not see how the killing had been done. In one or two cases the carcasses were sufficiently fresh for us to examine them carefully. One doe had claw marks on her face, but no fang marks on the head or neck; apparently the neck had been broken by her own plunging fall; then the cougar had bitten a hole in the flank and eaten part of one haunch; but it had not disemboweled its prey, as an African lion would have done. Another deer, a buck, was seized in similar manner; but the death wound was inflicted with the teeth, in singular fashion, a great hole being torn into the chest, where the neck joins the shoulder. Evidently there is no settled and invariable method of killing. We saw no signs of any cougar being injured in the struggle; the prey was always seized suddenly and by surprise, and in such fashion that it could make no counter-attack.

Few African leopards would attack such quarry as the big male cougars do. Yet the leopard sometimes preys on man, and it is the boldest and most formidable of fighters when brought to bay. The cougar, on the contrary, is the least dangerous to man of all the big cats. There are authentic instances of its attacking man; but they are not merely rare but so wholly exceptional that in practice they can be entirely disregarded. There is no more need of being frightened when sleeping in, or wandering after nightfall through, a forest infested by cougars than if they were so many tom-cats. Moreover, when itself assailed by either dogs or men the cougar makes no aggressive fight. It will stay in a tree for hours, kept there by a single dog which it could kill at once if it had the heart—and this although if hungry it will itself attack and kill any dog, and on occasions even a big wolf. If the dogs—or men—come within a few feet, it will inflict formidable wounds with its claws and teeth, the former being used to hold the assailant while the latter inflict the fatal bite. But it fights purely on the defensive, whereas the leopard readily assumes the offensive and often charges, at headlong, racing speed, from a distance of fifty or sixty yards. It is absolutely safe to walk up to within ten yards of a cougar at bay, whether wounded or unwounded, and to shoot it at leisure.

Cougars are solitary beasts. When full grown the females outnumber the males about three to one; and the sexes stay together for only a few days at mating time. The female rears her kittens alone, usually in some cave; the male would be apt to kill them if he could get at them. The young are playful. Uncle Jim once brought back to his cabin a young cougar, two or three months old. At the time he had a hound puppy named Pot—he was an old dog, the most dependable in the pack, when we made our hunt. Pot had lost his mother; Uncle Jim was raising him on canned milk, and, as it was winter, kept him at night in a German sock. The young cougar speedily accepted Pot as a playmate, to be enjoyed and tyrannized over. The two would lap out of the same dish; but when the milk was nearly lapped up, the cougar would put one paw on Pot's face, and hold him firmly while it finished the dish itself. Then it would seize Pot in its fore paws and toss him up, catching him again; while Pot would occasionally howl dismally, for the young cougar had sharp little claws.

Finally the cougar would tire of the play, and then it would take Pot by the back of the neck, carry him off, and put him down in his box by the German sock.

When we started on our cougar hunt there were seven of us, with six pack-animals. The latter included one mule, three donkeys—two of them, Ted and Possum, very wise donkeys—and two horses. The saddle-animals included two mules and five horses, one of which solemnly carried a cow-bell. It was a characteristic old-time Western outfit. We met with the customary misadventures of such a trip, chiefly in connection with our animals. At night they were turned loose to feed, most of them with hobbles, some of them with bells. Before dawn, two or three of the party—usually including one, and sometimes both, of the elder boys—were off on foot, through the chilly dew, to bring them in. Usually this was a matter of an hour or two; but once it took a day, and twice it took a half-day. Both breaking camp and making camp, with a pack outfit, take time; and in our case each of the packers, including the two elder boys, used his own hitch—single diamond, squaw hitch, cowman's hitch, miner's hitch, Navajo hitch, as the case might be. As for cooking and washing dishes—why, I wish that the average tourist-sportsman, the city-hunter-with-a-guide, could once in a while have to cook and wash dishes for himself; it would enable him to grasp the reality of things. We were sometimes nearly drowned out by heavy rain-storms. We had good food; but the only fresh meat we had was the cougar meat. This was delicious; quite as good as venison. Yet men rarely eat cougar flesh.

Cougars should be hunted when snow is on the ground. It is difficult for hounds to trail them in hot weather, when there is no water and the ground is dry and hard. However, we had to do the best we could; and the frequent rains helped us. On most of the hunting days we rode along the rim of the canyon and through the woods, hour after hour, until the dogs grew tired, or their feet sore, so that we deemed it best to turn towards camp, either striking no trail or a trail so old that the hounds could not puzzle it out. I did not have a rifle, wishing the boys to do the shooting. The two elder boys had tossed up for the first shot, the cousin winning. In cougar hunting the shot is usually much the least interesting and important part of the performance. The credit belongs to the hounds, and to the man who hunts the hounds. Uncle Jim hunted his hounds excellently. He had neither horn nor whip; instead, he threw pebbles, with much accuracy of aim, at any recalcitrant dog—and several showed a tendency to hunt deer or coyote. "They think they know best and needn't obey me unless I have a nosebag full of rocks," observed Uncle Jim.

Twice we had lucky days. On the first occasion we all seven left camp by sunrise with the hounds. We began with an hour's chase after a bobcat, which dodged back and forth over and under the rim rock, and finally escaped along a ledge in the cliff wall. At about eleven we struck a cougar trail of the night before. It was a fine sight to see the hounds running it through the woods in full cry, while we loped after them. After one or two checks, they finally roused the cougar, a big male, from a grove of aspens at the head of a great gorge which broke through the cliffs into the canyon. Down the gorge went the cougar, and then along the slope between the white cliffs and the red; and after some delay in taking the wrong trail, the hounds followed him. The gorge was impassable for horses, and we rode along the rim, looking down into the depths, from which rose the chiming of the hounds. At last a change in the sound showed that they had him treed; and after a while we saw them far below under a pine, across the gorge, and on the upper edge of the vermilion cliff wall. Down we went to them, scrambling and sliding; down a break in the cliffs, round the head of the gorge just before it broke off into a canyon, through the thorny scrub which tore our hands and faces, along the slope where, if a man started rolling, he never would stop until life had left his body. Before we reached him the cougar leaped from the tree and tore off, with his big tail stretched straight as a bar behind him; but a cougar is a short-winded beast, and a couple of hundred yards on, the hounds put him up another tree. Thither we went.

It was a wild sight. The maddened hounds bayed at the foot of the pine. Above them, in the lower branches, stood the big horse-killing cat, the destroyer of the deer, the lord of stealthy murder, facing his doom with a heart both craven and cruel. Almost beneath him the vermilion cliffs fell sheer a thousand feet without a break. Behind him lay the Grand Canyon in its awful and desolate majesty.

The boy shot true. With his neck broken, the cougar fell from the tree, and the body was clutched by Uncle Jim and the other boy before it could roll over the cliff—while I experienced a moment's lively doubt as to whether all three might not slip over. Cautiously we dragged him along the rim to another tree, where we skinned him. Then, after a hard pull out of the canyon, we rejoined the horses; rain came on; and, while the storm pelted against our slickers and down-drawn slouch hats, we rode back to our water-drenched camp.

On our second day of success only three of us went out—Uncle Jim, the other one of the two elder boys, and I myself. Unfortunately, the youngest boy's horse went lame that morning, and he had to stay with the pack train. For two or three hours we rode through the woods and along the rim of the canyon. Then the hounds struck a cold trail and began to puzzle it out. They went slowly along to one of the deep, precipice-hemmed gorges which from time to time break the upper cliff wall of the canyon; and after some busy nose-work they plunged into its depths. We led our horses to the bottom, slipping, sliding, and pitching, and clambered, panting and gasping, up the other side. Then we galloped along the rim. Far below us we could at times hear the hounds. One of them was a bitch, with a squealing voice. The other dogs were under the first cliffs, working out a trail, which was evidently growing fresher. Much farther down we could hear the squealing of the bitch, apparently on another trail. However, the trails came together, and the shrill yelps of the bitch were drowned in the deeper-toned chorus of the other hounds, as the fierce intensity of the cry told that the game was at last roused. Soon they had the cougar treed. Like the first, it was in a pine at the foot of the steep slope, just above the vermilion cliff wall. We scrambled down to the beast, a big male, and the boy broke its neck; in such a position it was advisable to kill it outright, as if it struggled at all it was likely to slide over the edge of the cliff and fall a thousand feet sheer.

It was a long way down the slope, with its jungle of dwarf oak and locust, and the climb back, with the skin and flesh of the cougar, would be heartbreaking. So, as there was a break in the cliff line above, Uncle Jim suggested to the boy to try to lead down our riding animals while he, Uncle Jim, skinned the cougar. By the time the skin was off, the boy turned up with our two horses and Uncle Jim's mule—an animal which galloped as freely as a horse. Then the skin and flesh were packed behind his and Uncle Jim's saddles, and we started to lead the three animals up the slope. We had our hands full. The horses and mule could barely make it. Finally the saddles of both the laden animals slipped, and the boy's horse in his fright nearly went over the cliff—it was a favorite horse of his, a black horse from the plains below, with good blood in it, but less at home climbing cliffs than were the mountain horses. On that slope anything that started rolling never stopped unless it went against one of the rare pine or pinyon trees. The horse plunged and reared; the boy clung to its head for dear life, trying to prevent it turning down hill, while Uncle Jim sought to undo the saddle and I clutched the bridle of his mule and of my horse and kept them quiet. Finally the frightened black horse sank on his knees with his head on the boy's lap; the saddle was taken off and promptly rolled down hill fifty or sixty yards before it fetched up against a pinyon; we repacked, and finally reached the top of the rim.

Meanwhile the hounds had again started, and we concluded that the bitch must have been on the trail of a different animal, after all. By the time we were ready to proceed they were out of hearing, and we completely lost track of them. So Uncle Jim started in the direction he deemed it probable they would take, and after a while we were joined by Pot. Evidently the dogs were tired and thirsty and had scattered. In about an hour, as we rode through the open pine forest across hills and valleys, the boy and I caught, very faintly, a far-off baying note. Uncle Jim could not hear it, but we rode towards the spot, and after a time caught the note again. Soon Pot heard it and trotted towards the sound. Then we came over a low hillcrest, and when half-way down we saw a cougar crouched in a pine on the opposite slope, while one of the hounds, named Ranger, uttered at short intervals a husky bay as he kept his solitary vigil at the foot of the tree. The boy insisted that I should shoot, and thrust his rifle into my hand as we galloped down the incline.

The cougar, a young and active female, leaped out of the tree and rushed off at a gait that for a moment left both dogs behind; and after her we tore at full speed through the woods and over rocks and logs. A few hundred yards farther on her bolt was shot, and the dogs, and we also, were at her heels. She went up a pine which had no branches for the lower thirty or forty feet. It was interesting to see her climb. Her two fore paws were placed on each side of the stem, and her hind paws against it, all the claws digging into the wood; her body was held as clear of the tree as if she had been walking on the ground, the legs being straight, and she walked or ran up the perpendicular stem with as much daylight between her body and the trunk as there was between her body and the earth when she was on the ground. As she faced us among the branches I could only get a clear shot into her chest where the neck joins the shoulder; down she came, but on the ground she jumped to her feet, ran fifty yards with the dogs at her heels, turned to bay in some fallen timber and dropped dead.

The last days before we left this beautiful holiday region we spent on the tableland called Greenland, which projects into the canyon east of Bright Angel. We were camped by the Dripping Springs, in singular and striking surroundings. A long valley leads south through the tableland; and just as it breaks into a sheer walled chasm which opens into one of the side loops of the great canyon, the trail turns into a natural gallery along the face of the cliff. For a couple of hundred yards a rock shelf a dozen feet wide runs under a rock overhang which often projects beyond it. The gallery is in some places twenty feet high; in other places a man on horseback must stoop his head as he rides. Then, at a point where the shelf broadens, the clear spring pools of living water, fed by constant dripping from above, lie on the inner side next to and under the rock wall. A little beyond these pools, with the chasm at our feet, and its opposite wall towering immediately in front of us, we threw down our bedding, and made camp. Darkness fell; the stars were brilliant overhead; the fire of pitchy pine stumps flared; and in the light of the wavering flames the cliff walls and jutting rock momentarily shone with ghastly clearness, and as instantly vanished in utter gloom.

From the southernmost point of this tableland the view of the Canyon left the beholder solemn with the sense of awe. At high noon, under the unveiled sun, every tremendous detail leaped in glory to the sight; yet in hue and shape the change was unceasing from moment to moment. When clouds swept the heavens, vast shadows were cast; but so vast was the canyon that these shadows seemed but patches of gray and purple and umber. The dawn and the evening twilight were brooding mysteries over the dusk of the abyss; night shrouded its immensity, but did not hide it; and to none of the sons of men is it given to tell of the wonder and splendor of sunrise and sunset in the Grand Canyon of the Colorado.

****

Ever a voracious reader, Roosevelt always took particular delight in works dealing with hunting, fishing, or natural history. As a youngster he had read William Elliott's Carolina Sports By Land and Water *(1859), although he gets the book's title wrong in the present piece. In Elliott's work, which is one of the early classics of American sporting literature, considerable space (pp. 11–104) is devoted to harpooning or spearing manta rays, and when TR had the opportunity for a similar experience in 1917, the chance was irresistible. Not even fears of German submarines could stay him from the chase.*

This piece, originally published in Scribner's Magazine *(vol. 62, no. 3 [1917]: 293–305), has never, to my knowledge, appeared anywhere else. It features TR the storyteller at his best and reveals that even in later years he was keen in the extreme for sport. Indeed, he handled the massive iron spears used to take the mantas, and he also did his part to work the ropes once the harpoon hit home.*

HARPOONING DEVILFISH

At the end of July, 1908, Mr. Russell Jordan Coles, by vocation a tobacco-dealer of Danville, Virginia, and by avocation a sportsman and field naturalist—especially an ichthyologist—was at Cape Lookout, North Carolina. A heavy gale blew up and several vessels were partly wrecked. The life-saving crew of the Cape Lookout Station, although hampered by an antiquated and outworn equipment, did everything possible to save them. However, despite their gallantry and efforts, one of the vessels—the *John Swann*—would have been abandoned and have become a wreck had not Coles been in the harbor. He was aboard his hired boat, and he called for volunteers and put out to the rescue. The captain and owner of the boat, Charles Willis, and five other men accompanied him. They were able to rescue the vessel after a very exhausting and dangerous struggle.

Coles was much impressed by the poorness of the equipment of the life-saving station and the neglect with which it had been treated by the government—unfortunately the life-saving service, of which there is nothing an American should feel more proud, has little political influence and is sometimes shamefully overlooked. Coles found that the senators and congressmen of the neighborhood had been either indifferent to, or unable to help in, the matter. He announced that he would write to the President direct. Everybody assured him that his letter would receive no attention; but, having been accustomed to dealing with the dangerous game of the sea, he was not much afraid of politicians on land, and he wrote direct to the President forthwith. Within less than a week he received a communication from the President that he had taken up the matter. In the same mail came a communication from the general superintendent of the life-saving service stating that he had been directed to see that the shortcomings were at once made good. Within sixty days the shortcomings *were* made good; and the devoted, uncomplaining, stalwart men of the life-saving station, who so willingly risked their lives in the performance of their duty, were, thanks to Coles, given the equipment necessary to put their efforts on the highest plane of efficiency.

I was the President in question. The incident passed wholly from my mind. Early in the fall of 1916 I came across Coles's account of his extraordinary experiences in securing with harpoon and lance the big manta, or devilfish, of the Gulf and South Atlantic, for the American Museum. Killing devilfish with the harpoon and the lance had always appealed to me as a fascinating sport, since as a boy I had read Elliott's account of it in his "Field Sports of South Carolina"; but nothing I had ever read approached in excitement and scientific interest Coles's really noteworthy article. He was evidently a man who, in addition to being a successful hunter of the big game of the sea, was also engrossed in their study from the standpoint of the biologist. I entered into correspondence with him. He remembered the life-saving incident which I had forgotten. The result was an invitation to me to come down the following spring for a month's work with the harpoon and the lance off the coast of southwestern Florida.

At the last moment the German submarine campaign stirred our dulled national conscience to the point of rendering necessary a special session of Congress on April 2. I was not willing to be absent when Congress assembled, and as this would cut down the trip to a week I notified Coles that it was not worth while going. But Coles telegraphed in response that his arrangements were such that he was confident that we could make our trip successful in a week. Later he told me that if I would come as agreed—leaving New York on March 23—by "thirty-five minutes of nine" (as he phrased it) on Monday the 26th I would have killed my devilfish. I did not believe that his optimism could be warranted. But it *was* warranted; being based on a first-hand field familiarity with the habits of the big game of the sea which we were after, and by his justified belief in the thoroughgoing nature of the preparations that he had made, and in the efficiency of the trained men upon whom he relied and whom he had brought together for the expedition. It is really an extraordinary thing; but exactly six minutes before the precise minute he had prophesied I struck the death-blow with the spade-lance into my first devilfish, after having harpooned it eleven minutes before. Fifty minutes later I struck, and killed in twenty-six minutes, a larger devilfish—indeed a devilfish of a size which two years before scientists believed to be non-existent, and second only to the largest of which we have authentic record—that was killed by Coles two years previously and now in the American Museum of Natural History, New York.

We reached Punta Gorda, Florida, at midday of March 25, 1917. That afternoon we boarded one of the Punta Gorda Fish Company's small steamboats and went down through bays and sound to where, off the eastern side of Captiva Island, we found our camp. It was afloat, consisting of a one-room house aboard a flat scow. The boat was about fifty feet by twenty, the house occupying all except a small space at the stern and another small space at the bow. We bunked, cooked, and lived comfortably in the one room. Our party consisted of seven, all told: Coles, myself, Coles's private secretary A. A. Rice from Danville, and the four veteran companions of his previous expeditions who were to help us in actual chase of the devilfish.

These four men, who composed the actual crew, were Americans of a kind that we like to regard as typical—the type welcome to the soul that has become heart-sick over the moral degeneracy implied in the decadent sentimentality of professional pacifism and the revolting and sordid gross-ness of its ally materialism. All four were professional fishermen, aver-aging fifty years of age. They were alert, weather-beaten men who all their lives long had wrought their livelihood by hard and hazardous labor on the sea. They were quiet, hard-working, self-reliant, utterly fearless. They had been trained by Coles until they were as letter-perfect in har-pooning devilfish as in working their light craft in a gale. Three came from North Carolina, being natives of Morehead City. Of these, tall Captain Charley Willis has been Coles's boat companion for twelve years, was equally at home with sails and a gasoline-engine, and was a natural leader of men. He was a skilled two-handed harpooner. Little Roland Phillips had worked in Charley's crew for nearly thirty years as second in command. He was as hard as iron and as quick as a cat, a skilled two-handed harpooner and an extraordinary lookout. Nothing on the surface of the sea escaped his eyes. He interpreted with instant sureness every swirl or stain on the water and every dim shadow beneath it. Tall, silent Mart Lewis had served under Charley for some fifteen years; he was fish-erman, engineer, cook—a first-class all-around man.

Mart had originally been trained in seamanship under the fourth mem-ber of our crew, Captain Jack McCann, who was born on the south Florida keys. He was a little man, quiet-mannered and steel-eyed, whose reputa-tion was that of being gentle with all well-behaved people and dangerous to all others. For over thirty years he has fished along the Gulf and South Atlantic coasts, usually beginning the season with a crew of raw men and boys whom at the end of the season he has turned into finished fishermen. There are hundreds of high-class native fishermen scattered along a thou-sand miles of coast-line who owe their original training to Captain Jack. At least half of the men whom Coles has had in his crews at Morehead City during the last twenty years were trained by Captain Jack. In addi-tion to being a veteran professional fisherman he possessed an excellent working knowledge of the botany and conchology of south Florida, always mentioning the different plants and shellfish by their scientific names. Fish he looked upon as a purely commercial proposition, but he was a keen and accurate observer, and was able to give information of value about the life histories of the creatures of the deep.

It would not have been possible to find four better men for their work, nor four better companions, from every standpoint, for an outing of this character.

The morning after we arrived the cook was stirring at dawn. Soon after sunrise we started in the heavy launch for the devilfish ground. Roland stood forward as lookout, Captain Jack steered, Charley was working on the harpoons, Mart ran the engine, while Coles and I had nothing to do until we sighted the devilfish. We were all dressed alike, for rough work in warm weather—thin, durable blue shirts and trousers, and broad-brimmed cabbage-palm hats.

We had a half-dozen harpoons with us. (By the way, "harpoon" is a term not used by those who use the weapon itself—it is called the "iron.") The harpoon consists of a wooden handle about eight feet long, the head being of the finest steel, with a long shank of very soft malleable iron. The head, or "shackle-iron," is fastened to the end of the iron shank by a fine steel pin on which it pivots freely; being kept in place during the thrust by a wooden pin the size of a match thrust through a small hole, and fastening the rear of the steel head to the iron shank. When thrust into as huge and tough a creature as the devilfish the harpoon, if properly hurled, drives deep into the body; the plunge of the stricken monster puts such a strain on the barbed head as to break the wooden pin; and the whole head, which is eight inches long, pivots until it is transverse to the shank, when, of course, it will endure a tremendous strain before drawing out. The rush of the fish bends the tough, malleable iron shank, which is loosely fixed to the handle by a rope. The handle usually comes loose during the fight and as a matter of fact is often smashed. The rope may be run through a groove (or with a thoroughly trained crew through the bow-ring), or it may have at its end a drogue, which is tossed overboard. This drogue consists of a thick, square board, with a stick through the middle, to one end of which the rope is attached, so that the flat board offers the maximum resistance to the water. Dragged at the end of a thirty or forty foot rope the drogue so hampers and retards the quarry that after a while it can be picked up. For the killing a lance is the weapon. Of lances we had in the launch three, one of which was an ordinary whale-lance, which we did not use, and the others spade-lances made for Coles, on his design, by a New Bedford whaling-smith, who also made his irons for him.

Excepting myself every man aboard the boat was a veteran, knowing exactly what to do and how to do it, never getting flustered and meeting every emergency with cool readiness. To men of experience it is hardly necessary to say that in this type of expedition there is almost as much need of efficient preparedness in advance as there is in war itself. There is, of course, a big element of luck; but this element is minimized if the organizer of the expedition knows by long field study the habits of the dangerous game of the sea, if he has organized and trained a group of hardy, fearless, and resourceful men for the actual work of the chase and the fight, and if he has provided in advance for those details—in weapons and in management—which it is so easy to overlook.

Our floating camp was moored on the eastern side of long, narrow Captiva Island, directly west of which lies the Mexican Gulf. There is only a little tide here—about eighteen inches or so—but this is quite enough in the shoal waters of the bays to make a real difference in ease of navigation. Our motor-boat chugged southward through a narrow, winding passage between bright-green banks. Palmettos, and graceful cocoanut-palms with fronds which waved ceaselessly, broke the thick growth of the mangroves which came down into the water. The number and tameness of the big birds showed what protection has done for the bird life of Florida of recent years. The plumed lesser blue herons, and more rarely the great blue heron and the lovely plumed white egret, perched in the trees or flapped across ahead of the boat. Shore birds ran along the beaches. Parties of big terns bleated and creaked as they flew overhead. Once or twice we saw parties of small gulls with black bills. But much the most noticeable birds were the pelicans. They swam in midstream, they stood in flocks on the sand-bars, and they perched on the dead snags. They seemed to be abroad at tall hours of the day and night. Parties of them flew by with their necks folded back like herons, not stretched out like cranes; they would all beat their wings regularly for several seconds and then for several seconds glide with their wings motionless. They showed little fear and often swam by the boat within easy gunshot; and their size and quaint ungainliness and distinctive individuality made them features of real attraction in the landscape.

Oysters grew in clusters on the rope-like branch-roots of the mangrove—these queer, water-loving trees send down pendent streamers from the branches which touch the water and then take root in the mud beneath. The mangroves are peculiar in more than one way; for, unlike most water-loving trees, their wood is hard and hence and not only makes excellent fuel but can be left under water for long periods without impairing its usefulness for the fire.

Here and there we passed houses where the forest had been cleared, and the saw-palm—the sabal palm—grubbed out of the soil, and plantations of oranges and grapefruit grown. When we walked through them the air was heavy with the fragrance of their blossoms. Interspersed among them were other fruits even more typically tropical—the sapodilla, the pawpaw, limes, and rough lemons. One house was picturesque. It stood at the water's edge behind a great Florida fig-tree, while to one side stretched a row of the beautiful ever-fruitful cocoanut-palms, the palms that bear all the year round.

Through these scenes, delightful in their strangeness and in their beauty, the boat went forward until we struck the main channel, Boca Ciego, the "hidden mouth." It is thus called because where it enters the Gulf the opening can hardly be made out from a distance of half a mile; for the sandy southern point of Captiva Island overlaps the end of its eastern neighbor Sanibel Island. Locally this is known as Blind Pass; the name Boca Ciego is a survival from the days of the pirates of the Spanish Main.

Out from Blind Pass went the launch, jumping in the short rollers on the bar and then turning northward into the wind-ripples Mexican Gulf. The breeze was light, the sky was glorious overhead, and as the sun rose higher the white radiance was blinding. The tepid waters teemed with life. The dark shadowlike places on the surface marked where schools of fish swam underneath; and to the trained eyes of the professional fishermen in our boat differences that were to me utterly indistinguishable, differences that I could not see even when pointed out, enabled them to tell the species of the fish beneath. Pompano, the most delicious of all food fishes, skipped like silver flashes through the air. Here and there porpoises rolled by.

Suddenly Roland, standing on the bow, pointed ahead, and immediately afterward the rest of us also was the devilfish. It was half a mile off, swimming rather slowly through the water, so near the surface that now and then its glistening black mass appeared for a moment above. The huge batlike wings flapped steadily; occasionally the point of one was thrust into the air. Roland slipped back and I clambered up in his place, while Coles stood beside me, each of us with a harpoon. I was to throw the harpoon to which the drogue was attached, he the harpoon to which the rope led out through the bow-ring. We stood on the balls of our feet with our knees flexed, taking the movement of the boat. The harpoon was poised in my right hand, which also held a single loop of the rope. Before making the cast I glanced down to see that the rope was not entangled in my feet and would run overboard freely. I steadied myself by gripping the painter, so that I could exert all my strength when I used the harpoon; for I threw with one hand, although the ordinary practice, and doubtless ordinarily the best practice, is to hurl with both hands.

However, this particular devilfish was not destined to be mine. He was travelling rather fast, about four feet under water, coming toward us. I missed him—darting behind him—not having allowed for the speed with which the boat and the fish were travelling in opposite directions. Of course, a skilled harpooner would have hit him.

There was scant time to mourn, however, for it soon became evident that we had struck a lucky day. We saw four or five of the great sea brutes on the surface ahead and to one side of us. These were not travelling; they were lying or moving slowly, almost on top of the water, occasionally throwing one wing above it. First rapidly and then slowly the launch surged through the light waves toward one of the strange water monsters—the survivors of a long-vanished elder world, for these devilfish belong among the fishes which at one time, a myriad ages ago, in the dim and shrouded earliest Mesozoic past, were the highest forms of life on the globe.

The black bulk of the manta was a couple of feet below the surface. It was swimming slowly away as the launch, its bow gently rising and falling, came within striking distance. "Iron him, colonel," said Captain Charley. This time I threw true, the iron going deep into the middle of the great body; and instantly afterward Coles fastened it with another iron, calling aloud that the time was just eight minutes past eight. With a tremendous flurry and a great gush of dark blood the devilfish plunged below and ahead, the drogue spinning along behind him, while the rope of the other harpoon ran like lightning through the ring. Our launch was heavy and the drogue by itself was a terrible hampering obstacle; yet the big fish towed us half a mile to windward before we began to haul in on him. Then we got the drogue aboard and with the two ropes we speedily brought him up near enough the bow for me to dart the big spade-headed lance into him; and the death flurry began as I stuck him the second time with the lance. Everything had been quiet and businesslike up to this moment, but as the great fish was drawn alongside and securely gaffed we shouted with exultation and Coles called out that the time was "eight nineteen." The fight had only lasted eleven minutes. Yet it was remarkable that it should have lasted as long, for, as we afterward found, my first harpoon had been driven into the body two feet and four inches, through tough hide, flesh, and bone, and had passed through the upper part of the heart. The iron had been bent into a complete semicircle by the furious struggles of the morally wounded fish.

Our prize was an adult male of fair but not extraordinary size. One of the others we had seen seemed larger, and we wished to get after it as soon as possible. Accordingly we headed the launch for the beach half a mile away, shoving our dead quarry before us. As soon as we reached the beach we jumped overboard, hauled the devilfish far enough up to be confident that it would not be swept away by the tide, pushed off again, and ten minutes afterward were in sight of another devilfish.

This was a bigger one. It was swimming head on toward the boat, two or three feet below the water. The grotesque black form flapped slowly, the horns were thrust forward; I struck it in the centre of the body almost in the exact spot that I had struck the first, and was drenched by the volume of water cast up by the great wing fins. Coles also made fast and the fish ran off sideways, pulled the boat around while it careened heavily, and towed us briskly out to sea against the wind. Although the blood left a dark wake, it swam very strongly and some minutes elapsed before we got the drogue inboard. It was lucky we did so, for shortly afterward Coles's iron pulled out. We now had only one iron in; so, bringing the rope home, we brought the boat close enough up to the monstrous creature for me to iron it again. This time the flurry was tremendous and we were drenched with water. We were in a heavy thirty-foot, five-ton launch; yet the devilfish, passing under us and rising, lifted the stern a foot or more upward, and then sounding, pulled the bow a couple of feet down; and for some little time it actually hauled the launch backward. Then it came to the surface again and towed us in a long three-quarter circle. We began to haul in on both ropes. At last it was near enough for me to dart the lance. As the wicked spade-head drove into its life the huge fish flapped and splashed with such vigor for a few seconds that I drove the lance into it twice again. Then its struggles ceased and once more we yelled as we brought the great carcass alongside for the gaff. The fight had lasted twenty-six minutes and the devilfish had towed us over two miles, and had left throughout the entire two miles a broad wake of blood. There had been no hitch in the handling of the ropes, which is one of the danger-points in such a fight.

This devilfish was a female, although much larger than the male. We drew both together up on the beach. The first had a breadth of thirteen feet two inches from tip to tip and the second a breadth of sixteen feet eight inches—flat measurements—not taken across the curve of the body. As far as I know, Coles's devilfish now mounted in the American Museum of Natural History, which was eighteen feet two inches from tip to tip, is the only captured individual of which we have authentic record that was larger. Doubtless larger ones have been captured, and there may be records of which I do not know. There are certainly devilfish with considerable more than twenty feet spread; but we have hitherto no authentic record of the capture of one of these exceptionally large animals.

The stomachs of these devilfish contained such completely digested liquid animal remains that we were unable to determine what they had been feeding on. This was a real disappointment, as there has been much discussion about the food of the big creatures. On the first devilfish were half a dozen small remora, from ten to fourteen inches long. They were slim, striped, active fish, which attached themselves to the body of their huge host by the flat, oval sucking cusp on top of the head. These fish similarly attach themselves to sharks, sawfishes, and turtles, offering as curious an example of parasitism as is found among vertebrates.

There were still devilfish in sight, lying on the surface of the water and offering chances such as Coles said he had never in all his previous experience witnessed. However, I did not care to kill any more of the huge, rare creatures. I much regretted that the two which were drawn up on the beach could not have been saved for scientific purposes, as they were unusually perfect specimens, both male and female, and as there is in the museums of the world but one specimen—the one killed by Coles previously mentioned—which is larger than my largest. We had offered the National Museum at Washington to get them not only specimens of this great devilfish but also of anything else that we obtained on the expedition, if they would send a taxidermist with us. But they notified us that they were unable to accept the offer. Therefore we did not make the full collections we otherwise would have made.

On a subsequent day—to settle some questions which we had been discussing—we decided to kill another manta; but our experiences this day made us realize how fortunate we had been on our first day. We did not decide to attempt the capture of the devilfish until so late that we lacked our full equipment of harpoons in the launch. The water was rather rough. We was only one rather small devilish, which was travelling fast; we lost sight of it on two or three occasions, and had a long chase before we finally overtook it. After first missing it I succeeded in ironing it; whereupon it jumped partly out of the water, making an awkward, sidewise, whirling leap, with a tremendous splash. Two-thirds of its body appeared above the surface. After letting it tow us for a quarter of an hour I hauled in one the rope until it was close up to the boat. We ought to have ironed it again; but there were no harpoons ready; and with a sudden twist and jerk my iron tore loose, although it was firmly fixed. The devilfish lay for a couple of minutes not far away before it once more started off at speed, its wings flopping so that it looked as if it was flying through the water instead of swimming in conventional fish fashion. On overtaking it again Roland ironed it. He struck two-handed with such force the wooden pole entered the devilfish just back of the brain. The fish made a tremendous flurry, smashing into the boat with sufficient force to have wrecked a smaller launch, and then passed astern. The rope did not play out freely, and as the boat had not lost its headway and was forging onward when the strain came, just as the devilfish was astern of us, this iron also pulled out. When it did so it must have inflicted a mortal wound, probably severing the backbone, for the fish sank. As it never again appeared, it doubtless lay dead at the bottom.

We had paid the proper penalty for not having prepared in advance. This devilfish was considerably smaller than either of the ones we had killed the previous day. But on the previous day we had prepared, and had safeguarded ourselves in advance against every untoward chance; whereas with this smaller devilfish we had shown a lack of forethought in preparation rather painfully suggestive of the national attitude in dealing with more serious enemies than devilfish.

The first two fish had been ironed at the beginning in a vital spot, so that they did not show the formidable fighting powers which these fish so often do show when the first iron does not itself weaken their vital force. If either of them had been ironed farther away from the vitals, and had then been treated as carelessly as we treated the last one, we should doubtless not have obtained either, and might have met with some rather unpleasant incident.

Coles's experiences in the past had been in a somewhat smaller launch than the one we were this time using and had therefore been more exciting. On one occasion, after ironing a big female her mate hung about and the boat was in some peril because of the rushes of the two great creatures. One of the members of his crew at the time was a Florida fisherman, a hard-bit man, entirely new to the work but possessed of a game soul. The launch listed heavily as one of the devilfish rose under it while they were fast to the other. Thereupon the new man called out with grim jocularity: "Iron the big bull and let us all go to hell in tow of a team of devils!"

The extraordinary shape, huge size, and vast power of the big devilfish, or manta, give him an evil reputation, which is heightened by his black coloring. A queer peculiarity of this coloring is that the black pigment comes off on anything touching it. Kneeling on one of the devilfish when it was drawn up on the sand I arose with my knee completely blackened. The skin is not only very tough, but is also very rough, being covered, like that of an old shark, with dermal denticles which scarify the skin if a naked arm of leg is drawn across it. The big mouth is practically tooth-less, entirely so as regards the upper jaw, while the lower jaw has a small dental plate which differs in the two sexes. In spite of its size the manta is in no way dangerous to man unless attacked; but when harpooned its furious energy, tenacity of life, and enormous strength render it formida-ble; for it can easily smash or overturn a boat which is clumsily handled, and if the ropes foul an accident is apt to occur.

Some months before our visit there had been a strange phenomenon, possibly due to some subterranean volcanic outburst rolling in from the Gulf; the water grew poisonous, killing enormous multitudes of fish and shell-fish. There had been time for only a partial recovery. Whether owing to this or to other causes sharks and skates were rarely seen, the few sharks being little bits of fellows. One skate was grained by Roland. When taken aboard it was found to weigh one hundred pounds. Its tail had been cut off by some previous fisherman so as to get rid of the sting. The fishermen hold the sting-ray in more dread than any other fish, and kill or cut the tail off of every specimen they catch. The spine is a weapon of defense, employed by the fish when angered or frightened. Coles, Captain Jack, Roland, and Captain Charley have been stuck by sting-rays. In the case of Captain Jack, the sting was driven through the rear end of his foot from side to side, pinning the shoe to the flesh and bone. In the case of Roland it was driven through the thickest part of the calf of the leg. Captain Charley had a sting driven clean through his heel. Coles was stuck in the thigh, the spine being driven in to the bone. All four men agreed that they never suffered such pain. Apparently this sting or spine is an irritant of the utmost violence, although examination has so far failed to reveal any poison in connection with it. Captain Jack had known one man who died as the result of a blow from the sting-ray. Still more remarkable is what happens in connection with sharks. These fish are sin-gularly callous to pain and indifferent to injuries. They habitually prey on sting-rays, seizing them by the head or side. Yet when sharks and sting-rays, as sometime occurs, are gathered together in a fisherman's net, num-bers of the sharks are killed by the sting-rays, which lash right and left; and the sharks show every symptom of great agony.

All of the trained and experienced observers with me agreed in saying that near our coast-line there was but little danger from sharks for a man swimming. Accidents do occur, but they are wholly exceptional—unlike what is true in the Indian Ocean and around Australia. The white shark is undoubtedly a man-eater, and Coles, who is probably more competent to pass judgment on the question than any other man in the United States, believes that the four bathers killed and partly eaten off the New Jersey coast in the summer of 1916 were all victims of one rather small straggler of this formidable species. When this straggler was captured it was found that there were human bones and flesh in it, and with its capture all attacks on swimmers ceased. Coles believes that under exceptional circumstances the leopard or tiger shark may also attack men. None of my companions, however, had personal knowledge of any man being killed by sharks, although Coles had for years made a practice of investigating all stories of fatalities of this kind alleged to have occurred at some near-by point. All of my companions, however, knew of instances where men had been bitten by sharks which they had handled carelessly when caught in nets. Captain Jack had once been bitten by a Moray eel, which is undoubtedly a savage creature. On another occasion, when out at night in his fishing-smack, having made an immense haul of fish, a large number of big sharks attacked the fish with such ravenous ferocity that he grew seriously concerned lest they should actually force their way into the boat, and was finally obliged to cut the net adrift before he had taken half the fish out of it.

All of my companions agreed that, for some reason, sharks were afraid of porpoises. The killer whale preyed on porpoises, seeming to prefer warm-blooded prey; but one of my companions mentioned an instance where a killer attacked and slew a big shark, and they agreed that sharks gave the killer a wide berth. The adroitness with which sharks prey on formidable creatures like sting-rays, seizing them so as almost invariable to avoid the sting, is paralleled by the mathematical nicety with which porpoises seize "crucifixion cats," so as just to avoid the spines which make these gregarious sea catfish so dangerous to handle. The spines stick out from the pectoral fins, and render it well-nigh fatal for anything that attempts to swallow them whole. But porpoises attack their schools at full speed, and with such precision that every catfish is cut through just behind the pectorals. All of my companions, including Coles, had at various times come across the wake of a party of porpoises which had assailed a school of crucifixion cats, and they described the sea as being, on each occasion, covered with the fore parts of the cats, each fish having lost all of its body back of the pectoral fins. The unerring, the automaton-like accuracy with which the feat was performed resembled the unerring automatism with which a hunting-wasp paralyzes its victims by stinging them in precisely the right nerve ganglion.

One day we visited an island game refuge which had been established as such when I was President, on the initiative of the Audubon Society. It was locally known as Hemp Island, but I think on the maps it appears as Cayatuna Island. It is fringed by a dense growth of mangroves, while various trees, including wild figs and native pawpaws and wild, native cotton-bushes, grow on the hillock which forms the centre. The birds were chiefly cormorants, pelicans, and Louisiana herons. All were nesting in the trees, and we found several heron eggs, so they had evidently begun to lay. The pelicans were the most numerous and the most conspicuous. To me they are always interesting and amusing birds, and I never get over the feeling of the unexpected about them; their size, shape, and relationship seem at variance both with their habit of diving headlong into the water like king-fishes and with their habit of perching in trees and nest-building therein. As we stood on the island many of the pelicans, soaring overhead, were carrying branches in their bills, and as they grew accustomed to our presence they lit with awkward flapping an balancing in the tree-tops and added sticks to the nests they were building. I believe that on the east coast of Florida they build on the ground instead of in the trees. They uttered queer hoarse croaks of protest as they left their nesting-sites. When on the fishing-grounds they swung around in circles overhead and came down into the water with a splash, disappearing bodily. When they reappeared their heads were pointing up-wind, although they had dived down-wind. They and the cormorants often sat on the spiles driven here and there in the broad, shallow bay.

Among the mangroves on this island were some small diamond-back terrapin, of which we got three for our supper. A more interesting capture was made on the hillock in the centre of the island. We found a hole obviously made by some living creature which Captain Jack at one pronounced to be one of the big Florida land-turtles. The burrow was shallow and we experienced little difficulty in digging out the turtle—the first of its kind I had ever seen. This specimen weighed over eleven pounds and was a regular land tortoise; although the plastron did not shut up tight, as in the case of the box-turtle. The species is purely a vegetable feeder and its meat is esteemed a great delicacy—we found it very good. In Florida it is called the gopher—a name reserved in the West for the burrowing pouched rat which in Florida is most inappropriately called the salamander. Captain Jack stated that he had once found one of these big land-turtles in the belly of a large diamond-back rattlesnake, which was a surprise to me; as I had supposed that the rattlesnake ate only birds and mammals.

On another island we found colonies of cormorants and of beautiful white ibises, together with Louisiana and little blue herons. The ibises had built nests but had not begun to lay. In some of the cormorant nests there were well-grown young and the old birds made guttural noises of indignation at our approach. Under on tree, on the ground, we found a scraped hollow in the dead leaves, in which were an egg and a newly hatched chick which seemingly belonged to a small black vulture which was perched overhead. The egg was greenish, speckled with brown, and the fluffy feathers of the noisome fledgling harmonized exactly in color with the brown leaves.

We had beautiful weather. From the western side of Captiva Island the sunsets were wonderful, across the Mexican Gulf. There was a growing moon and the nights were very lovely. The soft, warm water lapped against the side of the boat, while the soft, warm night air was radiant in the moonlight.

It was a thoroughly enjoyable trip. My success was, of course, entirely owing to the masterly efficiency of my host and of his four fine sailormen and killers of the big game of the seas. It was a delight to witness the cool, unhurried sureness of decision and power with which they met every labor, every emergency, and every hazard. It was an even keener delight to feel that they were my fellow Americans, and to know that the Americanism which they represented and typified was still a living force in the nation.

PART V
Readings,
Reflections, and Reminiscences

Introductory Note

In his later years, as is the wont of most humans as they age, Roosevelt became increasingly reflective. The pieces in this section belong to that part of his life. Most come from the pages of the *Outlook,* a magazine with which he held a masthead position for several years and for which he continued to write regularly even after concluding that arrangement. Most of his contributions were editorials or review essays, formats that suited the persona of a man who held strong opinions and expressed them just as strongly.

While he was always a staunch proponent of conservation, one senses that Roosevelt realized that he himself may have been prodigal to a certain degree. He is particularly culpable on that score in connection with his African trip, and a number of writers have criticized the record of carnage associated with that safari. To do so, however, is to overlook two considerations of note. First of all, one is judging Roosevelt by modern standards rather than those of his time, and that is unfair. Secondly, a convincing argument can be made that the animals he shot, virtually without exception, were used as food or as subjects of scientific study. As a hunter, I appreciate his sporting ethic and his recognition of the fact that sportsmen could be the finest of all conservationists.

In a sense TR was a prophet slightly before his time, although he had enough drive and sufficient political clout to inaugurate our system of national parks and forests. Similarly, he may well rank as the finest champion of conservation America has known, and some of that sense of loving the land and farsightedness shines through in these selections. That is particularly true of "Our Vanishing Wild Life," "The Conservation of Wild Life," and "A National Park Service." Likewise, in his pieces on John Muir and the writings of Charles Sheldon and Abel Chapman, TR shows a deep appreciation of the impact men of their ilk can have in directing the attention of others to the value of clean water and untrammeled wilderness.

****

This review essay, which originally appeared on pages 161–162 of the Outlook *(vol. 103 [1913]), ostensibly covers William T. Hornaday's* Our Vanishing Wild Life. *As was often the case at this period, Roosevelt uses the review of the book as a platform to appeal*

*for migratory-bird laws (effective regulations, at least in the case of
waterfowl, did not come until a generation later), game animals, and
the environment in general. When TR writes that "at last it looks as
if our people [are] awakening," he is perhaps being overly opti-
mistic. The passage of almost nine decades has still left most devoted conservationists believing much remains to be done, but this voice
crying in the wilderness for the wilderness was certainly heard.*

OUR VANISHING WILD LIFE

There has just been published an unusual book on the extermination
of the beautiful and wonderful forms of wild life which is now
going on with such appalling rapidity. It contains a discussion of
the methods to check this extermination and to preserve the birds and
mammals the loss of which can literally never be repaired. The writer, Mr.
Hornaday, is the director of the New York Zoölogical Park, a trained naturalist, an explorer of and dweller in the world's waste spaces, a man who
has been a mighty hunter in the proper sense of the word, but whose chief
work for many years has been the effort to preserve and not destroy wild
life. The foreword is written by Henry Fairfield Osborn, President of the
New York Zoölogical Society.

As President Osborn says in his introduction, the United States at this
moment occupies a lamentable position as being perhaps the chief offender
among civilized nations in permitting the destruction and pollution of
nature. Our whole modern civilization is at fault in the matter. But we in
America are probably most at fault. The civilized people of to-day look
back with horror at their mediæval ancestors who wantonly destroyed great
works of art, or sat slothfully by while they were destroyed. We have passed
that stage. We treasure pictures and sculptures. We regard Attic temples
and Roman triumphal arches and Gothic cathedrals as of priceless value.
But we are, as a whole, still in that low state of civilization where we do not
understand that it is also vandalism wantonly to destroy or to permit the
destruction of what is beautiful in nature, whether it be a cliff, a forest, or a
species of mammal or bird. Here in the United States we turn our rivers and
streams into sewers and dumping-grounds, we pollute the air, we destroy
forests, and exterminate fishes, birds, and mammals—not to speak of vul-
garizing charming landscapes with hideous advertisements. But at last it
looks as if our people were awakening. Many leading men, Americans and
Canadians, are doing all they can for the Conservation movement.

One phase of this Conservation movement is the preservation of the noble and beautiful forms of wild life in this country. It is to this phase that Mr. Hornaday devotes himself. As he points out, it is not merely folly, it is wickedness, to permit a small number of our people, perhaps two or three per cent, to destroy the animals and birds in which the other ninety-seven per cent have an equal ownership, and in which the posterity of all of them should have an equal interest. The true sportsman, the nature-lover, the humanitarian—in short, all good citizens of all types—should read this book and should respond to the appeal Mr. Hornaday makes. We need drastic action. Song-bird slaughter should be stopped absolutely, of course, and so should the slaughter of water-birds. For game the bags should be strictly limited by law, all spring shooting should be stopped, and in most places there should be long close seasons, and, as regards many birds and mammals, absolute prohibition of killing at all. Congress should protect all migratory birds.

This was once a great game country. It is now in large part an absolutely gameless country, a country with less game than is found in most European countries, and the game is rapidly disappearing even from where it still exists. The wild antelope and the prairie chicken are on the point of following the wild bison and the passenger pigeon into memory. A few States have done their duty as to a few animals. Sheep are protected in Colorado—really protected, not nominally protected only—and have increased in consequence. Moose have been protected and have increased in Maine and New Brunswick. Deer have been protected, and have increased astonishingly, in Vermont, and indeed throughout New England. The elk have been thoroughly, but unintelligently, protected in the Yellowstone Park. Additional winter grounds should be provided for these Yellowstone Park elk, and moreover, as Mr. Hornaday points out, it is imperatively necessary that provision should be made for hunting and killing cows and young bulls (not old bulls, of which there are now too few). The Vermont deer are now so plentiful that there should be more hunting of them permitted. The elk in the Yellowstone Park are the only North American animals which have been so well protected in our preserves that their increase has outstripped the food supply, and in consequence multitudes now perish in the most miserable way by starvation.

The National and State game reserves offer fine examples of what can be done by adequate legislation. The work of the Pennsylvania Game Commission is singled out by Mr. Hornaday for special praise; and it is worth remembering that only by such genuine game preservation by the State or Nation will it ever be possible to give to the farmer, the mechan-

ic, and the clerk the chance to do hunting which otherwise is strictly con-
fined to the millionaire and the market gunner.

The pleas made by Mr. Hornaday for the whooping crane, the upland
plover, the California condor, for grouse, egrets, the wood duck, the
blacktail deer, the California elephant seal, and other animals, are not
only convincing, but should excite our legislators, sportsmen, and nature-
lovers to active work. All our people should wake up to the damage done
by the migratory sheep bands which are permitted to pasture on, and to
destroy, the public domain. There should be international agreement to
put down the iniquitous feather trade. It seems inconceivable that civilized people should permit it to exist. Money is needed for the missionary work which Mr. Hornaday has started. Our rich men should realize
that to import a Rembrandt or a Raphael into this country is in no shape
or way such a service at this moment as to spend the money which such
a picture costs in helping either the missionary movement as a whole, or
else parts of it, such as the preservation of the prongbuck, or the activities of the Audubon Society on behalf of gulls and terns. The Ward-
McIlhenny bird preserve, recently given to Louisiana by Mr. Edward A.
McIlhenny and Mr. Charles Willis Ward, is already a nursery of priceless
value for the preservation of egrets.

This book should be studied in every legislature. I commend it to
women's clubs just as much as to farmers' associations. It should be read
by all intelligent, far-sighted, and public-spirited men and women
throughout the Union. Moreover, when they have read it, let them not be
content with impotent indignation, but let them do all they can to act on
the advice it contains.

****

*Today, John Muir is widely recognized as an icon of the natural
world. Groups like the Sierra Club have rightly touted his love of the
wilderness, and he ranks well to the forefront of our most eloquent
spokesmen for conservation, in company with Roosevelt, John
Burroughs, Aldo Leopold, Ben Hur Lampman, and Archibald
Rutledge. Interestingly, Roosevelt and Muir did not always see eye to
eye, as the former admits here. Perhaps John Burroughs, who knew
both men well, went to the heart of the matter when he wrote, "Both
are great talkers, and two talkers, you know, seldom get on well
together. Now he finds me an appreciative listener, and that suits him
better." Nonetheless, Roosevelt clearly appreciated what Muir stood*

for, as this little essay reveals. The profile originally appeared in the January 16, 1915, edition of the Outlook *(pp. 27–28) and was reprinted in* Wilderness Writings *(1986), edited by Paul Schullery.*

JOHN MUIR: AN APPRECIATION

Our greatest nature lover and nature writer, the man who has done most in securing for the American people the incalculable benefit of appreciation of wild nature in his own land, is John Burroughs. Second only to John Burroughs, and in some respects ahead even of John Burroughs, was John Muir. Ordinarily, the man who loves the woods and the mountains, the trees, the flowers, and the wild things, has in him some indefinable quality of charm which appeals even to those sons of civilization who care for little outside of paved streets and brick walls. John Muir was a fine illustration of this rule. He was by birth a Scotchman—a tall and spare man, with the poise and ease natural to him who has lived much alone under conditions of labor and hazard. His was a dauntless soul, and also one brimming over with friendliness and kindliness.

He was emphatically a good citizen. Not only are his books delightful, not only is he the author to whom all men turn when they think of the Sierras and northern glaciers, and the giant trees of the California slope, but he was also—what few nature lovers are—a man able to influence contemporary thought and action on the subjects to which he had devoted his life. He was a great factor in influencing the thought of California and the thought of the entire country so as to secure the preservation of those great natural phenomena—wonderful canyons, giant trees, slopes of flower-spangled hillsides—which make California a veritable Garden of the Lord.

It was my good fortune to know John Muir. He had written me, even before I met him personally, expressing his regret that when Emerson came to see the Yosemite, his (Emerson's) friends would not allow him to accept John Muir's invitation to spend two or three days camping with him, so as to see the giant grandeur of the place under surroundings more congenial than those of a hotel piazza or a seat on a coach. I had answered him that if ever I got in his neighborhood I should claim from him the treatment that he had wished to accord Emerson. Later, when as President I visited the Yosemite, John Muir fulfilled the promise he had at that time made to me. He met me with a couple of pack-mules, as well as with riding mules for himself and myself, and a first-class packer and cook, and I spent a delightful three days and two nights with him.

The first night we camped in a grove of giant sequoias. It was clear weather, and we lay in the open, the enormous cinnamon-colored trunks rising about us like the columns of a vaster and more beautiful cathedral than was ever conceived by any human architect. One incident surprised me not a little. Some thrushes—I think they were Western hermit-thrushes—were singing beautifully in the solemn evening stillness. I asked some question concerning them of John Muir, and to my surprise found that he had not been listening to them and knew nothing about them. Once or twice I had been off with John Burroughs, and had found that, although he was so much older than I was, his ear and his eye were infinitely better as regards the sights and sounds of wild life, or at least of the smaller wild life, and I was accustomed unhesitatingly to refer to him regarding any bird note that puzzled me. But John Muir, I found, was not interested in the small things of nature unless they were unusually conspicuous. Mountains, cliffs, trees, appealed to him tremendously, but birds did not unless they possessed some very peculiar and interesting as well as conspicuous traits, as in the case of the water ouzel. In the same way, he knew nothing of the wood mice; but the more conspicuous beasts, such as bear and deer, for example, he could tell much about.

All next day we traveled through the forest. Then a snow-storm came on, and at night we camped on the edge of the Yosemite, under the branches of a magnificent silver fir, and very warm and comfortable we were, and a very good dinner we had before we rolled up in our tarpaulins and blankets for the night. The following day we went down into the Yosemite and through the valley, camping in the bottom among the timber.

There was a delightful innocence and good will about the man, and an utter inability to imagine that any one could either take or give offense. Of this I had an amusing illustration just before we parted. We were saying good-by, when his expression suddenly changed, and he remarked that he had totally forgotten something. He was intending to go to the Old World with a great tree lover and tree expert from the Eastern States who possessed a somewhat crotchety temper. He informed me that his friend had written him, asking him to get from me personal letters to the Russian Czar and the Chinese Emperor; and when I explained to him that I could not give personal letters to foreign potentates, he said: "Oh, well, read the letter yourself, and that will explain just what I want." Accordingly he thrust the letter on me. It contained not only the request which he had mentioned, but also a delicious preface, which, with the request, ran somewhat as follows:

"I hear Roosevelt is coming out to see you. He takes a sloppy, unintelligent interest in forests, although he is altogether too much under the influence of that creature Pinchot, and you had better get from him letters to the Czar of Russia and the Emperor of China, so that we may have better opportunity to examine the forests and trees of the Old World."

Of course I laughed heartily as I read the letter, and said: "John, do you remember exactly the words in which this letter was couched?" Whereupon a look of startled surprise came over his face, and he said: "Good gracious! there was something unpleasant about you in it; wasn't there? I had forgotten. Give me the letter back."

So I gave him back the letter, telling him that I appreciated it far more than if it had not contained the phrases he had forgotten, and that while I could not give him and his companion letters to the two rulers in question, I would give him letters to our Ambassadors, which would bring about the same result.

John Muir talked even better than he wrote. His greatest influence was always upon those who were brought into personal contact with him. But he wrote well, and while his books have not the peculiar charm that a very, very few other writers on similar subject have had, they will nevertheless last long. Our generation owes much to John Muir.

****

One of Roosevelt's most lasting contributions was the creation of our national park system. Beginning with Yellowstone, important natural areas were set aside for the enjoyment of the public. Here TR writes in favor of creating an administrative agency to oversee the parks. The piece originally appeared on page 246 of the February 3, 1912, edition of the Outlook *and can also be found in* Wilderness Writings *(1986), edited by Paul Schullery.*

A NATIONAL PARK SERVICE

The American people have been gradually awakening during the past few years to the idea of the city park as not merely an adornment, but an instrument of social service to the community. We are coming more and more to realize that life is better worth living in those cities which have relatively large park areas effectively developed not only as beauty spots but as recreation centers and playgrounds for all classes in the community. But we have not yet made effective application of the same idea to our National parks. It is true that we have an ample measure of them in area, but we are not yet sure as a people just what we want them for; and we have as yet given them no efficient and intelligent administration. There are in the United States thirteen National parks, embracing over four and a half million acres. At present, as the Secretary of the Interior has pointed out in his annual report, each of these parks is a separate and distinct unit for administrative purposes. Special appropriations are made for each park, and the employment of a common supervising and directing force is impossible. As the President of the American Civic Association said in his address at the Association's recent convention, "Nowhere in official Washington can an inquirer find an office of the National parks, or a desk devoted solely to their management. By passing around through their departments, and consulting clerks who have taken on the extra work of doing what they can for the Nation's playgrounds, it is possible to come at a little information." A bill is before Congress for the creation of a Bureau of National Parks, the head of which shall have the supervision, management, and control of all the National parks and National monuments in the country, and shall have the duty of developing these areas so that they shall be the most efficient agencies possible for promoting public recreation and public health through their use and enjoyment by the people. We have a single amendment to propose to the bill. The new bureau should be called the National Park Service, in conformity with the custom already established in naming the Forest Service. The establishment of the National Park service is justified by considerations of good administration, of the value of natural beauty as a National asset, and of the effectiveness of outdoor life and recreation in the production of good citizenship.

*****

This review essay reiterates some of the same themes expressed in the first selection in part 5, but it does so in considerably more detail. Loosely based on three books — Wild Life Conservation, by William T. Hornaday; Alaskan Bird Life, edited by Ernest Ingersoll; and Deutsche Verlags-Anstalt, by Adolf Fische — the piece argues eloquently for conservation laws. Some steps in this direction had been taken by this time, but TR realized that much more needed to be done. It is also interesting to note that at this point, well before the United States entered World War I, he comments on the tragedy of

World War I, though without revealing that he is a strident Anglophile. We also notice the intellectual powers of Roosevelt, not only in the ease with which he read German but also in the manner he readily moves from one continent to another while embracing various aspects of conservation. This piece comes from the Outlook (vol. 109 [1915]: 159–162).

THE CONSERVATION OF WILD LIFE

F orty years ago John Ruskin gave a series of lectures on "Greek and English Birds," which he later gathered into a volume under the title of "Love's Meinie"—a title showing affectation of course, for Ruskin was as affected as Carlyle; and no small part of the contents of the volume exhibits affectation carried to the verge of mental unsoundness. But it is beautifully written—else would it not be Ruskin's. It shows the delight in nature which can never be felt save by the man whose pulses throb with sheer delight in the spring scents of budding things, in the music of birds, the rustling of trees, the running of brooks, and in the wind-flaws on glassy lakes; a delight which can never be interpreted to others unless by one who is also master of the great art of putting fine thoughts into simple, clear, and noble words.

It also contains a characteristically amusing, and by no means wholly unjust, attack on modern science. In comparing it with the crass ignorance of the average upper-class Englishman he says: "It is vulgar in a far worse way by its arrogance and materialism. In general the scientific natural history of a bird consists of four articles—first, the name and estate of the gentleman whose game-keeper shot the last that was seen in England; secondly, two or three stories of doubtful origin, printed in every book on the subject of birds for the last fifty years; thirdly, an account of the feathers, from the comb to the rump, with enumerations of the colors which are never more to be seen on the living bird of English eyes; and, lastly, a discussion of the reasons why none of the twelve names which former naturalists have given to the bird are of any further use, and why the present author has given it a thirteenth, which is to be universally, and to the end of time, accepted."

With the stricture on modern scientific terminology contained in the last clause I cordially agree. But of far greater practical importance is the lesson to be inferred from the first and third "articles." It is deeply discreditable to the people of any country calling itself civilized that as regards many of the grandest or most beautiful or most interesting forms of wild life once to be found in the land we should now be limited to describing, usually in the driest of dry books, the physical characteristics which when living they possessed, and the melancholy date at which they ceased to live.

Ever since man in recognizably human shape made his appearance on this planet he has been an appreciable factor in the destruction of other forms of animal life, and he has been a potent factor ever since he developed the weapons known to the savages of the last few tens of thousands of years. But modern weapons have given a tremendous impetus to this destruction. Never before were such enormous quantities of big beasts and large birds slain as in the nineteenth century. Never before was there such extensive and wasteful slaughter of strange and beautiful forms of wild life as in the century which saw the greatest advance in material civilization and the most rapid spread of the civilized peoples throughout all the world.

Towards the end of that century a few civilized nations wakened to a sense of shame at what was going on. Enlightened men and women here and there began to take efficient action to restrain this senseless destruction of that which, once destroyed, could never be replaced. Gradually they roused a more general sentiment, and now there is a considerable body of public opinion in favor of keeping for our children's children, as a priceless heritage, all the delicate beauty of the lesser and all the burly majesty of the mightier forms of wild life. We are fast learning that trees must not be cut down more rapidly than they are replaced; we have taken forward steps in learning that wild beasts and birds are by right not the property merely of the people alive to-day, but the property of the unborn generations, whose belongings we have no right to squander; and there are even faint signs of our growing to understand that wild flowers should be enjoyed unplucked where they grow, and that it is barbarism to ravage the woods and fields, rooting out the mayflower and breaking branches of dogwood as ornaments for automobiles filled with jovial but ignorant picnickers from cities.

In the present century the new movement gathered head. Men began to appreciate the need of preserving wild life, not only because it was useful, but also because it was beautiful. Song birds, shore birds, water-fowl, birds of all kinds, add by voice and action to the joy of living of most men and women to whom the phrase "joy of living" has any real meaning. Such stately or lovely wild creatures as moose, wapiti, deer, hartebeeste, zebra, gazelle, when protected, give ample commercial returns, and, moreover, add to the landscape just as waterfalls and lofty pine trees and towering crags add to the landscape. Fertile plains, every foot of them tilled, are of the first necessity; but great natural playgrounds of mountain, forest, cliff-walled lake, and brawling brook are also necessary to the full and many-sided development of a fine race. In just the same way the homely birds of farm and lawn and the wild creatures of the waste should all be kept. It is utterly untrue to say, as demagogues and selfish materialists sometimes unite in saying, that "the game belongs to the people"— meaning the loafers and market gunners who wish to kill it, and the wealthy and lazy gourmands who wish to eat it, without regard to the future. It is true that the game belongs to the people; but this rightly means the people who are to be born a hundred years hence just as much as the people who are alive to-day. In the same way, persons who own land, and, above all, persons who merely visit or pass through land, have no more right wantonly or carelessly to destroy birds or deface scenery than they have to pollute waters or burn down forests or let floods through levees. The sooner we appreciate these facts, the sooner we shall become a really civilized people.

Laws to protect small and harmless wild life, especially birds, are indispensable. Such laws cannot be enacted or enforced until public opinion is back of them; and associations like the Audubon Societies do work of incalculable good in stirring, rousing, and giving effect to this opinion; and men like Mr. Hornaday render all of us their debtors by the way they efficiently labor for this end, as well as for what comes only next in importance, the creation of sanctuaries for the complete protection of the larger, shyer, and more persecuted forms of wild life. This country led the way in establishing the Yellowstone Park as such a sanctuary; the British and German Empires followed, and in many ways have surpassed us. There are now many such sanctuaries and refuges in North America, middle and South Africa, and even Asia, and the results have been astounding. Many of the finer forms of animal life, which seemed on the point of vanishing, are now far more numerous than fifteen years ago, having by their rapid increase given proof of the abounding vigor of nature's fertility where nature is unmarred by man. But very much remains to be done, and there is need of the most active warfare against the forces of greed, carelessness, and sheer brutality, which, if left unchecked, would speedily undo all that has been accomplished, and would inflict literally irreparable damage.

The books before me are powerful weapons in this warfare for light against darkness. Mr. Hornaday's volume, in which he has been assisted by Mr. Walcott, consists chiefly of lectures delivered before the admirable Forest School of Yale University. It is really a full technical treatise which should be owned and constantly used by every man and woman who is alive to our needs in this matter. He shows how much has been accomplished in creating the right type of popular opinion. He is able to tell what we have accomplished in the creation of great National playgrounds, the National parks, which are National game preserves. The Yellowstone, Glacier, Mount Olympus, Grand Canyon, Sequoia, and other parks represent one of the best bits of National achievement which our people have to their credit of recent years. The National forests should also be made game reserves. No sale of game or market hunting should be allowed anywhere; fortunately, the infamous traffic in millinery feathers has now been forbidden. The Federal migratory bird law is a capital piece of legislation. Mr. Hornaday shows the imperative need of protecting our shore birds; he shows the economic value of birds to the farmer; he deals with what must, alas! be called just severity with the attitude of the average "sportsman" toward wild life.

One of the most interesting and pleasant phases of the movement of which Mr. Hornaday is one of the leaders is that which deals with the rapidity with which animals accustom themselves to protection and multiply when given the chance to do so. In New York and New England white-tail deer have enormously increased in numbers during the last thirty years. In Vermont the deer were absolutely exterminated forty years ago. Then a dozen were introduced from the Adirondacks. These have thriven and multiplied literally over a thousandfold. In forty years the original twelve individuals have increased to such an extraordinary degree that at present hunting under proper restriction is permitted, and five or six thousand deer are killed annually; without diminution of the stock. Mr. Hornaday is an entirely sane and rational man; he heartily approves of hunting, of sport carried on in legitimate fashion, as it can be, without any diminution of the amount of game. He shows that in the case of the Yellowstone elk it is urgently desirable that there should be a great increase in the killing, especially of cows; for in the absence of a sufficient number of natural foes they have increased until they now die by thousands each winter of starvation. (By the way, I venture to point out that when the cougars in the Yellowstone dwell away from the deer, antelope and sheep, and prey only on elk, they do no damage.) Our prime duty, at present, as regards the immense majority of large or beautiful or useful mammals and birds, is to protect them from excessive killing, or, indeed, from all killing. But when genuinely protected, birds and mammals increase so rapidly that it becomes imperative to kill them. If, under such circumstances, their numbers are not kept down by legitimate hunting—and some foolish creatures protest even against legitimate hunting—it would be necessary to have them completely exterminated by paid butchers. But the foolish sentimentalists who do not see this are not as yet the really efficient foes of wild life and of sensible movements for its preservation. The game hog, the man who commercializes the destruction of game, and the wealthy epicure—all of these, backed by the selfish ignorance which declines to learn, are the real foes with whom we must contend. True lovers of the chase, true sportsmen, true believers in hunting as a manly and vigorous pastime, recognize these men as their worst foes; and the great array of men and women who do not hunt, but who love wild creatures, who love all nature, must discriminate sharply between the two classes.

The Audubon Societies, which have done so much good work, have rarely done a better piece of work than in publishing the charming little book on "Alaskan Bird Life" which has been edited by Ernest Ingersoll. It has been prepared for free distribution among the people of Alaska. Surely, societies that do such work are entitled to the heartiest support from all good citizens. But something ought to be charged for the book. Let school-teachers have it free by all means; give it as a prize to exceptional pupils; but let the average man or woman pay something for such a first-class little volume. It is a book of really exceptional merit; no bird lover in the United States or Canada—not to speak of Alaska—can afford not to have it in his or her library. It is all excellent; but best of all are the portions contributed by Mr. E. W. Nelson. Mr. Nelson is one of our best field ornithologists, and also one of our best closet scientific systematists; and to extraordinary powers of observation, and intense love of the wilderness and of wild creatures, he adds the ability to write with singular power and charm. Nothing better of its kind has ever been done than his account in this little volume of the bird life, at all seasons of the year, in the Yukon Valley and on the islands and along the seacoast. His ear is as good as his eye. He is the first writer to do justice to the musical notes, especially the love notes, of the "sou-sou-southerly" duck, which in winter we know so well on Long Island Sound. He tells of the Lapland longspur, singing on the wing like a bobolink; and of the noisy cock ptarmigan crowing his challenge as he springs a few yards in the air when he is still the dominant figure on the snowy spring plains, before the hosts of water-fowl arrive. Mr. Nelson is the first observer graphically and fully to portray the life history of the strange emperor goose.

He is almost the first observer to describe the songs—for they are songs—of the shore birds; and particularly attractive is his description of the aerial love dance and love song of the tiny and gentle semi-palmated sandpiper. I cannot forbear quoting his account of the bird chorus that greets the oncoming of one of the spring storms:

"The evening before the onset of one of these spring storms was commonly heralded on the tundra, even in the clearest weather, by wonderful outbursts of cries from the larger water-fowl, and these would continue for half an hour before the birds settled down for the night. Thousands of birds took part in producing the tremendous chorus. It was made up of the notes of numberless loons in small ponds joined with the rolling cries of cranes, the bugling of flocks of swans on the large ponds, the clanging of innumerable geese, the hoarse calls of various ducks, and the screams of gulls and terns, all in a state of great excitement, apparently trying to outdo one another in strength of voice. The result was a volume of wildly harmonious music, so impressive that these concerts still remain among my most vivid memories of the north."

These ornithological sketches by Mr. Nelson are masterpieces of vivid and truthful portrayal of wild nature. They are as well done, from the standpoint of the nature lover and the man of letters, as Hudson's delightful "Naturalist in La Plata" and "Idle Days in Patagonia." These two volumes of Hudson's are literature, just as White's "Selborne" and Burroughs's writings are literature. Nelson writes with as strong charm as Hudson; he has the same love and understanding of wild life, and in addition he is a trained scientific man of the first class and an adventurous wanderer in the wilderness. A man who combines such qualities is very rare, and it is a pity not to utilize him to the utmost. Some first-class publishing firm, like Scribners, should insist upon Mr. Nelson's writing an American ornithology which would take rank as both a literary and a scientific classic.

The third volume is Mr. Fischer's sketch of men and beasts in German southwestern Africa. He describes the fell destruction, the almost complete annihilation, of the wonderful big game fauna of these southwestern African wastes by the white hunters and the black and yellow men whom they armed in the nineteenth century. It was a butchery so appallingly wasteful that it is melancholy to read of it. He also describes the steps taken by the German Government during the last decade to undo this wrong, especially by the establishment of carefully guarded game reserves. As in our country, as soon as the effort was seriously made it was entirely successful; eland, kudu, wildebeests, zebras, and many other wild creatures have once again begun to grow plentiful, and on these reserves are gradually losing their fear of man. Mr. Fischer's account of the desert and its dwellers shows keen sympathy and understanding. The mighty wilderness creatures of Africa surpass those of all the other continents in size, beauty, strangeness, number, and variety; and to allow this magnificent fauna to be needlessly butchered to satisfy the ignoble greed of hide and trophy hunters is a crime against our children's children. There are vast tracts of country that are useless for agriculture and of most use as game preserves managed in the interest of all people, both those existing and the unborn. England and Germany have done a fine work in the interest of civilization by their preservation of the African fauna in sanctuaries and by good game laws well enforced.

This is one of the many, many reasons why the present dreadful war fills me with sadness. The men, many of whom I have known—Germans, Englishmen, Frenchmen, Belgians—who have been opening the Dark Continent to civilization, and who on the whole and of recent years have done their work so wisely, are now destroying one another and ruining the work that has been done. I knew many of the men, Englishmen and Germans, who have done most for the creation and success of these game preserves—Schilling, Hamilton, Jackson, Götzen, Harry Johnson, Buxton. In all essentials they resembled one another. The admirable work they did was of the same character, alike in the British and in the German possessions. It is cruel to think that their splendid purposes and energies should now be twisted into the paths of destruction.

****

Charles Sheldon, whose book The Wilderness of the Upper Yukon *forms the basis of this article, was, as Roosevelt says, "a capital representative of the best hunter-naturalist type." Strangely, Roosevelt makes no mention of Fred Selous, a great friend of TR's who hunted with Sheldon in the Yukon. While Roosevelt rightly praises Sheldon as a hunter, he is most impressed by his work in natural history. Others have since concurred, and in recent years considerable attention has been devoted to Sheldon's journals of his travels not only in the Arctic but in the high country of Mexico. Perhaps no American hunter, with the possible exception of Jack O'Connor, did more sheep hunting, and here Roosevelt provides a useful appreciation of the skills and endurance this demanding sport required. The piece appeared in the* Outlook *(vol. 99 [1911]: 854–856).*

THE AMERICAN HUNTER-NATURALIST

I t has been wisely said that the most valuable work done by any individual in a nation, from the standpoint of the nation itself, is apt to be, from that individual's own standpoint, non-remunerative work. The statesmen and soldiers who have really rendered most service to the country were not paid, and indeed, according to our theories, ought not to have been paid, in a way that represented any adequate material reward as compared, for instance, to the sums earned by the most successful business and professional men. Great scientists, great philosophers, great writers, must also get most of their reward from the actual doing of the deed itself; for any pay they receive, measured in money, is of necessity wholly inadequate compared to the worth of the service. Finally, there are certain kinds of work in which the man not merely gets no adequate remuneration, but is obliged to spend far more than he receives, so that he actually pays for the privilege of rendering the public a service. This is peculiarly apt to be the case with explorers and with those adventurous naturalists whose love for their pursuit takes them into lands difficult and dangerous of access. From the days of Lewis and Clark to the days of Peary our greatest explorers have not only made no money out of their explorations, but have had to pay heavily for the privilege of doing work of incalculable risk and hardship; and their sufficient reward has been that the result of their work added materially to the record of honorable achievement of the American people.

Mr. Charles Sheldon is a capital representative of the best hunter-naturalist type of to-day. During the century and a half that have elapsed since tranquil Mr. White of Selborne began to correspond with Pennant the love and appreciation of wild things have grown wonderfully. The Gilbert White type of writer and observer has probably reached its highest expression in John Burroughs. But during the last thirty or forty years one of the most interesting developments of this type—foreshadowed in Waterton—has been the wilderness wanderer, who to the hardihood and prowess of the old-time hunter adds the capacity of a first-class field naturalist, and also, what is just as important, the power of literary expression. Such a man can do for the lives of the wild creatures of the wooded and mountainous wilderness what John Muir has done for the physical features of the wilderness; what John Burroughs has done for field and grove and farm land, and the birds and little beasts that dwell therein. It must always be remembered that in order to make such writings of the highest value they must have the quality of literary interest which we demand in really first-class history and first-class fiction no less than the power of accurate observation and the strict fidelity to truth which the historian must exhibit. Owen Wister's account of his white goat hunting is not only accurate, but is also as amusing and as interesting as his account of the adventures of the Virginian and Linn MacLean and Honey Wiggin, and of what befell the Pilgrim on the Gila, and the story of the worried Territorial officials and competent officers and enlisted men of the regular army who brought about the Second Missouri Compromise.

Exactly as every modern historian now recognizes the elementary fact that history means documents, so the man interested in biology, and especially in the life histories of living creatures—the study of which is certain to receive a constantly increasing appreciation by scientific men—must always remember that observations are useless unless they are written down and ultimately published. It is exasperating to think of certain of our naturalists and hunter-naturalists the value of whose really extraordinary achievements will wholly or in part die with them unless they realize the need of putting them on paper in proper form. Taking him all in all, from the standpoint of field study and closet study, from the standpoint of scientific investigator and of observer in the open, there is no mammalogist in the world who stands quite on a level with Hart Merriam, of the National Museum at Washington. He has written innumerable pamphlets which are excellent in their way, he has done an extraordinary amount of genuine scientific work; but, though there is this sum of real achievement to his credit, it is not a tenth or a twentieth as important as what he could put to his credit—and incidentally to our credit, to the credit of the American people—if only he would do so; for he could, and ought to, write a work on the mammals of North America which would literally be monumental, which would last indefinitely. He has written such a book about the mammals of the Adirondacks, and, though this book was written many years ago when he was only a young man, it is the best thing of its kind that has ever been done in this country; and it will be a real misfortune if Mr. Merriam does not repeat it on a great scale by writing such a book for all the mammals of the continent north of Mexico, or even including Mexico.

Mr. Shiras and Dr. Abbott are two men with experiences so remarkable that it is really lamentable that they should not understand that in the last analysis all that distinguishes civilization from savagery rests on the written word, and that the lack of will to write is always likely to make even the best work of ephemeral value. Dr. Abbott's feats as a naturalist and explorer in Africa and in Asia have been extraordinary, but they have not been of more than the smallest fraction of the value that they should have been, simply because they have not been recorded. There are very few men alive whose experiences would be of more value than his, if only they were written out. Mr. Shiras has done extraordinary work in the woods with a camera as well as with the notebook. He is a great hunter, but he has finally almost abandoned hunting and become a great field naturalist and observer of wild life. His photographs are extraordinary, his note-books are filled with matter of extraordinary interest; but he will not pub-lish them! He comes out of the wilds and gives his photographs to some daily paper and talks about his experiences to a reporter. He might exact-ly as well talk about them and show his photographs in a smoking-car, so far as any real value in the way of recording what he has seen is con-cerned. If he could or would put into book form his experiences, thus pre-serving his written notes and his pictures, he would render a very real service to the cause of science, he would confer a boon upon lovers of nature; and, unless he does so, his experiences will really amount to very little excepting in so far as they have given him personal gratification.

Mr. Sheldon has now for many years hunted in the wilderness, and most carefully studied in a state of nature at first hand the wild animals of this continent which are best worth studying. He is a hardy and adven-turous hunter and a trained faunal naturalist. What he has to say is of high value, and he has the power so to say it as to bring out this value to the full. This is only the first of the books which we have a right to expect from him. His experiences in Alaska, and indeed in the entire Northwest, are such as no other man has had; and no other writer on the subject has ever possessed both his power of observation and his power of recording vividly and accurately what he has seen. The present volume is fascinat-ing reading from every standpoint. It is all good, from the dedication to the illustrations. The dedication is to one of the best outdoor and indoor naturalists in America, Mr. Edward W. Nelson, and it is phrased so as to show a genuine appreciation of Mr. Nelson's services; and the illustrations include capital photographs and some good reproductions of the striking animal paintings of the animal artist Carl Rungius.

Mr. Sheldon is not only a first-class hunter and naturalist but passion-ately devoted to all that is beautiful in nature, and he has the literary taste and ability to etch his landscapes into his narratives, so that they give to the reader something of the feeling that he must have had when he saw them—and that this is no mean feat is evident to every one who realizes how uncommonly dreary most writing about landscape is, for the average writer either treats the matter with utter bareness, or, what is worse, indulges at much length in "fine writing" of the abhorrently florid and prolix type.

Mr. Sheldon hunted in the tremendous Northern wilderness of snow-field and torrent, of scalped mountain and frowning pine forest; and in all the world there is no scenery grander in its lonely desolation than that which he portrays. He is no holiday hunter. Like Stewart Edward White, he is as skillful and self-reliant a woodsman and mountaineer as an old-time trapper, and he always hunts alone. The chase of the Northern mountain sheep, followed in such manner, means a test of every real hunter's quality—marksmanship, hardihood and endurance, nerve and skill as a cragsman, keen eyesight, and high ability as still hunter and stalker. Mr. Sheldon possesses them all. Leaving camp by himself, with a couple of crackers and a piece of chocolate and perhaps a little tea in his pocket, he would climb the mountains until at last he saw his game; and then might have to spend twenty-four hours in the approach, sleeping out overnight and not returning to camp until late the following evening, when he would stagger downhill through the long sub-arctic dusk with the head, hide, and some of the meat of his game on his back. This kind of hunting is the kind that really speaks well for the hunter's bodily prowess and moral qualities.

But the most important part of Mr. Sheldon's book is that which relates not to hunting but to natural history. No professional biologist has worked out the problems connected with these Northern mountain sheep as he has done. He shows that they are of one species; a showing that would have been most unexpected a few years ago, for at one extreme this species becomes the black so-called Stone's sheep, and at the other the pure white, so-called Dall's sheep. Yet, as Mr. Sheldon shows in his maps, his description, and his figures, the two kinds grade into one another without a break, the form midway between having already been described as Fannin's sheep. The working out of this fact is a matter of note. But still more notable is his description of the life history of the sheep from the standpoint of its relations with its foes—the wolf, lynx, wolverine, and war eagle.

A very interesting side of Mr. Sheldon's study is his careful examination of the actual facts as to the methods of attack upon the sheep by their various foes. Closet theorists, many of them wholly without any knowledge of the actual life histories of the animals they describe, have of recent years carried the doctrine of concealing coloration to a preposterous extreme, and they have applied it to these sheep heedless of the fact that one extreme form is black and the other extreme form white, although they are living under practically similar conditions. Mr. Sheldon's first-hand studies in the field show that concealing coloration is a practically negligible factor in the lives of the sheep, that the coloration is of negligible consequence in protecting them from their foes; it is advertising rather than concealing.

In short, this volume is one of the rare volumes which should be in the library of every man who cares for stories of adventure, of every man who cares for natural history and big-game hunting, and, finally, of every man who cares to read of outdoor nature in the wilderness, described with truthfulness, with power, and with charm.

****

Abel Chapman was a noted African hunter, a first-rate field naturalist, a keen waterfowler, and an authority on birds. In his two works of autobiography, Retrospect: Reminiscences and Impressions of a Hunter Naturalist in Three Continents, 1851–1928 *(1928) and* Memories of Fourscore Years Less Two *(1930), Chapman provides one of the finest examples of the meaning of a life devoted to outdoor pursuits. Those works were published well after the five volumes reviewed below by Roosevelt. Roosevelt always appreciated fellow toilers in the wild world, and he particularly admired Chapman's exceptional attention to detail and powers of observation. The two never hunted together, but as TR makes clear, they were kindred spirits as hunter-naturalists. This selection originally appeared in the* Outlook *(vol. 99 [1911]: 110–114).*

A HUNTER-NATURALIST IN EUROPE AND AFRICA

As any literature develops, there necessarily comes the differentiation and specialization which mark development. Just as poetry, religion, and history were originally all one so far as literature was concerned, so the comparatively late literary development which treats of wild nature has tended of recent years to specialize along a score of different lines. The hunting book proper goes back at least to Xenophon, and was continued from classic times through the Middle Ages—witness Gaston de Foix and the Duke of York—receiving its greatest development within the last century. Scientific zoölogy started, in very rudimentary shape, with Aristotle and Pliny; unfortunately, these great men were succeeded for between fifteen hundred and two thousand years by pupils with that utterly worthless type of mind which makes the owner content only to copy the teacher in servile fashion instead of extending and developing the teacher's work. It has only been within the last two or three centuries that we have gradually developed great faunal naturalists. The nature book proper, which treats with power and charm of outdoor life and of the smaller wild things, from the standpoint, not of the mere hunter or mere zoologist, but of the man of letters and learning who is in love with nature, may be said to have begun with Gilbert White, a century and a quarter ago, and it has received its highest expression in John Burroughs—I sympathize too much with Lowell's view of Thoreau to put the latter in the direct line of descent between the two.

Specialization is a good thing, but it may readily be carried too far; and after it has reached a certain point it is well to try to develop again, and on a larger scale, the man who has a special side, but who possesses broader instincts also, and who is able to combine the peculiar aptitudes of the specialist with the larger power that belongs to the man with a broad grasp of the general subject. Half a century or so ago it looked as if we would develop hunters who knew nothing whatever of anything except hunting, zoölogists who knew life only from musuem specimens, and outdoor lovers of nature who were not competent to make additions to scientific truth, nor yet to deal with and describe nature in its wilder and more imposing forms, animate and inanimate. Nowadays, however, we are tending to develop much higher types of all of these; and also a type which includes them all. The man who is to do the best work as a zoölogist must be an out-of-doors man of the fields as well as a man of the laboratory, book-shelf, and microscope. The big-game hunter cannot possibly be of much use from a serious standpoint unless he is a keen naturalist. The outdoor man who writes, the nature writer proper, should not only be a keen observer and a man of genuine literary capacity, absolutely trustworthy and able to tell with interest and charm what he has seen, but ought also to have the power to utilize, and to add to, what science can teach; and he ought to be able not only to describe what goes on in our gardens, fields, and woods, but also to tell of the great epic tragedy of life which is unfolded in the stark wilderness. Finally, while each man will still tend to put most emphasis on his work in some one of these three special lines, the really great writer and observer ought to combine something of all of them; and the writer on big game, in particular, falls far short of the proper standard unless he is also a good field naturalist and lover of nature, who has the power to see what is of most interest and then to put before our eyes in vivid shape what he has himself thus seen.

Mr. Abel Chapman's books are good from every standpoint I have mentioned. He is a sportsman who knows how to observe and how to tell what he sees; he is a big-game hunter of renown; and on every hunt he watches with keen interest all the small life of the wilderness. He can both write and draw. There is not one of his books, whether dealing with the land or water fowl of Northumberland, with wild Norway and wilder Spain, or with the giant fauna of equatorial Africa, which a man who cares for outdoor natural history, or for small-game shooting, or for big-game hunting, can afford to be without. The volumes on Spain by Messrs. Chapman and Buck have an especial charm because the authors penetrated into out-of-way corners of one of the oldest and least-known portions of Europe, a land that in its past and present, in its greatness and in its weakness, offers one of the most puzzling of all possible problems to the student. In Spain they did original zoölogical work of high value. They gave us our first adequate knowledge of the Spanish ibex; and they point out that this beast of the high peaks sometimes dwells in thick scrub on low mountains—just as I have found white goats on certain ranges living all the year round on mountains timbered to their tops. They first revealed the truth about the nesting habits of the flamingo. Their account of the big bustard is of extreme interest. In the haunts of the flamingo, the wide, marshy marismas, they found wild—or rather feral—camels; and it is an extraordinary thing that these camels should have become marsh beasts. The observations on the birds of prey and water-fowl are of especial value.

Not since Lloyd has as good a book appeared about the Scandinavian Peninsula as Chapman's "Wild Norway," and Lloyd was by no means as competent to tell us about the smaller forms of life, which are of such interest to the naturalist. The Northumberland book, excellent from every standpoint, shows how much room there is for the best kind of work of this nature near home. Mr. Chapman's books on Spain derive part of their interest from the fact that he went where practically no one else had gone. But he wrote about Northumberland simply as Jefferies could and did write about Devon, and Colquhoun and St. John about the Highlands of Scotland. There is ample room for just such a book about Alaska, for instance—which, by the way, Mr. Sheldon could write if he would; there is real need for such a book on American big game, and on the smaller wild creatures to be found in the haunts of American big game; a book for which Mr. Shiras has such ample material in photographs and notes as would enable him to make a literally priceless contribution to our nature writings, if he would only take the time and trouble to do what I really think is his plain duty.   Maine, Pennsylvania, Texas, Arizona, Washington—there is hardly a State about which it would not be possible to produce a book as interesting as that of Mr. Chapman about Northumberland, if only there were produced in each case the man combining, as Mr. Chapman combines, the abilities of sportsman, naturalist, and writer.

Mr. Chapman's "On Safari"—a capital title—must be numbered among the best books that have been written about African big game, and this although Mr. Chapman has not had one-tenth or one-hundredth part of the experience that many of the great African hunters have had. A few of these great African hunters—Gordon Cumming, Cornwallis Harris, Samuel Baker, Stigand, Arthur Neuman, and, above all others, Selous— have given us much that we wish to know concerning the huge or beautiful or formidable creatures of the plains, the forests, and the mountains. But the average big-game hunter writes a book about as interesting as a Baedeker, and nothing like as useful. I doubt if there is a less attractive type of literary output than an annotated game bag, or record of slaughter, from which we are able to gather nothing of value as to the lives of the animals themselves, and very little even from the dreary account of the author's murderous prowess. Some of the books by the best men err in exasperating fashion owing to a morbid kind of modesty which makes the writer too self-conscious to tell frankly and fully what he himself has done. This is sometimes spoken of as a good trait, but it is not a good trait. It is not as repellent as conceit or vulgarity, separate or combined, or as that painful trait, the desire to be "funny;" but it is a very bad trait, nevertheless. If a hunter thinks he ought not to tell what he himself has done, then he had much better not write a book at all. There is scant use in his joining the inarticulate mob which Carlyle praised with such verbose insincerity and unveracity. If the hunter does write, and is a keen observer, he should remember that, if he is worth listening to at all, his listeners will be particularly interested in hearing of any noteworthy experience that has happened to him personally.   Having just re-read Captain Stigand's otherwise admirable book, I am writing with a keen sense of personal injury, because, while from allusions in the book I gather that Captain Stigand was once tossed by rhinoceros and once mauled by a lion, I am wholly unable to get any full and satisfactory information as to these thrilling incidents, and accordingly I feel just as I would feel if the last chapters had been omitted from "Guy Mannering," and Meg Merrilies barely mentioned. I wish a good hunting book to be as interesting as a good novel! I have read Patterson's "Man-eaters of Tsavo" again and again, just because the lions *were* man-eaters, and because Patterson killed them, and because (with evident accuracy and truthfulness) he gives all the details of his failures and of his ultimate success. I read the book, among other reasons, because it is interesting—just as "Nicholas Nickleby," and "The Murders of the Rue Morgue," and Macaulay's "Essays," and Parkman's "Montcalm and Wolfe" are interesting. Of course a hunting book must be absolutely true, just as much so as a history; the quality of interest cannot supply the lack of accuracy; but unless the book has interest it is a poor book.

Mr. Chapman in "On Safari" puts before our eyes a vivid picture of the great game of East Africa, such as hardly any other writer, except the German Schilling, paints for us; and when we follow his hunts we do it with thorough sympathy and understanding, because, without useless detail, he yet tells us everything essential that happened, so that we can see it all with our eyes. We know just how the rhinoceros looked and how he acted; we see the hartebeest overcome by pride in his position as he leads the files of wildebeest down to the water; we know how the hunter himself feels on the march, in his different camps, and when he is breakfasting at dawn while his tent is being struck. Moreover, with pen and pencil Mr. Chapman brings before us pictures of many of the striking birds which are a delight to the eyes of the African hunter who loves nature. Mr. Chapman is a thorough sportsman. He is free from that besetting desire to make record bags[1] which is, to my mind, one of the most curious and unpleasant, and indeed unhealthy, developments of the otherwise excellent English sportsmanship; and what he preaches about the preservation of game and wild things could be preached with even more advantage in our own country than in his.

There are two or three specific points made by Mr. Chapman which are directly applicable to our needs over here. He speaks with proper condemnation, not only of we would call the "game hog," but of the mere collector, the man who is not a naturalist at all, and who collects rare species as a professional stamp-collector would collect stamps, for sale, heedless of the fact that he may be doing irreparable harm. Game heads and antlers which represent merely the owner's money make that owner look absurd; trophies, save in rare cases when they are gifts, should be proofs of the owner's prowess. Here in America a dozen birds have vanished or their

---

[1] But when among Spanish wild flow Mr. Chapman could have afforded to be more moderate.

numbers have been so thinned out that they are on the point of vanishing. The passenger pigeon, paroquet, whooping crane, Eastern prairie hen, trumpeter swan, Labrador duck, and ivory-billed woodpecker are among them; and the butchery of terns and herons for "fun," or for woman's headgear, has been atrocious—I can use no other word. It would, of course, be as great an absurdity to stop all killing of game birds as to stop all killing of barnyard fowls; but it is no less an absurdity to kill beyond the point where they can reproduce themselves. Birds that are useless for the table and not harmful to the farm should always be preserved; and the more beautiful they are, the more carefully they should be preserved. They look a great deal better in the swamps and on the beaches and among the trees than they do on hats. There are certain species in certain localities which it is still necessary to collect; but no really rare bird ought to be shot save in altogether exceptional circumstances and for public museums, and the common birds (which of course should also be placed in public museums) are entirely out of place in private collections; and this applies as much to their eggs and nests as to their skins. The proper way to study these birds is to study them as Mabel Osgood Wright studies them; and we should all endeavor to preserve them in our own gardens and fields and woods, just as she has succeeded in preserving them.

Again, I cordially agree with what Mr. Chapman says about photography. He fully appreciates its great importance in the study of nature. The photographs of big game by Schilling, Dugmore, Kearton, Delamere; the photographs of wild birds by Kearton, Job, Findley, Frank T. Chapman, and many others, represent an immense addition to our knowledge. But it is a mistake to suppose that photographs can ever supply the place of good letterpress or of good pictures—pictures like those in Millais's "Breath from the Veldt." It is only under exceptional circumstances that photographs can be treated as in themselves an end; normally they are only a means to an end. As Mr. Chapman says, pictures of out-of-door life must be both accurate and artistic—qualities which were formerly held to be mutually exclusive.

Mr. Chapman appeals to those of us who are not past-masters in all branches of the difficult art of the wilderness hunter, because he takes pride in just the same modest feats in which we also take pride. For instance, Captain Stigand, who is a very exceptionally skillful hunter and hardy wilderness wanderer, expresses the utmost contempt for people who take any pride in killing game on the open plains; whereas to men of humbler powers it is comforting to their self-respect to find that that good hunter and fine naturalist ex-Governor Jackson, of British East Africa, devotes much space to the description and praise of precisely this open plains shooting.

Finally, Mr. Chapman's observations on natural history should be held up as an example to those writers who make observations only with the deliberate purpose of twisting them into the support of some theory. Mr. Chapman applies the doctrine of concealing coloration much more widely than I do, and I differ with him as regards some of the examples he gives in this matter, just as I differ with him as to certain of his observations on African big game—as, for instance, his belief that African game rarely lies down when resting, and his belief in the excessively dangerous character of the rhinoceros. But honest differences of opinion, honest differences in seeing and interpreting facts, are helps and not hindrances to getting at the truth.

Such differences of opinions, and conflicts in recorded facts, there must be, and it is right that there should be. What is essential is that they should be based on a desire actually to see facts and truthfully to record them. A thousand fantastic laboratory experiments about concealing coloration are not worth a single observation based on intelligent experience in the field, truthfully recorded and interpreted.   The following remark by Mr. Chapman, in connection with shooting the great bustard, applies universally among the hunted as well as the hunters: "Immobility is tenfold more important than color. A pure white object that is quiescent is overlooked, where a clod of turf that *moves* attracts instant attention." So, in speaking of grouse and wild fowl, he acutely distinguishes between the period when they have dull-colored plumage patterns and seek and profit by concealment, and the period when they are in their full vigor, have advertising coloration patterns, and make no effort to hide. (I condense.) "During the second half of October a marked change will be observed in the habits of the moorland game and wild fowl. The grouse sit boldly conspicuous on the open ground. The mallard drakes, having acquired their glossy green heads and chestnut breasts, show up boldly on the open waters instead of skulking in reeds or sedge. All the strong willed-birds, in fact, having attained their full feather and beauty, now assume the full measure of confidence—not to say defiance—that marks their winter habit. They no longer seek a delusive security in concealment. Early in the season such tactics were intelligible enough with immature poults, or with ragged old birds still in full molt. But with increasing strength their former devices are cast aside; they now sit bare and conspicuous on hillside, knowe, or lough, confident in their own keen instincts and powers of wing and eye to keep themselves beyond the reach of danger." All of which is commended to the prayerful consideration of the well-meaning but slightly absurd faddists who believe that the male mallards and wood ducks when in full winter or spring plumage are "concealingly colored." Many wading birds are concealingly colored at certain seasons, and at other seasons have a highly advertising coloration—the male often assuming such a coloration at the very time that it is most dangerous for him.

There is no more fascinating study than that of bird migration; and Mr. Chapman touches on the subject again and again, and he brings up one of the most difficult puzzles connected with the subject when he describes how, in many species of water birds, the young come down from their Arctic birthplaces in advance of their parents, and yet, although unguided, and never having been near the places before, appear in the exact haunts that their forebears have frequented for countless generations.

Bibliography

Introductory Note

As a literary figure Roosevelt's legacy focuses primarily on his books, and as subscribers to the Roosevelt Classics Library know well, that legacy is a rich one. Inasmuch as the Library, in its totality, provides readers full access to all of TR's major books on the outdoors, they are included in this bibliography without any annotation or further mention (citations are for the first editions, although most have been reprinted a number of times). Worthy of note in this regard, however, is the fact that TR did contribute essays, introductions, and the like to a number of other books, and those efforts of this nature which seem relevant have been provided.

Sometimes the fact that TR, as a staunch conservationist and intrepid outdoorsman, wrote frequently (and well) on all aspects of the outdoors is overlooked, at least to the extent of assuming his contributions in this subject field were limited to books. Such is definitely not the case. The information offered here is intended to serve as a reasonably comprehensive guide to the literature by and about Roosevelt which relates to any aspect of conservation, natural history, hunting, or wilderness life.

While the bibliography comes from extensive reading and research, it should by no means be considered complete. This holds particularly true for works relating to Roosevelt. He continues to be the focus of keen interest on the part of historians and others, and at best the books and articles listed which relate to his career as an outdoorsman should be viewed as merely representative of the vast corpus of available literature.

****

ROOSEVELT'S ARTICLES ON THE OUTDOORS

As Edward Wagenknecht suggested, in his fine work *The Seven Worlds of Theodore Roosevelt* (New York: Longmans, Green & Company, 1958), "TR's articles in newspapers and magazines are like the sands of the sea in number." The listing which follows comprises most of his significant pieces dealing with outdoor-related matters, but unquestionably there are oversights, particularly when it comes to contributions to newspapers. Serious students of TR's work will also notice that several of these entries subsequently appeared in his books, a consideration which mitigated against them being incorporated into this anthology. Indeed, virtually the entire text of *African Game Trails* first appeared as a series of articles in *Scribner's Magazine*, beginning with the October 1909 issue and continuing for the next year, concluding with the twelfth and final supplement in September 1910. Similarly, the "Life History" series in the same magazine in 1913 formed an important part of *Life Histories of African Game Animals* which he co-authored with Edmund Heller.

The citations below refer, in each instance, to the original source of publication. In addition to those which appeared in TR's own books, several have been reprinted or included in other anthologies. Those selected for inclusion here follow the criteria delineated in "A Note of Selection and Organization" which appears at the beginning of the present volume. They are indicated by boldface. I have not been able to consult a few of the listed entries, and when this is the case, the designation "*Not Seen*" appears at the end of the citation.

"Across the Navajo Desert," *The Outlook*, Volume 105 (1913), 309-317.

"The American Hunter-Naturalist," *The Outlook*, Volume 99 (1911), 854-856.

"The Bear's Disposition," *Trail and Camp-Fire* (New York: Forest and Stream Publishing, 1897), 230-237. Reprinted in *American Bears*, edited by Paul Schullery (Boulder: Colorado Associated University Press, 1983), 59-64.

"Big Game Disappearing in the West," *The Forum*, Volume 15, Number 6 (August, 1893). *Not Seen*

"Bird Refuges of Louisiana," *Scribner's Magazine*, Volume 59 (1916), 261-280.

"Bison," in *The Encyclopedia of Sport*, 2 volumes, edited by Hedley Peek, earl of Suffolk and Berkshire, and F. G. Aflalo (New York: G. P. Putnam, 1898), Volume I, 116-118.

"Books on Big Game," in *Trail and Camp-Fire*, edited by George Bird Grinnell and Theodore Roosevelt (New York: Forest and Stream Publishing, 1897), 321-335. Although this article is unsigned, it bears the unmistakable stamp of TR's style.

"The Boy Roosevelt Self-Revealed; Excerpts from the Journal Which He Kept When He Was Ten Years Old," *The Outlook*, Volume 148 (1928), 529-530.

"Caribou," in *The Encyclopedia of Sport*, 2 volumes, edited by Hedley Peek, earl of Suffolk and Berkshire, and F. G. Aflalo (New York: G. P. Putnam, 1898), Volume I, 180-181.

"A Christmas in Mid-Africa," *The Outlook*, Volume 96 (1910), 1000-1001.

"The Conservation of Wild Life," *The Outlook*, Volume 109 (1915), 159-162.

"A Cougar Hunt on the Rim of the Grand Canyon," *The Outlook*, Volume 105 (1913), 259-266.

"Coursing the Prongbuck," in *American Big-Game Hunting*, edited by Theodore Roosevelt and George Bird Grinnell (New York: Forest and Stream Publishing, 1893), 129-139.

"Frederick Courteney Selous," *The Outlook*, Volume 115 (1917), 410-411.

"Grand Canyon, 1903," *New York Sun*, May 6, 1903. Reprinted in *Theodore Roosevelt: Wilderness Writings*, edited by Paul Schullery (Salt Lake City: Peregrine Smith Books, 1986), 217.

"Harpooning Devilfish," *Scribner's Magazine*, Volume 62 (1917), 293-305.

"A Hunter-Naturalist in Europe and Africa," *The Outlook*, Volume 99 (1911), 110-114.

"Hunting in the Cattle Country," in *Hunting in Many Lands*, edited by Theodore Roosevelt and George Bird Grinnell (New York: Forest and Stream Publishing, 1895), 278-317.

"Hunting Letters," *Country Life*, Volume 41 (1921), 54-55.

"In the Louisiana Canebreaks," *Scribner's Magazine*, Volume 43 (1908), 47-60. Reprinted in *Theodore Roosevelt: Wilderness Writings*, edited by Paul Schullery (Salt Lake City: Peregrine Smith Books, 1986), 86-110.

"John Muir: An Appreciation," *The Outlook*, Volume 109 (1915), 27-28. Reprinted in *Theodore Roosevelt: Wilderness Writings*, edited by Paul Schullery (Salt Lake City: Peregrine Smith Books, 1986), 143-146.

"The Life-History of the African Buffalo, Giant Eland, and Common Eland," *Scribner's Magazine*, Volume 54 (1913), 681-693.

"The Life-History of the African Elephant," *Scribner's Magazine*, Volume 54 (1913), 432-442.

"The Life-History of the African Lion," *Scribner's Magazine*, Volume 54 (1913), 279-298.

"The Life-History of the African Rhinoceros and Hippopotamus,"

Scribner's Magazine, Volume 54 (1913), 580-594.

"Literature of American Big-Game Hunting," in *American Big-Game Hunting*, edited by Theodore Roosevelt and George Bird Grinnell (New York: Forest and Stream Publishing, 1893), 319-325. Unsigned, but clearly TR's work.

"My Life as a Naturalist," *The American Museum Journal*, Volume 18 (1918), 321-330.

"A National Park Service," *The Outlook*, Volume 100 (1912), 246. Reprinted in *Theodore Roosevelt: Wilderness Writings*, edited by Paul Schullery (Salt Lake City: Peregrine Smith Books, 1986), 141-142.

"The Need of Trained Observation," *Outing*, Volume 37 (1900-01), 631-633.

"On the Little Missouri," in *Trail and Camp-Fire*, edited by George Bird Grinnell and Theodore Roosevelt (New York: Forest and Stream Publishing , 1897), 204-220.

"Opossum and Raccoon," in *The Encyclopedia of Sport*, 2 volumes, edited by Hedley Peek, earl of Suffolk and Berkshire, and F. G. Aflalo (New York: G. P. Putnam, 1898), Volume II, 62-63.

"Our Forests," *Journal of Education*, Volume 68 (1908), 169.

"Our Vanishing Wild Life," *The Outlook*, Volume 103 (1913), 161-162.

"Peccary," in *The Encyclopedia of Sport*, 2 volumes, edited by Hedley Peek, earl of Suffolk and Berkshire, and F. G. Aflalo (New York: G. P. Putnam, 1898), Volume II, 79.

"Prairie Chicken," in *The Encyclopedia of Sport*, 2 volumes, edited by Hedley Peek, earl of Suffolk and Berkshire, and F. G. Aflalo (New York: G. P. Putnam, 1898), Volume II, 131-132.

"Pronghorn," in *The Encyclopedia of Sport*, 2 volumes, edited by Hedley Peek, earl of Suffolk and Berkshire, and F. G. Aflalo (New York: G. P. Putnam, 1898), Volume II, 137-138.

"Puma," in *The Encyclopedia of Sport*, 2 volumes, edited by Hedley Peek, earl of Suffolk and Berkshire, and F. G. Aflalo (New York: G. P. Putnam, 1898), Volume II, 154-155.

"Rocky Mountain Goat," in *The Encyclopedia of Sport*, 2 volumes, edited by Hedley Peek, earl of Suffolk and Berkshire, and F. G. Aflalo (New York: G. P. Putnam, 1898), Volume I, 455-456.

"Small Country Neighbors," *Scribner's Magazine*, Volume 42 (1907), 385-395. Reprinted in *Theodore Roosevelt: Wilderness Writings*, edited by Paul Schullery (Salt Lake City: Peregrine Smith Books, 1986), 219-236.

"Tales Told by a Ranch Fireside: A Man-Killing Bear," *The Youth's Companion*, July 13, 1893, 354. Reprinted in *American Bears,* edited by Paul Schullery (Boulder: Colorado Associated University Press, 1983), 117-222.

"Tales Told by a Ranch Fireside: Wolfish Marauders," *The Youth's Companion*, June 22, 1893, 318.

"Three Capital Books of the Wilderness," *The Outlook*, Volume 102 (1912), 712-715. A review essay on J. Stevenson-Hamilton's *Animal Life of Africa,* Charles Sheldon's *The Wilderness of the North Pacific Coast Islands,* and Stewart Edward White's *The Land of Footprints.*

"Turkey," in *The Encyclopedia of Sport,* 2 volumes, edited by Hedley Peek, earl of Suffolk and Berkshire, and F. G. Aflalo (New York: G. P. Putnam, 1898), Volume II, 501-502.

"Wapiti," in *The Encyclopedia of Sport,* 2 volumes, edited by Hedley Peek, earl of Suffolk and Berkshire, and F. G. Aflalo (New York: G. P. Putnam, 1898), Volume II, 528-530.

"The Wild Animals of North America," *The Outlook*, Volume 120 (1918), 342-343.

"Wild Man and Wild Beast in Africa," *National Geographic*, Volume 22 (1911), 1-33. *Not Seen*

"Wild Ostrich," *Atlantic*, Volume 121 (1918), 755-757.

"Wolf-Coursing," in *The Encyclopedia of Sport,* 2 volumes, edited by Hedley Peek, earl of Suffolk and Berkshire, and F. G. Aflalo (New York: G. P. Putnam, 1898), Volume II, 540-541.

"A Zoological Trip Through Africa," *Bulletin of the Throop Polytechnic Institute,* Volume 20, Number 51 (July, 1911). *Not Seen*

ROOSEVELT'S BOOKS ON THE OUTDOORS

African Game Trails. New York: Scribner's, 1910.

A Book-Lover's Holidays in the Open. New York: Scribner's, 1916.

The Deer Family (with T. S. Van Dyke, D. G. Eliot, and A. J. Stone). New York and London: Macmillan, 1902. TR wrote the section on "The Deer and Antelope of North America."

Good Hunting: In Pursuit of Big Game in the West. London and New York: Harper, 1907.

Hunting Trips of a Ranchman. New York: G. P. Putnam, 1885.

Life-Histories of African Game Animals (with Edmund Heller). 2 volumes. New York: Scribner's, 1914.

Outdoor Pastimes of an American Hunter. New York: Scribner's, 1905.

Ranch Life and the Hunting Trail. New York: The Century Company, 1888.

Through the Brazilian Wilderness. New York: Scribner's, 1914.

The Wilderness Hunter. New York: G. P. Putnam, 1893.

The Winning of the West. 4 volumes. New York: G. P. Putnam, 1889, 1894, 1896. Not primarily on the outdoors, but the way to the West involved a great deal of hunting and life in the wilderness.

OTHER OUTDOOR-RELATED MATERIAL

"Foreword" to *African Adventure Stories*, by Alden J. Loring (New York: Scribner's, 1914).

"Foreword" to *African Nature Notes and Reminiscences*, by Frederick C. Selous (London: Macmillan, 1908).

"Foreword" to *Animal Life in Africa*, by James Stevenson-Hamilton (London: Heinemann, 1912).

"Foreword" to *The Master of Game*, by Edward, Second Duke of York (London: Ballantyne, Hanson & Company, 1904).

"Introduction" to *Camera Shots at Big Game*, by A. G. Wallihan (New York: Doubleday, Page & Company, 1901).

"Introduction" to *Hoofs, Claws and Antlers of the Rocky Mountains*, by A. G. Wallihan (Denver: Frank S. Thayer, 1894).

"Introduction" to *Hunting the Elephant in Africa*, by Chauncey H. Stigand (New York: Macmillan, 1913).

"Introduction" to *Lassoing Wild Animals in Africa*, by Guy H. Scull (New York: Frederick A. Stokes, 1911).

"Introduction" to *Tropical Wild Life in British Guinea*, by William Beebe, G. Inness Hartley, and Paul G. Howes (New York: The New York Zoological Society, 1917).

"Introduction" to *Wild Life Across the World*, by Cherry L. Kearton (London: Hodder & Stoughton, 1913).

"Introductory Letter" to *The Book of the Lion*, second edition, by Alfred E. Pease (New York: Scribner's, 1914).

"Introductory Letter" to *Wild Wings*, by Herbert K. Job (London: Constable, 1905).

"Preface" to *Wild Bird Guests*, by Ernest Harold Baynes (New York: E. P. Dutton, 1915).

ARTICLES ON ROOSEVELT AS AN OUTDOORSMAN

The essence of TR's character ensured that he would be the subject of extensive research and writing. That applies to his endeavors as an outdoorsman as well as to other aspects of his life as varied as politics, the study of history, diplomacy, and literary undertakings. Offered here is a sampling of contributions to periodicals which constitute, in my personal opinion, some of the most meaningful efforts focusing on TR's outdoor pursuits. It is by no means complete. Indeed, assiduous research would reveal scores if not hundreds of additional articles, but the listings below provide, at the least, an index to the sort of material available on the subject. As was the case with articles by Roosevelt, those which I have not personally consulted are denoted by "*Not Seen*."

Anonymous, "African Trophies of Theodore Roosevelt," *Country Life,* March, 1920. *Not Seen*

Anonymous, "Hunting Bear with T. R. and Uncle Holt," *Literary Digest*, Volume 112 (1972), 32-34.

Anonymous, "Theodore Roosevelt—An Outdoor Man," *McClure's Magazine*, Volume 26 (1906), 231-252.

Anonymous, "Theodore Roosevelt's Wilderness Legacy," *National Geographic*, Volume 162 (1982), 340-362. *Not Seen*

John Burroughs, "With Roosevelt at Pine Knot," *The Outlook*, Volume 128 (1921), 170-171. TR and the noted nature writer camp together.

Lindsay Denison, "President Roosevelt's Mississippi Bear Hunt," *Outing*, February, 1903. *Not Seen*

W. R. Foran, "With Roosevelt in Africa," *Field & Stream,* October, 1912, 591-597.

John B. Goff, "The Roosevelt Lion Hunt," *Outdoor Life*, 1901. *Not Seen*

George Bird Grinnell, "Theodore Roosevelt as a Sportsman," *Country Calendar*, November, 1905, 623-626, 666.

Roy H. Mattison and Olaf T. Hagen, "Pyramid Park—Where Roosevelt Came to Hunt," *North Dakota History*, Volume 19 (1952), 215-239.

J. A. McGuire, "Governor Roosevelt's Colorado Lion Hunt," *Outdoor Life*, March, 1901. *Not Seen*

C. Hart Merriam, "Roosevelt the Naturalist," *Science,* New Series Volume 75 (1932). *Not Seen*

John M. Parker, "Hunting with Col. Roosevelt," *Outers' Book-Recreation,* September, 1919.

Charles R. Podmore, "Theodore Roosevelt's African Journey," *African Wild Life,* Volume 13, Number 3 (September, 1959), 235-241.

D. Shaw, "TR's Last Hunt," *Field & Stream,* Volume 62 (1958), 35-38.

BOOKS ON ROOSEVELT
AS AN OUTDOORSMAN

Several full-length studies focusing exclusively or in large part on TR as an outdoorsman have been published over the years. They range from "pot boilers" (his African journey alone produced a dozen or more of these) to serious, carefully researched works which should be read by anyone keenly interested in just how TR lived the strenuous life. Taken a step further, mention of Roosevelt in writings by his contemporaries can be overwhelming. As Aloysius Norton puts it so vividly in his excellent *Theodore Roosevelt* (1980), "If there really are more stars in the heavens than there are grains of sand on all the beaches of the world, then their number can be rivaled by the seemingly infinite number of allusions to Roosevelt in the memoirs, autobiographies, biographies, and letters of his time." With an eye to offering some guidance through this wealth of literature, critical annotations accompany many of the listings below. Those which I consider essential reading are marked by an asterisk with the entry.

*Gilbert J. Black, *Theodore Roosevelt, 1858-1919, Chronology, Documents, Bibliographical Aids.* Dobbs Ferry, New York: Oceana Publications, 1969. An important reference source.

*William T. Cobb, *The Strenuous Life: The Oyster Bay Roosevelts in Business and Finance.* New York: William E. Rudge's Sons, 1946.

*Paul Russell Cutright, *Theodore Roosevelt, the Naturalist.* New York: Harper & Brothers, 1956. A solid contribution by a trained academic zoologist which attempts to place TR's eminence as a naturalist on a par with his political and military achievements. The bibliography accompanying the work is a bit disappointing, and Cutright seems to have made only selective use of the vast corpus of extant manuscript material bearing on his subject.

*Hermann Hagedorn, *The Roosevelt Family of Sagamore Hill*. New York: Macmillan, 1954. Somewhat gossipy, but lots of useful anecdotal material on TR's youth.

*Hermann Hagedorn, *Roosevelt in the Bad Lands*. Boston: Houghton Mifflin, 1921. One of the best treatments of Roosevelt's years in the Dakota Badlands. Hagedorn knew TR well and was the individual who edited and compiled what is generally considered the best edition of his works, the 24-volume "Memorial Edition" (1923-26). It should be noted, incidentally, that the Memorial Edition not only printed the vast majority of TR's writings. The volumes also included commentary and other information from friends and students of the man.

Edwin P. Hoyt, *Teddy Roosevelt in Africa*. New York: Duell, Sloan and Pearce, 1966. A juvenile, but with useful anecdotes.

Lincoln Lang, *Ranching with Roosevelt*. Philadelphia: Lippincott, 1926. On the author's experiences with Roosevelt in the Dakota Badlands.

*J. Alden Loring, *African Adventure Stories*. New York: Scribner's, 1927. Loring was the field naturalist to the Roosevelt expedition. The book includes a brief Introduction by TR.

Axel Lundeberg and Frederick Seymour, *The Great Roosevelt African Hunt and the Wild Animals of Africa*. Chicago: D.B. McCurdy, 1910. Essentially a pot boiler.

John T. McCutcheon, *In Africa: Hunting Adventures in the Big Game Country*. Indianapolis: Bobbs-Merrill, 1910. Another pot boiler, although it is an item coveted by collectors of African big game books.

*Aloysius Norton, *Theodore Roosevelt*. Boston: Twayne, 1980. A vital guide to Roosevelt the writer and scholar.

John Callan O'Laughlin, *From the Jungle Through Europe with Roosevelt*. Boston: Chapple Publishing Company, 1910. O'Laughlin was the Washington correspondent of the *Chicago Tribune*.

*Gifford Pinchot, *Breaking New Ground*. New York: Harcourt Brace, 1947. Pinchot's autobiography, with much on his forest-related work with Roosevelt. The book is interesting but not always reliable.

*Carleton Putnam, *Theodore Roosevelt: The Formative Years*. New York: Scribner's, 1958. Perhaps the best treatment of TR's youth.

William W. Sewall, *Bill Sewall's Story of T. R.*. New York: Harpers, 1919. On the Dakota period of TR's life.

*Paul Schullery (Editor), *American Bears: Selections from the Writings of Theodore Roosevelt*. Boulder: Colorado Associated University Press, 1983. This work brings together a dozen selections from Roosevelt's writings on bears, most of which (nine of the twelve entries) are excerpted from his hunting books. Of particular note is Schullery's lengthy Introduction, which covers pages 1-23 and delves deeply into the fascination he had for bears and his ethic as a conservationist.

Howard Smith, *Roosevelt in the Rough*. New York: Washburn, 1931. The author knew TR in the Dakota Badlands.

Frederick W. Unger, *Roosevelt's African Trip*. Washington: W.E. Scull, 1909. Yet another pot boiler.

*John Hall Wheelock, *A Bibliography of Theodore Roosevelt*. New York: Scribner's, 1920. An early reference source on TR's writings, it is exceedingly rare thanks to the fact that only 500 copies were printed.

*G. Edward White, *The Eastern Establishment and the Western Experience: The West of Frederic Remington, Theodore Roosevelt, and Owen Wister*. New Haven and London: Yale Univ. Press, 1968. Includes a most useful bibliography.

*Farida A. Wiley (Editor), *Theodore Roosevelt's America: Selections from the Writings of the Oyster Bay Naturalist*. New York: The Devin-Adair Company, 1955. A volume in the American Naturalists Series, this work consists of somewhat fragmented selections from Roosevelt arranged in chronological order and spanning virtually all of his adult years. Strangely, his great African adventure, which TR himself saw as the high point of his career as a naturalist, is completely ignored. The most notable portions of the book are the opening section, which offers the views of four contemporaries on "Roosevelt as a Naturalist," Chapter VII, "In Defense of Our Natural Heritage," and a chronology, "Important Events in the Life of Theodore Roosevelt."

*R. L. Wilson, *Theodore Roosevelt, Outdoorsman*. New York: Winchester Press, 1971. Recently reprinted by Trophy Room Books. Written by a well-known and widely published student of firearms history, this work is a curious blend of strengths and weaknesses. The illustrations are excellent, as is the textual material on guns. On the other hand, the handling of source citations is irritating in the extreme, and a single page of "Credits and References" leaves the reader scratching his head and wondering: "Is that all there is?" What the work does make clear — and this has not changed in the passage of almost three decades since its appearance — is that the definitive work on Roosevelt as an outdoorsman is yet to be written.

****

In addition to the above, Roosevelt figures prominently in a number of anthologies on sport. Among these is Michael Brander's *The Big Game Hunters* (London: Sportsman's Press, 1988), which devotes pages 135-41 to TR and Sam Fadala's *Great Shooters of the World* (South Hackensack, NJ: Stoeger Publishing, 1990), which covers TR on pages 223-232.